Economic Models

AN EXPOSITION

NEW YORK · JOHN WILEY & SONS, INC.

LONDON · SYDNEY

by E. F. BEACH
Professor of Economics
McGill University

Economic Models

A N   E X P O S I T I O N

FIFTH PRINTING, SEPTEMBER, 1966

Library of Congress Catalog Card Number: 57–10800

Printed in the United States of America

To my mother

Preface

In recent years there has been a great increase in the use of mathematics in the development and application of economic theory. Indeed, the concepts of economic theory have become so intimately related to mathematics that no student should now consider working in economic theory unless he has a fairly good grounding in mathematics.[1] But this development has presented us with two problems. On the one hand, there are many good theorists whose knowledge of mathematics is limited and who have difficulty in following the very active leaders in this field. They would like to be able to do so, and their critical appraisal of the newer developments is very much needed. Professor J. M. Clark has issued a plea for more communication between these two groups.[2]

The second problem arises in the education of the students. A number of our ablest economic theorists have come to this field after having achieved a competence in the quantitative disciplines, but many students become interested in economic theory only after they have left the study of mathematics at an early stage some years previously. It is rather difficult for them to return to the study of mathematics when they are rather fully occupied with the requirements of advanced degrees.

This second problem has been met in some universities by a rearranging of the courses and requirements so as to make the study of mathematics a more integral part of the curriculum in economics. The former problem is more difficult. An adequate knowledge of mathematics is acquired only with serious and extended study.

[1] J. A. Schumpeter, *History of Economic Analysis* (N. Y. Oxford University Press, 1954), p. 956.

[2] *Econometrica, 15:* 75–78. See also the critical items in *Econometrica:* (1) *16:* 216; (2) *17:* 90–92; (3) *17:* 251–252; and (4) *18:* 173.

This book is a contribution to the solution of both of these problems. There is no attempt to add to current knowledge of mathematical economics or statistics, but great care has been taken to put this knowledge in a form that can be readily digested by beginners. Much can be learned from the book, it is hoped, if the student has no more than some very elementary algebra. It would be better, however, if he had a brief introduction to calculus, and for Part II a beginning course in the theory of statistics is highly desirable.

It is intended to avoid advanced mathematical devices such as the manipulation of determinants and matrices. There is a growing number of books available for instruction in such techniques. We attempt to present the essential ideas with less elaborate machinery. This policy leaves us facing the criticism that students will not be able to go directly to much of the current literature. We reply that, when they finish reading this book, they should know whether they want or need to go further into that literature.

The first chapters of this book will be found to be very simple, even to be laboring the obvious. This is a matter of deliberate policy since it has been found that only a very few students can absorb a new idea upon first being introduced to it. Pedagogically each idea should be discussed at least twice, preferably from a slightly different point of view the second time. Some ideas, like that of interdependence of variables, require even more reiteration. The later chapters become more difficult, so that there is not a uniform level of difficulty maintained; indeed, it would be impossible to develop the ideas of the later chapters with the simplicity of the first three chapters. Increasing difficulty is to be expected, and each student is to try his own strength by going as far as he can. He will find, however, that even when he reaches some sticky areas, he will be able to learn something by skipping over these parts, and continuing into some of the later chapters. The ideas are presented in such a way as to minimize difficulty of understanding. Those who wish advice on methods of computation should look elsewhere.

The title of the book is not ideal, but the alternative "Economic Systems" has connotations in economic literature that are less appropriate for our purposes. It is intended that the discussion be primarily directed to the mathematics and statistical theory of the subject, and hence not much time is spent on the direct application in terms of the institutions of a particular time or country, nor with the sometimes more decorative models of a mechanical or hydraulic type.

Professors J. C. Weldon and M. C. Kemp have read much of the manuscript and made very helpful comments. A considerable number of students have suffered the trials of my pedagogy, and their responses, both positive and negative, are appreciated. Suggestions by other students are invited. Finally I wish to express appreciation to the John Simon Guggenheim Memorial Foundation, the Cowles Commission, and the staff and students at McGill University, the University of Chicago, and the University of Minnesota.

E. F. BEACH

Montreal, Canada
January, 1957

Acknowledgments

Thanks are due to the Cambridge University Press for a quotation from pages 295 and 296 of *The Measure of Consumers' Expenditure and Behavior in the United Kingdom 1920–1938*, Volume I, by Richard Stone, and to the Royal Statistical Society for a quotation from an article by the same author entitled "The Analysis of Market Demand" (Volume 108, 1945). We thank also the Universities National Bureau Committee for Economic Research for permission to quote from the paper by C. Christ published in the *Conference on Business Cycles* (1951), and Professor R. A. Fisher, author, and Oliver and Boyd, publishers, of *Statistical Methods for Research Workers*, 6th edition, for Student's t and the χ^2 distribution tables.

Contents

CHAPTER 1

Introduction

THE PURPOSE OF MODELS

The devising of simplified skeletal systems generally called models has become a conspicuous part of the writings on economic theory in recent years. This is evidence of a desire to be more systematic in tracing theoretical relationships. Such increased thoroughness is very much needed in economics,[1] but it is not easy to achieve because of the large number of variables that seem to be relevant, and the variety of relationships.

This statement implies that we shall be concerned in this book with that part of economic theory that can be expressed in quantitative terms. Clearly this is not the whole of economic theory; but equally clearly it is an essential part of it. Furthermore, it should be noted that the ingenuity of the mathematicians is constantly increasing the area of quantitative methods.

It is recognized that the utility of mathematics extends beyond purely quantitative concepts. The methods of symbolic logic are not restricted to quantifiable entities, and indeed promise a considerably broader approach to many problems.[2]

In this book, however, it will be convenient to limit ourselves to the consideration of quantifiable entities which may be either variables or

---

[1] See the "Editorial" in *Econometrica, 1:* 1–4; and also J. A. Schumpeter, "The Common Sense of Econometrics," pp. 5–12 of the same issue; also Ragnar Frisch, "The Responsibility of the Econometrician," *Econometrica, 14:* 1–4.

[2] J. C. Weldon, "On the Problem of Social Welfare Functions," *Canadian Journal of Economics and Political Science, 18:* 452–463; K. J. Arrow, "Mathematical Models in the Social Sciences," Chap. VIII of *The Policy Sciences,* ed. by Daniel Lerner and Harold D. Lasswell, Stanford University Press, Stanford, California, especially pp. 129–130.

constants, and to relations among them which will be expressed generally in the form of equations. This we shall call a model.[3]

MATHEMATICAL MODELS

A distinction may be drawn between a mathematical model and an econometric model. The former is merely a set of relations among a number of economic variables. The "Marshallian demand curve" is such a model. It deals with a single relation between two variables, and it has proved to be extremely valuable in analyzing price changes. The "Marshallian cross," consisting of two relationships, a demand curve, and a supply curve, is another valuable model which is only slightly more complicated. It has been extraordinarily useful.

In much the same way, we need merely mention the Keynesian models to realize the value of such constructions in the understanding of economic theory. Indeed, in the discussions following the appearance of Keynes's *General Theory* the construction of models played an especially important part in explaining Keynesian ideas.[4] Conversely, the development of Keynesian theory played an important part in the acceptance of the model as a significant tool in economic theorizing. Emphasis was laid on a small number of key variables whose interrelations could be displayed in a model much more adequately than in written form. If Keynes had himself specifically constructed a model in mathematical terms, his ideas might have been appreciated more quickly, but probably the book would have been limited to a much smaller circulation, and it might indeed have taken longer for the ideas to be so generally understood!

Further examples of mathematical models can be found in the works of Quesnay, Cournot, Walras, Edgeworth, Fisher, Pareto, J. B. Clark, Chamberlin, Mrs. Robinson, Frisch, Harrod, and Kalecki, to mention only some of the outstanding contributors to economic theory. Hence models play an essential part in portraying economic relationships. Part I of this book is devoted to an understanding of such mathematical models.

---

[3] We shall not be particularly concerned in this book with mechanical models such as the "moniac," or with quasi-mechanical models such as Boulding's "bathtub theorem" (*Economic Analysis*, Harper, 3rd ed., p. 108) or Samuelson's income flow model (*Economics*, McGraw-Hill, 3rd ed., pp. 185, 232). These mechanical and quasi-mechanical models are especially useful in exposition. Basically they are mathematical models and as such are included in the discussion.

[4] J. R. Hicks, "Mr. Keynes and the 'Classics'; a Suggested Interpretation," *Econometrica, 5:* 147–159; and Franco Modigliani, "Liquidity Preference and the Theory of Interest and Money," *Econometrica, 12:* 45–88.

ECONOMETRIC MODELS

Mathematical models are theoretical constructions which are tested against reality mainly on grounds of consistency and reasonableness. Only partial information about the real world is brought forth in their support. The econometric models, on the other hand, are designed to make more systematic use of statistical data in assessing their adequacy. H. L. Moore was one of the first to attempt such constructions. His pupil, Henry Schultz, carried his method to fruition, devoting his life to assembling masses of data, and fitting demand and supply curves. E. J. Working and R. Frisch were the most notable critics, the latter devising his "confluence analysis" as an alternative and supplement to the Fisher probability theory which was clearly inadequate in these circumstances.

Tinbergen explored new paths. He laboriously fitted many equations that he assumed to hold simultaneously, and thus formed a model of a whole economy with which he could test economic theories. Haavelmo took the next step, in making use of newer developments in probability theory to reformulate the concept of an econometric model, and this has been the basis of much of the work of the Cowles Commission. Examples can be found in the writings of Marschak, Koopmans, Klein, Christ, and others. These people suggest that we should be wary of fitting equations individually unless they are carefully formulated. This careful formulation entails a knowledge of the purely mathematical models discussed in Part I; but a considerable knowledge of statistical theory is required as well. Research in this area has been moving rapidly, and it is notable that no longer is it merely a matter of adapting statistical theory to the needs of economics, but the needs of economic theory are causing an important development of statistical theory.

How useful the econometric models can be in terms of policy or prediction is still a matter of considerable doubt. The Dutch and the Canadian Governments have been making use of the techniques in careful co-operation with other approaches and with some success. In the United States and the United Kingdom, however, the governments are apparently content to let private organizations experiment with the techniques a bit longer. This is unfortunate because it has already become clear that the building of useful models requires much re-working of the basic data, and close co-operation with those who provide the data. It is perhaps too much to expect to achieve a single good model of a whole economy; it has proved to be advisable to construct a series of models for different purposes, and to understand the strengths and the weaknesses of each. The techniques are flexible enough to allow a considerable variety of models.

Much of the work on econometric models has to date been negative in the sense that it has shown what we should not do in drawing inferences from statistical data. But this has had a healthy influence on economic theory. Positively, it has provided some usable estimates of quantities such as elasticities,[5] and has begun to show some promise of use for Governmental purposes.[6]

[5] Arnold C. Harberger, "On the Estimation of Economic Parameters," paper delivered at meetings of American Statistical Association, Montreal, September 1954.

[6] T. M. Brown, "Habit Persistence and Lags in Consumer Behavior," *Econometrica*, *20:* 355–371.

PART I

MATHEMATICAL MODELS

CHAPTER 2

The Elements of Model Construction

The concept of a model as used in economic theory implies a set of relations among a group of variables. These relations are usually presented in the form of equations, though they are sometimes shown in the form of a graph or chart. The elements of model construction to be studied in this chapter are therefore the idea of a variable, and the idea of an equation or relation. First let us consider the concept of a variable.

VARIABLES

A variable is a quantity that may vary over a range.[1] It may take on any value within this range, like the height of the mercury in a thermometer, or it may take on only certain particular values in the range, like the number of children in a family, when only whole numbers may be used. In the former example the variable is said to vary continuously. In the latter it is noncontinuous, and is sometimes said to be discrete. For many purposes the latter may be regarded as a special case of the former. We shall first treat the more general case, returning to the discrete variables at a more advanced level. Much of the statistical material used in economics is in this discontinuous form, but the mathematical machinery that has been developed makes it easier to handle the continuous variables.[2]

The use of variables implies the ability to measure, which is true in relation to height and weight, though perhaps less so in relation to "intelligence." Things that cannot be measured cannot be taken into

[1] Alternatively we may say that we are concerned with a set or class of values, any one of which may be considered at any particular time.

[2] Samuelson made a point of considering discrete variations with care, but found very little difference in many theorems. *Foundations of Economic Analysis* (Harvard University Press, Cambridge, 1947).

account directly, though they can, of course, be taken into account in the final assessment of any results. Attitudes over the bargaining table would be a good example. Frequently some immeasurable aspect of a situation can be brought into consideration by the measuring of some related aspect. But this lack of ability to measure a part of our causal factors does not seem to be the most troublesome problem we have. There remains a great deal that is measurable, and we have not yet learned how to handle well those materials that we have at hand.[3]

Some measurements are not made with great accuracy. They are statistical estimates, sometimes based on arbitrary definitions. But the development of national accounts in the major countries of the West since 1935 should make us optimistic. As such measurements came to be so important their definitions were sharpened, and the estimates improved. Similar improvement is likely to take place whenever a measurement becomes important; and an increasing number of aspects of the major Western economies are being measured, or at least estimated. It would be foolish to deny the use of mathematical tools when measurements are imprecise, though the interpretation of the results must be made with care.

Some economists feel more comfortable with less exact formulations to which they have become accustomed. The haziness allows them to interpret the analysis in different ways for different conditions. But surely progress in this field as in others implies a continual searching after more precise and correct formulations.

It is not claimed that the whole of economics or even the whole of economic theory can be encompassed in a model or a set of models. But it is claimed that a well-devised model can bring out certain features of interdependence among economic quantities that are not easily comprehended without its help. It makes the assumptions more precise, the relationships more evident, and allows the theory to be tested for logical consistency. An illustration is the use of abstract models to portray the essence of the Keynesian ideas.[4] Such models played a large part in the understanding, the use, and the improvement of these ideas.[5]

But the negative side should also be heard. Models can be misunderstood, and misapplied. At the very worst, it can be said that there has been more than one Euler proving the existence of God with a formula.

[3] R. Stone, *The Measurement of Consumers' Expenditure and Behaviour in the United Kingdom, 1920–1938*, I (Cambridge: At the University Press, 1954).

[4] J. A. Schumpeter, *History of Economic Analysis* (N. Y., Oxford, 1954), gives marginal utility as an example.

[5] S. E. Harris, *The New Economics* (N. Y., Knopf, 1947), especially Chap. XIII, by P. A. Samuelson, on p. 146.

The most frequent error is, of course, the attempt to use a model where it does not fit. The history of economic thought is cluttered with such misadventures. Indeed, the history of economic thought could be thought of to a very large extent as a history of misapplied models.

The model builder can quite easily err in this way. Certain operations in mathematics are much simpler than others. Hence the model builder is inclined to adjust the model just a bit in order to take advantage of these simple mathematical operations. One of the most common examples is the use of straight lines when curved lines are indicated by the context. Straight lines are so very much easier to handle in groups; indeed, nonlinear relations can become so complicated that often there is little or no advantage in building a model at all.

Other disabilities may be cited. When we cannot find a suitable series of measurements for a desired variable, we use an alternative, or omit the variable completely. Klein's *Economic Fluctuations in the United States* gives many examples of the bold assumptions necessary in creating any comprehensive model, such as the assumption that all labor is assumed to be homogeneous.

The problems facing those who try to devise actually descriptive econometric models from economic data are obviously tremendous. Some of these problems will be examined in Part II. But the use of mathematical models to assist in our thinking can be very helpful. No man would attempt to weigh himself on a small table scales, taking one part of his body at a time; yet the effects of a particular change on the economy as a whole may be quite as inseparable, and hence the total effect should be estimated as a whole from a model that is as complete as possible.

EQUATIONS

Frequently we designate a variable with the letter x and a second variable with the letter y. Consider a demand relation for sugar in the United States estimated by Schultz:[6]

$$y = 70.62 - 2.26x \tag{1}$$

The letter y stands for the per capita consumption of sugar in the United States in any year. The period considered was 1875–1895, during which period y varied from 35 to 70. The letter x stands for the

[6] H. Schultz, *The Theory and Measurement of Demand* (Chicago, University of Chicago Press, 1938), p. 196. There is also a time variable in Schultz's equation which is ignored here. It would be more proper to speak of this equation as relevant to the year 1885, the middle of the period.

deflated wholesale price in cents of a pound of sugar, which varied during this period from 2 cents to 16 cents.

This equation could have been stated differently, as

$$x = \frac{70.62}{2.26} - \frac{1}{2.26} y \tag{2}$$

i.e.,

$$x = 31.25 - 0.44y \tag{3}$$

Equations 1 and 3 are equivalent mathematically, but there is usually a different connotation in relating the equation to the economic situation. In the first equation, y is said to depend upon x; y is said to be the *dependent* variable and x is said to be the *independent* variable. In equation 3 the roles are reversed. Equation 1 would be the appropriate version in considering the demand for sugar by an individual consumer who could have no influence on the market price by varying his consumption. For him the price is independent of his consumption behavior; it is fixed by the market, whereas the amount of his consumption would depend upon this price, and is therefore a dependent variable.[7] In considering a market demand relation, however, price and quantity are interdependent, and either variable may be regarded as the independent one for purposes of that equation, according to circumstances. Schultz used price as the independent variable along with other more truly independent variables such as time; but other authors have chosen to think of price as the dependent variable, and quantity as the independent variable.[8]

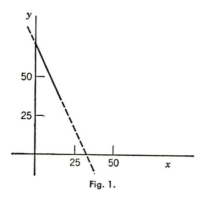

Fig. 1.

An equation is an algebraic method of expressing a relation among variables. For some purposes a geometrical expression is better. The straight line that is plotted in Fig. 1 is equivalent to equation 1, and is therefore another way of expressing Schultz's relation between consumption and price. The line is solid over the range that covers the variation in the variables during the period under study.

[7] In terms of the jargon to be adopted subsequently, equation 1 can be considered as a one-equation model with x as an exogenous variable.

[8] Karl A. Fox, "Structural Analysis and the Measurement of Demand for Farm Products," *Review of Economics and Statistics, 31*: 57–66. Incidentally, the difficulty that has been disclosed here may be taken as a hint as to why models are needed—a single equation is not enough to take into account the possibility of joint dependence.

It may be well to give a little attention to the actual plotting of such an expression as equation 1. The easiest way to do this is to compute the intercepts, that is, the points at which the line cuts the two axes. This is done by noting the value of y when x is zero, that is, 70.62, and the value of x when y is zero, which is 31.25. The y intercept is 70.62, which is the constant term in equation 1. The x intercept is 31.25, which is the constant term in equation 3.

We may now mark off these two intercepts, or, what is the same thing, plot the two points (0, 70.62) and (31.25, 0) and join them. If these two points are fairly close to- gether, the line may not be accurately plotted, and should be checked by find- ing another point some distance away: give x a value of 10 or 100, and com- pute the value of y from the equation.

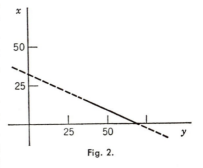
Fig. 2.

A geometric presentation is some- times more suggestive, and for many people it is more easily understood. Furthermore, charts can easily give effect to subtle changes in the shapes of the curves, changes which are generally more difficult to handle algebra- ically. But they are limited in the number of variables, i.e., dimensions, which they can present, whereas algebraic methods can easily be gener- alized to many variables. In general, algebra is the more powerful tool, and hence the student should learn to use both, moving from one to the other as circumstances suggest.

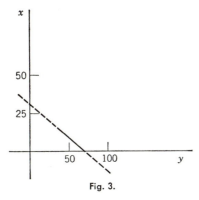
Fig. 3.

Just as an algebraic expression can be presented in more than one way, so a geometric relation can be presented in a variety of ways. The straight line in Fig. 2 is equivalent to equation 3. The axes have been interchanged from their position in Fig. 1, and the line appears at first glance to have a different slope. It is thus wise, in describing a slope, to mention the axis to which it is relevant.

It is necessary, also, to take note of the scale. Figure 3 is equivalent to Fig. 2, but the scale of the y axis has been changed so that the slope of the line with respect to the y axis appears to be steeper. Mathe- matically the line is the same.

A few words about the concept of slope will doubtless not be amiss.

Consider equation 1 again. A textbook on calculus would define slope as the rate of change of one variable (y) with respect to another (x). In other words, for a certain (small) change in x, the slope tells how much y will change. Fortunately, a straight line is one for which the slope is constant throughout; this makes the question quite simple, and we can calculate the slope by increasing x by 1 unit, and computing the amount by which y will then increase. From equation 1 this is clearly -2.26, which is the slope of this line with respect to the x axis. From equation 3 we can see that the slope of this line with respect to the y axis is -0.44.

Engineers are wont to say that the slope is the "rise over the run." In Fig. 1, while the line runs in the x direction from 0 to 31.25, the value of y falls from 70.62 to 0, or, in other words, rises an amount of -70.62. Hence the rise/run is $-70.62/31.25 = -2.26$, which is seen to be the value of the coefficient of x in equation 1. Similarly, the coefficient of y in equation 3 is the slope of the line with respect to the y axis; in this case, the run is 70.62 and the rise is -31.25. If the equation is not given and we have only the graph, the intercepts can be estimated from the chart and the slope computed from their ratio.

The value of the slope depends on the units in which the variables are quoted. If the price had been quoted in a different monetary unit, the scale of the price axis would have to be changed appropriately. The transformation of cents to dollars would, of course, be simply a matter of moving the decimal points two places to the left, and this is indeed what would be required of the coefficient of x in equation 1. If the price of sugar were quoted in dollars per pound, this coefficient would become -226. The quotation in terms of French francs, Italian lira, or British pounds would each require a different transformation. Furthermore, if we kept to the same country but quoted dollars per ton of sugar, the slope would have to change, because the transformation from cents to dollars requires our dividing by 100, but the transformation from pounds to (short) tons requires our dividing our figures by 2000. Hence our slope would be transformed as follows: $-2.26 \times (100/2000) = -0.113$.

GENERAL EQUATIONS

A more general formulation of a relation is required frequently. In discussing linear relations between two variables, a general equation may be written thus:

$$y = \alpha + \beta x \tag{4}$$

The Greek letters α and β are known as *parameters*. For a particular equation they may take on specific numerical values, as in equation 1, where $\alpha = 70.62$ and $\beta = -2.26$. They are sometimes known as *constants* because they have constant values for any particular equation.

It may be noted that, when x is given a value of 0, then y equals α. Thus α, the constant term in the equation, is known as the intercept, because it is the value at which the line cuts the y axis, as seen in Fig. 1. The other constant of the linear equation, β, is known as the slope, because, as x increases, y increases β times as much. Or, in other words, when x increases by 1, y increases by β; when x increases by 10, then y increases by 10β. In Fig. 1, the slope is negative, so that y decreases at a rate of 2.26 per unit of x, since $\beta = -2.26$. It may be remembered that a straight line is by definition one whose slope is constant throughout, and hence is easy to handle. When discussing more complicated curves, the interpretation of the constants other than the intercept is not a simple matter.

A general linear relation is sometimes expressed as

$$y = l(x) \tag{5}$$

where the letter l stands for "some linear function of." It is therefore equivalent to equation 4. This simpler type of expression is particularly helpful when there are several variables entailed, for example:

$$y = l(x, w) \tag{6}$$

which is equivalent to

$$y = \alpha + \beta x + \gamma w \tag{7}$$

meaning that the dependent variable, y, is a linear function of the two independent variables, x and w. α is the y intercept (i.e., when both x and w are zero), β is the slope with respect to the x axis, and γ is the slope with respect to the w axis.

The charting of such an expression is instructive. Three axes, or dimensions, are entailed, one for each variable. Consider the following particular equation:

$$d = 70.62 - 2.259p + 0.837t \tag{8}$$

This is another version of Schultz's demand relation for sugar.[9] The dependent variable is d, the number of pounds per capita consumed in a year. The independent variables are p, the price per pound in cents, and t, the time variable, expressed in years, starting with the origin at July 1, 1885. That is, the value of t at July 1, 1885 is 0; the value of t one year later is 1; and so on. The parameters are $\alpha = 70.62$,

[9] Schultz, *op. cit.*, p. 187.

$\beta = -2.259$, and $\gamma = 0.837$. In this equation we can express the coefficients of the independent variables with one more decimal point than the constant term, because these coefficients are multiplied by the values of the independent variables before being added to the constant term, and hence the total value, expressed to two decimals, will have greater accuracy than if all parameters were given to two decimal points. If one of the independent variables varied over a wide range, or were expressed in large numbers, then its coefficient should have more decimals.

We have already explored the relation between d and p while t was assumed to be 0, since this is equation 1. Now, we can obtain a relation between d and t by assuming $p = 0$, or letting p take on some average value, say $p = 10$, getting a new constant term. The equation then becomes

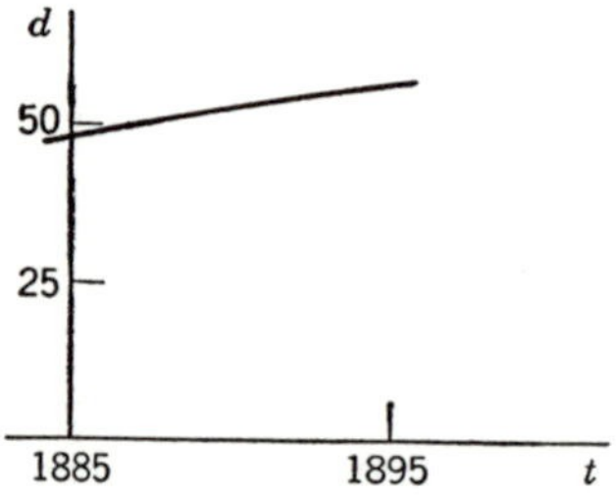

Fig. 4.

$$d = \alpha' + \gamma t \qquad (9)$$

where

$$\alpha' = 70.62 - (2.259)10 = 48.03 \qquad (10)$$

Thus

$$d = 48.03 + 0.837t \qquad (11)$$

which equation is represented in Fig. 4.

We may now proceed to chart the whole equation in three variables, using three dimensions. This is done in Fig. 4, Chap. 3, which is a sketch of a somewhat more pictorial chart to be found in the Schultz book.[10]

It will be seen that the linear function represents a flat plane surface which does not pass through the origin (the d intercept is not 0). It slopes downward as p increases, but slopes upward with t. In general, a linear function may include any number of variables. If there are more than two variables, the function can no longer be represented by a line—it becomes a flat plane surface with as many dimensions as there are variables. The function remains "linear" or, more strictly, completely linear, as long as the slope with respect to each one of the variables remains constant for all values of that variable. An expression may also be only partly linear, like the following

$$y = 10 + \tfrac{1}{2}x - 2w + w^2$$

which is linear in x, but quadratic in w. The student should amuse

[10] See also B. S. Keirstead, *Essentials of Price Theory* (Toronto, The University of Toronto Press, 1942).

himself by charting such a relation. In particular he will see that linear relations are always single valued, whereas nonlinear relations may not be. That is, letting $w = 0$, for any particular value of x, there is one and only one value of y; and, for any particular value of y, there is one and only one value of x. But, if we let $x = 0$, then a particular value of y will allow us two possible values of w.

A general linear relation has been expressed in equations 5 and 6. A still more general functional relation may be written as

$$y = f(x) \tag{12}$$

where $f(x)$ means "some function of x." This function might be linear as in (5), or it might be parabolic, as

$$y = \alpha + \beta x + \gamma x^2 \tag{13}$$

or logarithmic, as

$$y = \alpha + \beta \log x \tag{14}$$

or some other type of relation, perhaps involving trigonometric functions, roots, or powers, or some combination of these. Similarly, a general formulation of a functional relation among three variables is

$$y = f(x, w) \tag{15}$$

A still more general statement of this function is

$$\phi(y, x, w) = 0$$

where all the variables, y, x, and w, appear on the left-hand side, and on the right-hand side there is only a zero. Treating equation 1 in this fashion, we get

$$y + 2.26x - 70.62 = 0$$

It happens that the first variable, y, has a coefficient of 1, but this need not be so, for the whole expression could be multiplied by a constant without changing its value; that is, each term could be multiplied by this constant. For some mathematical operations it is helpful to select one of the variables, place it first, and divide through by the appropriate constant to make its coefficient equal to 1. This is called "normalizing" the expression.

The concept of a functional relation, or a *function*, need not detain us long at this point, though it should be considered. A mathematical function is what we mean by a relation. If two variables are related by a mathematical function, a given value of one implies a value or a set of values for the other. A linear relation is a single-valued function; that is, any given value for one of the variables implies a single value for the other. If the function entails powers or roots, then a given value for one of the variables may imply more than one value for the other.

Mathematicians must concern themselves with a great many different kinds of functions, some of them with curious kinks or twists in them, but in econometrics we seldom have any use for such complicated relations. We tend to restrict our attention to relatively simple functions.

A more troublesome problem for econometricians is the definiteness or sharpness of the relation. We are concerned with relations like that of Schultz between the amount of sugar consumed and its price. There are, of course, many other factors that affect the consumption of sugar besides its price. By introducing the time factor, Schultz is able to take into account some of these factors, like the change in tastes. But there are always more that we cannot take into account for one reason or another. In Part II, we shall see how the statistical techniques attempt to meet this problem. In the meantime we proceed as if there were, at any point of time, a clear and definite relation, though it may shift its position or even change its shape over time.

TYPES OF MODELS

We have examined the elements of model construction, to wit, variables and relations. In Chap. 3, we proceed to examine some simple *linear models,* and in later chapters some more complicated ones. The first complication is to introduce a nonlinear equation, producing a *nonlinear model.* Next, we differentiate between *static models* and *dynamic models.* We shall define a dynamic model as one involving time explicitly. Although this definition differs from current practice,[11] it simplifies our approach.

In Part II, the *stochastic model* is examined; this is a model that entails the theory of probability and the use of random variables. In Part I, the models are all *nonstochastic,* or exact, using no random variables. We prefer to call them mathematical models.

Finally, we may distinguish between a *micro model* and a *macro model.* The former is a model of some small segment of the economy, or some substantial segment of it, such as the banking sector, or a geographical region. A macro model refers to a whole economy. It implies the use of aggregated variables, but this is not a precise distinction, because a single industry usually implies an aggregation of firms, and a market demand schedule an aggregation of individual demands. Both micro and macro models will be used throughout this book.

[11] W. J. Baumol, *Economic Dynamics* (N. Y., Macmillan, 1951).

EXERCISES

1. From the relation 1, compute the values of y for each of the following values of x: 1, 10, 20, 35, $5\frac{1}{2}$, 7.23.

2. In equation 4, plot the line indicated by giving α the value of 3 and β the value of 5. Then compute the values of y which result from the following values of x: 1, 3, 17, 2.3.

3. Try to draw your own demand curve for some commodity that you buy regularly such as cigarettes, cups of coffee, or candy bars.

4. Plot the planes indicated by (7) when $\alpha = 2$, $\beta = 0.5$, and $\gamma = 1.2$; and when $\alpha = 1$, $\beta = -0.5$, and $\gamma = 1.2$.

5. Draw up a list of types of functional relations that might be included in (12).

6. Write out explicitly a linear equation involving four variables, such as would be indicated by $d = l(p, Y, n)$ where n stands for the number of people, Y stands for average disposable income, and d stands for the total amount demanded.

7. Attempt to plot the nonlinear function

$$d = 10pY$$

8. Explore the nature of logarithmic and exponential relations by plotting some particular examples.

READINGS

A. SOME SIMPLE EXPOSITIONS OF MATHEMATICS

1. A. N. Whitehead, *An Introduction to Mathematics* (Home University ? 1911, revised 1948, Oxford). A concise and readable discussion for n? maticians by an outstanding authority.
2. Richard Courant and Herbert Robbins, *What is Mathematics?* (Lon? University Press, 1941). An extremely good book for those with ? matical training who would like to have a clearer picture of the ? This is a good reference even for fairly advanced parts of the ? can also be dipped into or glanced over with profit.
3. Lancelot T. Hogben, *Mathematics for the Million* (ill. by J. F. ? G. Allen & Unwin Ltd., 1936). A book with much the same p? and Robbins.
4. W. W. Sawyer, *Mathematician's Delight* (Penguin Books, ? introduction to mathematical reasoning for which no pr? assumed. From simplest beginnings we are taken int? and calculus.
5. G. L. S. Schackle, *Mathematics at the Fireside* (Cam? Press, 1952). This is an interesting attempt to pres? but the concepts tend to get beyond the compre? should be useful for adults who lack regular train?

6. Gerard Piel, "Mathematics Comes out of the Classroom," *Yale Review, 39:* 132–141 (1949–1950). This interesting article discusses the practical uses of mathematics.

B. MATHEMATICS FOR ECONOMISTS

7. R. G. D. Allen, *Mathematical Analysis for Economists* (Macmillan & Co., London, 1942). The standard work for economists who wish to have enough mathematics for handling economic theory. A minimum would be Chapters I through VIII.
8. W. L. Crum and J. A. Schumpeter, *Rudimentary Mathematics for Economists and Statisticians* (McGraw-Hill, 1946). The first chapters are an excellent presentation of the fundamental ideas of infinitesimal calculus for those whose studies have to be brief and hurried.
9. Jan Tinbergen and J. J. Polak, *The Dynamics of Business Cycles: A Study of Economic Fluctuations* (Chicago, The University of Chicago Press, 1950). First published in Dutch in 1942, translated by Polak. Shows the use of elementary mathematics in discussing some economic variations.
10. Jan Tinbergen, *Econometrics* (New York, Blakiston, 1951), translated from the Dutch by H. Rijken van Olst. Tinbergen has a remarkable ability to explain his econometrics in simple terms. Almost all of this book is readable by the nonmathematician.
11. P. A. Samuelson, "Economic Theory and Mathematics—An Appraisal," *Papers and Proceedings, American Economic Review, XLII*, No. 2: 56–66 (May 1952); and discussion by Fritz Machlup, *ibid.*, 66–69. This paper should be read by every student.
12. "The Mathematical Training of Social Scientists," Report of the Boulder Symposium, *Econometrica, 18:* 193–205.
13. Jan Tinbergen, "Reformulation of Current Business Cycle Theories as Refutable Hypotheses," *Conference on Business Cycles*, National Bureau of Economic Research, N. Y., 1951, pp. 131–141. See also comments by T. C. Koopmans (pp. 141–145) and D. M. Wright (pp. 145–148).
14. T. Wilson, "Some Reflections of the Business Cycle," *The Review of Economics and Statistics*, 1953, especially pp. 246–247.

CHAPTER 3

Linear Models

An economic model will be taken to mean a set of relations among a set of economic variables. For some purposes a single relation can be regarded as a model, as for example a demand curve. But the interesting problems arise from the existence of a set of relations holding simultaneously. If all the relations are linear, the name *linear model* is given. If one or more of the relations is nonlinear, the model is no longer a linear one because the solution will entail nonlinear relations. Some of the simpler nonlinear models will be examined in Chap. 4.

The manipulation of linear equations is a much easier matter than the manipulation of nonlinear relations, and, since the mathematical difficulties can soon mount fabulously, it behooves us to see what can be done with a more manageable set of relations. Hence much interest has centered on linear relations. Furthermore, linear models are not without practical importance, for, as econometricians have pointed out,[1] linear relations can give good approximations to more complicated functions if they are used within a limited range.

SHORT–RUN MARKET MODEL

A simple linear model of a commodity market will be used for illustration:[2]

$$d = \alpha + \beta p \tag{1}$$

$$s = \gamma + \delta p \tag{2} \text{ I}$$

$$d = s \tag{3}$$

---

[1] Jan Tinbergen, *Statistical Testing of Business Cycle Theories*, 2 vols. (Geneva, League of Nations, 1939); and G. U. Yule, *An Introduction to the Theory of Statistics* (London, Charles Griffiths & Co., 1932).

[2] Mathematical models will be given Roman numerals and numbered consecutively throughout the book. The component equations will be numbered consecutively with all other equations in each chapter separately.

This is a three-equation linear model. The variables are: d, the amount demanded, s, the amount supplied, and p, the price. The parameters are $\alpha, \beta, \gamma, \delta$. The first equation is a demand relation, so that we may suppose that β will be negative ($\beta < 0$). The second equation is a supply relation, and for present purposes we can suppose that δ is positive ($\delta > 0$). The third equation is sometimes called an equilibrating equation. It indicates that, for equilibrium to exist in this market, the amount demanded must equal the amount supplied.

Specific numerical values can be given to the parameters represented by the Greek letters, and the nature of any such relation could be explored by plotting the equations. Alternatively, the parameters could be estimated for a particular commodity for a particular period, as has been done by Schultz and others. This problem of fitting an equation or model to a set of data will be examined in Part II.

SOLVING THE EQUATIONS

The question to be explored now is the existence of and the nature of a solution of the model. In economic terms, this is the question of the existence of and the nature of an equilibrium, i.e., an equilibrium value for each of the variables entailed. Clearly it will not be possible to have an equilibrium for every set of values that we might assume for the parameters, and we shall want to know, first of all, what conditions are necessary for an equilibrium of any kind, and secondly what conditions give us an equilibrium that is reasonable.

Let us assume that there is a solution to model I. Then, by combining equations 2 and 3, we obtain

$$d = \gamma + \delta p \tag{4}$$

thus eliminating one equation and one variable. Now, by combining this equation with (1), we get

$$\alpha + \beta p = \gamma + \delta p \tag{5}$$

which is one equation in one variable. Re-writing it, we get

$$p = \frac{\alpha - \gamma}{\delta - \beta} \tag{6}$$

which is an expression for p in terms of the parameters alone. This is a solution for p in terms of the parameters. Similar expressions for the other variables are

$$d = s = \frac{\delta \alpha - \beta \gamma}{\delta - \beta} \tag{7}$$

We have thus found it possible to express each variable in terms of the parameters alone. If a specific numerical value had been given to each of the parameters, we should thus have a specific numerical value for each of the variables. A solution thus seems to be possible so long as δ does not equal β. Now it should be recalled that we have already imposed some limitations on two of the parameters, to wit $(\beta < 0, \delta > 0)$, so that these two parameters cannot be equal. Indeed, if they were equal, it would imply that the supply relation and the demand relation were parallel, which would be a most unusual economic situation. Thus we can assume that a solution exists.

Next we wish to know the conditions that are required to give us a plausible solution. An important implausibility to be ruled out is negative values for prices and quantities. Now a knowledge of the geometry of these two relations, the supply line and the demand line, will allow us to conclude that the intercept of the demand curve should be larger (higher on the q axis) than the intercept of the supply line, assuming that both are positive. Hence $\alpha > \gamma$ which, together with the restrictions mentioned above, implies that $\delta\alpha > \beta\gamma$, and all of these together will assure that the equilibrium p and q values will be positive.

It is helpful to attempt to disentangle the mathematics from the economics. This is especially useful to beginners who have difficulty in understanding what they are doing when performing mathematical tricks like solving equations. But it is a policy that should be used quite generally in teaching economics, as it could save one from some questionable activities.[3] When an applied mathematician can be sure that his mathematical model fits his particular problem well, he can make use of all the powerful devices that the pure mathematicians put in his hands. However, when he is not at all sure that the fit is good, he must be more careful to examine each step in the operation, to see what economic interpretation, if any, can be given to the operation.[4] We should not exclude the use of the wonderful mathematical methods just to explore the consequences, but the results will carry much more conviction if they can be supported by economic reasoning. This general point of view will be used in the application of calculus in later chapters. We turn now to its use in examining the process of solving a set of equations.

Equations 1 and 2 have clear economic meanings, as has been pointed

---

[3] E. F. Beach, "Market Theory of Walras and Marshall," *Jahrbücher für National-ökonomie und Statistik, 165:* 279–284.

[4] This seems to be the import of Alfred Marshall's distrust of "long trains of deductive reasoning," *Principles of Economics* (London, Macmillan, 8th ed., 1930), p. 781.

out. Equation 3, the equilibrating equation, is needed to complete the model, and it has a precise economic interpretation. The model might be more understandable to some if, instead of "amount demanded," the expression "amount that might be demanded" were used. Similarly, instead of "amount supplied," the expression "amount that might be supplied" could be understood. The restrictions $\beta < 0, \delta > 0$ have clear economic meaning, and indeed have been the subject of much discussion.[5]

The mathematical "solving" of equations has its own peculiarities. If there is to be a solution, it is required that the equations hold simultaneously and be consistent and independent. The matter of simultaneity needs, perhaps, no explanation. This is clearly a necessary condition of any solving procedure, as any textbook on elementary algebra emphasizes. The questions of consistency and independence are generally discussed at a more advanced level, and we shall postpone their consideration for a page or two.

Let us assume for the moment that our model I does consist of consistent and independent equations holding simultaneously. Then, as mathematicians have proved, a solution exists. This means that there is a set of values for the variables that satisfies all three equations (simultaneously). The solving operation seeks out these values. Thus equations 4, 5, 6, and 7 all hold at this point of equilibrium. We can reason as follows: if there is a point of equilibrium, then, at that point of equilibrium,

$$d = \gamma + \delta p \tag{8}$$

and similarly for the other equations until we come to the final equation which is the solution for the variable in that equation.

A GEOMETRIC INTERPRETATION

The treatment of model I has, so far, been in terms of algebra. The ideas introduced will be better understood if a somewhat comparable treatment is given in terms of geometry. For this purpose we need particular numerical values for the parameters. Let us take

$$d = 10 - 0.5p \tag{9}$$

$$s = 2 + p \tag{10} \text{ IA}$$

$$d = s \tag{3}$$

[5] E. J. Working, "What do Statistical Demand Curves Show?" *Quarterly Journal of Economics 41:* 212 ff.

The solution of this system is

$$p = 5\tfrac{1}{3}$$

$$s = d = 7\tfrac{1}{3}$$

The system is displayed in Fig. 1. The demand and supply lines are straight, of course, and meet at the point $(5\tfrac{1}{3},\ 7\tfrac{1}{3})$. Demand and supply curves are usually charted with price measured along the vertical axis, but Fig. 1 reverses this procedure in order to correspond more closely to the equations in which p is the independent variable. The concept in geometry that corresponds to a "solution" in algebra is a point at which the lines meet.[6] Only at this point can the variables satisfy both the demand and the supply conditions simultaneously. And obviously, since the lines are not parallel, they must meet once. Hence there will be one and only one solution in this case; furthermore, if the resulting solution is to be plausible economically, the meeting point will be in the first quadrant.[7]

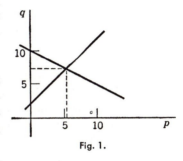

Fig. 1.

CONDITIONS FOR A SOLUTION

It is appropriate now to explain the important conditions of independence and consistency. We consider them in order. If each of the numerical coefficients of one equation is a fixed multiple of the corresponding coefficient of the other, then these two equations can be represented by the same line. In mathematical terms they meet at an infinite number of points, and have an infinite number of solutions. For example, take

$$2x + 3y = 5 \tag{11}$$

$$4x + 6y = 10 \tag{12}$$

More generally, whenever one equation of a group can be obtained by taking a linear combination of some other equations in the group, we

[6] In terms of mathematics a point is a set of values, one value for each variable. Thus an equilibrium point in a market model is a set of equilibrium values, one equilibrium value for each variable in the model.

[7] We do not need to exclude negative values for these variables, but they are seldom used in economics.

say that they are linearly dependent.[8]   For example,

$$x + y + z = 2 \tag{13}$$

$$3x + 2y + z = 3 \tag{14}$$

$$5x + 4y + 3z = 7 \tag{15}$$

The third equation of this group is obtained by taking twice the first, and adding the second. That is, the coefficient 5 is obtained by taking the coefficient of x in the first equation, multiplying it by 2, and adding the coefficient of x in the second equation. The coefficient of y in the third equation is obtained by taking the coefficient of y in the first equation, multiplying it by 2, and adding the coefficient of y in the second equation. Similarly, for the coefficient of z and also for the constant term. Now, in solving these three equations, we find that there is not a unique solution but an infinite number of solutions, forming the line where the planes represented by the first two equations meet. Thus, if we are to allow only a single solution, we must rule out cases of linear dependence.

Now turn to the second question. The matter of consistency arises when any two equations have coefficients of which all but the constant terms bear the same ratio to each other, as

$$2x + 3y = 5 \tag{16}$$

$$4x + 6y = 8 \tag{17}$$

These equations are said to be inconsistent because if $2x + 3y$ equals 5, then it cannot at the same time equal 4, as the second equation implies. In geometrical terms we have here two parallel lines, which, of course, have no meeting point, and hence have no solution. We find therefore, that inconsistent equations have no solution, and linearly dependent equations have too many solutions.

We are now in a position to give the precise conditions necessary for one and only one solution for a set of n equations in n variables. In geometrical terms, the lines or planes must not be parallel, and must all be distinct (i.e., no two are allowed to coincide). In algebraic terms the equations must be consistent and linearly independent. The

---

[8] Throughout this chapter the terms "dependent equation" and "independent equation" are to be taken to mean "linearly dependent equation" and "linearly independent equation." Indeed, a nonlinear dependence would necessarily entail nonlinear equations, and, since we are limiting ourselves to linear equations in this chapter, we need merely to speak of "dependence" and "independence." It should be noted also that the concept of linear independence of an equation is very different from the concept of an independent variable discussed above on page 10.

student should now refer to page 20 and examine the limitations imposed upon the parameters there in the light of this rule.

These conditions seem almost trivial when we are considering a simple model of two or three equations, but for larger models it is not so easy to take them into account, or even to appreciate their significance. We should not assume that these rules of reasonableness will be obeyed by all models that we may see fit to construct, though in general they should be, because of the economic nature of the functions that would make up a model.

EQUILIBRIUM VALUES

We turn now to the nature of the equilibrium (i.e., solved) values of the variables. In doing so we employ a simplifying device. Since the equilibrium value of s is equal to the equilibrium value of d, we use the variable q in their stead. Clearly a lower value for the slope of the supply curve with respect to the p axis (i.e., smaller δ) will imply a higher equilibrium value for p and a lower equilibrium value for q. A larger value for the intercept of the demand line (α) implies a larger value for both p and q. This, of course, can be seen from equations 6 and 7. In this way each of the parameters can be examined, and the results can be arranged in a table or a matrix as follows:

	α	β	γ	δ
p	$+$	$+$	$-$	$-$
q	$+$	$+$	$+$	$+$

Each sign shows the direction of the movement of the solved value of the variable indicated, resulting from an increase in each of the parameters. In the case of the slope of the demand line, which is negative, an increase is a flattening of the line with respect to the p axis; that is, an increase in an algebraic sense.

By examining the algebraic relations more closely, we can find not merely the direction of change but also the amount of change. Presenting equation 6 a little differently, we have

$$p = \left(\frac{1}{\delta - \beta}\right)\alpha + \left(\frac{-1}{\delta - \beta}\right)\gamma \qquad (18)$$

Thus, if α increases by one unit, and all other parameters remain unchanged, p increases by $1/(\delta - \beta)$ units. Similarly, if γ increases by one unit, and all the other parameters remain unchanged, p increases by $-1/(\delta - \beta)$ units. This is, of course, really a matter of taking first derivatives, as learned in calculus,[9] and for more complicated relations it will be necessary to refer to that mathematical technique. Thus we can write

$$\frac{\partial p}{\partial \alpha} = \frac{1}{\delta - \beta} \tag{19}$$

Differentiating equations 6 and 7 with respect to each parameter in turn, we obtain the following dependence matrix:

	α	β	γ	δ
p	$\dfrac{1}{\delta - \beta}$	$\dfrac{\alpha - \gamma}{(\delta - \beta)^2}$	$\dfrac{-1}{\delta - \beta}$	$-\dfrac{\alpha - \gamma}{(\delta - \beta)^2}$
q	$\dfrac{\delta}{\delta - \beta}$	$\dfrac{\delta(\alpha - \gamma)}{(\delta - \beta)^2}$	$\dfrac{-\beta}{\delta - \beta}$	$\dfrac{-\beta(\alpha - \gamma)}{(\delta - \beta)^2}$

This table is to be interpreted as follows: for an increase in α of one unit, there will be an increase in q of $\delta/(\delta - \beta)$ units. For an increase of one unit in γ, there will be a decrease in p of $1/(\delta - \beta)$. And so on. Thus we can see how the equilibrium values of the variables will change when the parameters are changed. This type of analysis has been called "comparative statics," since it entails a comparison of one static situation with another.

An examination of the dependence matrix brings out some interesting points. It may be noted that every one of these derivatives is a fraction, and that the expression $(\delta - \beta)$ appears in each denominator, and furthermore it appears always in the denominator. In half of the cases, those dealing with the slopes β and δ themselves, the quantity is squared. This quantity $(\delta - \beta)$, which is the difference between the slopes, can be called the *stability factor*,[10] since the greater it is, the smaller will be the changes in the equilibrium values for any of the variables resulting from a change in any of the parameters. Under the conditions assumed in the opening paragraphs of this chapter ($\beta < 0, \delta > 0$), this factor is necessarily positive. Thus great stability requires that the demand and supply lines be steep. This analysis should be compared by the reader with the analysis of the stability of price and quantity in many

---

[9] See Appendix to this chapter.

[10] More accurately, it should be called "the stability factor in comparative statics" so as to differentiate it from the related concept of stability in a dynamic sense, which is discussed in a future chapter.

elementary textbooks based usually and quite wrongly on elasticity rather than slope.[11]

Two further points should be made here. When the student is in doubt as to whether it is the slope or the elasticity that is the relevant aspect of the problem under discussion, he should move one of the axes parallel to itself. This movement changes the elasticities of the curves, but it does not change their slopes. If the analysis remains unchanged under such a transformation, then slope and not elasticity is the relevant consideration.

The second point to be added here is a further comment on the general statement made above that the stability is greater, the greater the difference between the slopes of the curves. This conclusion contrasts with the results of the geometric treatment which shows that the steeper the curves, the more stability given to p and the less stability given to q (recall that we are here considering that p is measured along the horizontal axis). Now, referring to the dependence matrix again, we notice that the bottom row has an additional slope parameter in each numerator, and hence in order to increase the difference between the slopes we must take account of the change in the numerator, too. Thus, to take $\delta/(\delta - \beta)$, if we double δ and β, the value of $\delta/(\delta - \beta)$ is unchanged (recall that β is negative). We may, however, steepen the demand curve, increasing the numerical value of β, leaving δ unchanged.

DETERMINATION

We consider next the numbers of equations and variables in any model. It will be assumed that all equations are linear, that the coefficients are numerical values, and that the equations are consistent and independent. In model I, the number of equations equals the number of variables, and the process of solving consists of a series of steps, each step being the elimination of a variable by using one of the equations. Clearly this is a general procedure. Whenever the number of equations equals the number of variables we can proceed until we end with one equation in one variable which is, by definition, a solution for that variable. Thus, solving for the other variables is straightforward, and the result will be the same, regardless of the choice of variables to be eliminated first.

If the number of variables is greater than the number of equations, we shall always have variables left in the final equation after all the elimination possible. There will then be an infinite number of solutions

[11] See, for example, Boulding, *Economic Analysis* (New York, Harper, 1948, 2nd ed.), Chap. 8.

to such a set of equations. Suppose, for example, we have left a single equation in two unknowns. There is more than one point along this line, indeed there are many points that fulfill the conditions. We can say that there are not enough conditions or restraints on the variables to give us a single solution. This is a case of lack of determination.

If the number of equations is greater than the number of variables, then we shall obtain a number of different solutions, depending on which of the variables we eliminate first. There are too many restraints on the variables. The model is said to be *overdetermined*. To take a simple geometrical illustration, consider three equations in two variables. In general there will be no single solution. With three straight lines there will normally be three meeting places, and hence three solutions for the two variables (Fig. 2). There is one special case in which

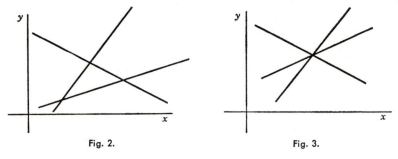

Fig. 2.   Fig. 3.

all the lines do happen to pass through a single point, and when this happens there is a special relationship among the equations (Fig. 3). In this special case any one of the equations can be derived by taking a linear combination of the other two. (See Exercise 4.) This is a case of linear dependence and has therefore been excluded.

It may thus be stated as a general rule that:[12] *A set of n consistent and independent linear equations in n unknowns will have one and only one solution. If the number of such equations is greater than the number of unknowns, there will be no unique solution—this is the case of overdetermination. If the number of such equations is less than the number of unknowns, there will be an infinity of solutions—this is the case of lack of determination.*

Thus, if we want a linear model that will yield a single set of equilibrium values, we must fulfill the three following conditions:

(a) The number of variables must be just equal to the number of equations.

[12] L. Dickson, *First Course in Theory of Equations* (New York, Wiley, 1922), Chap. VIII; or M. Bocher, *Introduction to Higher Algebra* (New York, Macmillan, 1907), Chap. IV.

(*b*) The equations must be consistent.

(*c*) The equations must be independent.

Such a linear model is said to be exactly determined or, simply, determinate. The first condition is easy to check, and commonly it is the only one overtly considered in econometric work. But this need not cause concern. When each equation contains a different set of variables, these conditions are almost[13] automatically fulfilled, since the coefficients of the nonappearing variables are zero, and these zero coefficients will occur at different places in each equation. We should be more concerned when the same variables appear in any two equations, as when we have a supply and a demand equation for a given commodity in only two variables, p and q, and even then it would be regarded as most unusual economic theory to suppose that these two linear relations were parallel or coincident.

SECOND MARKET MODEL

Let us now consider a slightly different model:

$$d = \alpha + \beta p \tag{1}$$

$$s = \gamma + \delta p + \epsilon r \tag{20) II}$$

$$d = s \tag{3}$$

Model II is the same as model I except that in the second equation an additional variable r appears together with an additional parameter ϵ. This new variable entering the supply equation is, let us say, the number of inches of rainfall during the growing season. It is a different kind of variable from the others. It is not one whose value we should expect to obtain by solving the model, but rather one whose value we insert for any given year, having obtained it from the meteorological records. It is known as an *exogenous* variable, whereas the others are *endogenous*, or jointly dependent variables. The endogenous variables are the ones whose values are determined by the model; the values of the exogenous variables are determined outside the model.

It is sometimes said that exogenous variables are "noneconomic" variables and hence they are the concern of other people like meteorologists in the case of rainfall, or psychologists in the case of demand preferences. But the decision as to what is an economic variable is a rather arbitrary one. The level of population may be taken as an exogenous variable for some models; that is, its value is determined by

[13] The possibility is not ruled out, but cases of dependence would then usually be quite obvious.

factors outside the model being considered at the moment. For other models it may be regarded as a variable whose value is determined by the economic forces under consideration in the model; i.e., it is one of the jointly dependent variables, the value of which is presumably to be determined along with the values of the other endogenous variables by the conditions and relations of the model. Each model will therefore have a certain span or coverage indicated by the variables included. It can be a "partial equilibrium" model, including only a few endogenous variables and ignoring the other variables in the economy. Of course, if the model is a good one, it must be possible to ignore the movements in the other variables as part of the *ceteris paribus* for the approximation desired. If we find that one of the ignored variables is of considerable importance to the model, then it should be taken into the model; i.e., the span of the model should be increased to include this variable either as an endogenous variable or as an exogenous one, depending on its relation to the system. The Walrasian model was the other extreme in that it purported to include all economic variables as endogenous variables, and all other variables that were ignored, or used as exogenous, were such noneconomic variables as technological production or supply factors, or psychological demand factors.

An exogenous variable is treated like a parameter in the solving of the equations. But its nature is somewhat different from that of a parameter. When a parameter is fixed, so that the equations become explicit numerical functions, the exogenous variable is still free to take on any set of values. For example, the rainfall in a certain district in a certain period was, say, r_1 inches. This rainfall varies from year to year, but presumably the model would not have been changed if the rainfall had been some other figure, say r_2. Thus, the quantity of rainfall will have an effect upon the equilibrium values of the endogenous variables, but none of the endogenous variables can affect the amount of rainfall.

The solution of model II is

$$p = \frac{\gamma - \alpha}{\beta - \delta} + \frac{\epsilon}{\beta - \delta} r \tag{21}$$

$$d = s = \frac{\gamma\beta - \alpha\delta}{\beta - \delta} + \frac{\epsilon\beta}{\beta - \delta} r \tag{22}$$

For any given value of r, a single determinate solution is obtained, as in model I; but the solved values are dependent on the value of the exogenous variable.

In the same way, another exogenous variable Y indicating the total national income, determined outside our model, could be added to the demand equation. There would still be three equations in three endogenous variables,[14] but the solved value for any of them would depend upon the values of r and Y. This dependence could be shown in the form of a matrix such as that used on page 26 to show the dependence of the solved values of the variables on the parameters. When given the following model:

$$d = \alpha + \beta p + \zeta Y \qquad (23)$$

$$s = \gamma + \delta p + \epsilon r \qquad (20) \quad \text{III}$$

$$d = s \qquad (3)$$

we get the dependence matrix:[15]

	r	Y
p	$\dfrac{\epsilon}{\beta - \delta}$	$\dfrac{-\zeta}{\beta - \delta}$
q	$\dfrac{\beta\epsilon}{\beta - \delta}$	$\dfrac{-\delta\zeta}{\beta - \delta}$

REDUCED FORMS

When there are exogenous variables in a model, we must take note of alternative ways of expressing the model. All our models have been originally expressed in terms of autonomous equations;[16] that is, each equation has an independent existence in terms of economic theory. If one of them were to be altered, there is no reason why any of the others should be. These equations indicate structural relations, and they may be of various kinds, indicating behavior (as a demand equation), technological relations (production functions), institutional relations (equations dealing with money supply), and definitional equations, identities, or equilibrating equations. When these equations have been solved so that each endogenous variable is expressed in terms of the parameters and the exogenous variables, it is said to be in its *reduced* form. Thus equations 21 and 22 are the reduced form of model

---

[14] It is to be noted that it is only the endogenous (also called internal) variables that are to be considered in relation to the number of equations. We may have as many exogenous variables as we wish.

[15] The existence of a "stability factor" here may be noted.

[16] T. Haavelmo, "The Probability Approach in Econometrics," *Econometrica, 12* (1944), supplement.

II. For model III, the reduced form is:

$$p = \frac{\gamma - \alpha}{\beta - \delta} + \frac{\epsilon}{\beta - \delta} r - \frac{\zeta}{\beta - \delta} Y \tag{24}$$

$$d = s = \frac{-\delta\alpha + \beta\gamma}{\beta - \delta} + \frac{\beta\epsilon}{\beta - \delta} r - \frac{\delta\zeta}{\beta - \delta} Y \tag{25}$$

The reduced form of a model will be found to have considerable importance when we consider the problem of fitting our relations to actual data. At the moment it can be seen that they would be useful in predicting a change in any of the variables resulting from a change in one of the exogenous variables.

Finally, we return to the definition of a *model*. A model is seen to be a set of relationships among a set of variables, the relationships being specified in the form of equations. When parameters of the equations are given numerical values, we have a particular *structure*. A model is therefore a class of structures.[17]

A MACRO MODEL

All the models discussed so far in this chapter have been models of a single market. Let us consider now a simple macro model:[18]

$$C = \alpha + \beta Y \tag{26}$$
$$Y = C + I + G \tag{27}$$

IV

where the endogenous variables are:

C: amount consumed
Y: amount of national income

And the exogenous variables are:

I: amount of investment
G: amount of government deficit

All variables are in billions of dollars per annum.

[17] J. Marschak, "Economic Measurements for Policy and Prediction," Chap. 1 of *Studies in Econometric Method*, ed. by Wm. C. Hood and T. C. Koopmans (New York, Wiley, 1953), Cowles Commission for Research in Economics, Monograph 14.

[18] A simple model somewhat like this one is to be found in S. E. Harris, *The New Economics* (New York, Knopf, 1947), Chap. XVIII, written by J. Tinbergen.

The reduced form of this model is

$$Y = \frac{\alpha}{1 - \beta} + \frac{1}{1 - \beta} I + \frac{1}{1 - \beta} G \tag{28}$$

$$C = \frac{\alpha}{1 - \beta} + \frac{\beta}{1 - \beta} I + \frac{\beta}{1 - \beta} G \tag{29}$$

The dependence matrix is clearly, as follows:

	I	G
Y	$\dfrac{1}{1 - \beta}$	$\dfrac{1}{1 - \beta}$
C	$\dfrac{\beta}{1 - \beta}$	$\dfrac{\beta}{1 - \beta}$

This dependence matrix can be called a *policy matrix* because the exogenous variables are here ones that might be directly (or indirectly) affected by government policy; and the matrix shows us the effects of changes in these exogenous variables on the endogenous variables.

An important theoretical point may be made here. Looking at equation 27 alone, it would seem that an increase in G of one unit would increase Y by one unit. But such a conclusion is too naive. From equation 26 it can be seen that, if Y is increased, C is also increased, and C is also an element in Y, as seen from equation 27. This is a case of interdependence which nonmathematical theory has difficulties in handling. It has even been called "circular reasoning" by some.[19]

It should be made clear from studying this model that the total effect on Y of a change in G can be measured only when all the relations of the model are taken into account.[20] This total effect can then be seen in the reduced-form equation 28, or in the dependence matrix which has been derived from the reduced-form equations.[21]

A further question may be raised as to whether all the effects of a real

[19] This question of "feed-back" is well presented in A. Tustin, *The Mechanism of Economic Systems* (London, Heineman, 1953), Chap. II.

[20] In an important article in the *Quarterly Journal of Economics, 41*, E. J. Working pointed out that a demand curve could not be established without some assumption about the supply curve.

[21] Model IV is essentially the model used by Mosak and Salant in showing that income is a determinate variable even though it is interdependent with consumption expenditure. See J. L. Mosak and W. S. Salant, "Income, Money and Prices in Wartime," *American Economic Review, 34*: 828–839.

world are taken into account here. This implies the question of the adequacy of the model, and clearly a model as simple as model IV must be far from completely adequate. There is no easy answer to this question of the adequacy of the model, and its treatment will have to be postponed until the student has learned more about models.

Equation 27 of this model should be examined further. It is not simply an equation; it is an *identity*. Here, Y is defined as the sum of the other three variables, and it cannot conceivably be anything else. Mathematicians prefer to write identities as

$$Y \equiv C + I + G \qquad (30)$$

In contrast, the consumption function may be thought of as an approximation of a curved line; or it may be that other variables that have been neglected by the model have enough effect to cause the relation 26 to be inexact. The deviations from the exact relation will be considered in handling the econometric models in Part II. Equation 27, however, can have no exceptions or deviations; it is an exact relationship. Other identities will occur from time to time in other models.[22]

Students frequently have difficulty in wrestling with questions of causation. The techniques of model building are not to be implied as a substitute for the consideration of such a philosophical question, but rather as a method of approach to it. Thus we must decide which variables are to be considered as endogenous, and which can be regarded as exogenous. This is partly a matter of convenience, since we desire a model that can be treated without too much trouble, and partly a matter of circumstance, since we start with some ideas of the variables whose movements we wish to explain, and the variables that can be considered as being determined essentially by factors that we are not at the moment considering, such as sociological conditions. The building of useful models is therefore, like the development of economic theory of which it is a part, largely an artistic achievement.

SECOND MACRO MODEL

Liu and Chang have used the following model for the United States:

$$C = aY + bP + c \qquad (31)$$

$$I = dY + eF + i \qquad (32) \quad \text{V}$$

$$Y = C + I + G \qquad (27)$$

[22] J. Marschak, "Identity and Stability in Economics: A Survey," *Econometrica*, *10*: 61–74.

where the variables are designated as follows:

$$\text{Endogenous} \begin{cases} C\colon & \text{Consumption expenditure} \\ I\colon & \text{Gross private domestic investment} \\ Y\colon & \text{Gross national product} \end{cases}$$

$$\text{Exogenous} \begin{cases} F\colon & \text{Corporation profits after taxes} \\ G\colon & \text{Government purchases of goods and services plus} \\ & \quad \text{net foreign investment} \\ P\colon & \text{Consumers' price index} \\ & \quad \text{(all variables except the last one are} \\ & \quad \text{annual figures in billions of current dollars)} \end{cases}$$

With the use of data for the years 1930–1948 they estimated[23] the constants as follows:

$$C = 0.535Y + 0.214P - 3.06 \qquad (33)$$

$$I = 0.221Y + 0.339F - 11.20 \qquad (34) \ \ \text{VA}$$

$$Y = C + I + G \qquad (27)$$

The student should solve the equations of model V, getting a reduced-form equation for C in terms of the exogenous variables and parameters. He can then substitute the values of the parameters given in model VA, and find, for example, that an increase of 1 million dollars in G would, according to this model, imply an increase of 2.2 million dollars in C.

THE CLARK MODEL OF THE UNITED STATES 1921–1933[24]

This model employs six endogenous variables and four exogenous variables. There are therefore six equations. One feature of this model is the use of *predetermined* endogenous variables. These are values of certain endogenous variables at some time previous to that under consideration. For example, considering the Clark model for the year 1921, the values of X for the previous periods are already determined and fixed, and can be taken as data. Similarly, for the year 1922, the values of X during 1921 are fixed. Thus we have here a type of dynamic model. Equations 38 and 39 show that the values of J

---

[23] The problem of estimation will be examined in Part II.

[24] Colin Clark, "A System of Equations Explaining the United States Trade Cycles, 1921–41," *Econometrica*, 17: 93–124.

and X are functions of these predetermined variables. (All quantities are measured in billions of wage units per quarter.)

$$C' = 0.550Y + 0.322M - 8.16 \tag{35}$$

$$G = 0.120Y - 0.0061\bar{G} - 2.32 \tag{36}$$

$$H = 0.255Y - 0.0142\bar{H} - 3.57 \tag{37}$$

$$J = -0.5X + F_j \tag{38}$$

$$X = 0.925Y + F_x \tag{39}$$

$$Y = X + J \tag{40}$$

VI

F_j, called "factors of J," is a combination of predetermined[25] variables:

$$-0.113J' + 0.119 \sum_{1}^{5} X_{-t} + 0.186 \left(\sum_{1}^{3} X_{-t} - \sum_{4}^{6} X_{-t} \right) \tag{41}$$
$$+ 0.136B' - 4.72$$

F_x, called "factors of X," is a combination of predetermined variables:

$$P + E + 0.322M - 0.0061\bar{G} - 0.0142\bar{H} - 14.05 \tag{42}$$

Endogenous Variables:

C' = $C - I$, where C represents personal consumption expenditures and I represents imports.

G represents producers' durable equipment gross.

H represents new private constructions gross.

J represents net change in inventories.

X represents outlay or sales.

Y represents gross national product or income (including transfer payments).

Exogenous Variables:

P represents government purchases of goods and transfer incomes.

E represents exports and net balance of invisible transactions.

B represents amount of bank cash at the beginning of the quarter.

B' represents the difference between B and an upward trend line (representing apparently a greatly increased financial caution, or demand for liquid assets in relation to business done).

---

[25] Predetermined variables are either exogenous variables or lagged endogenous variables. That is, at any moment of time when the interdependence of endogenous variables is being considered, these predetermined variables have fixed values.

Lagged Endogenous Variables:

X_{-t} represents X at t quarters previously.

$\bar{G}$ represents cumulated value at the beginning of the quarter of G for the past *ten* years.

$\bar{H}$ represents cumulated value at the beginning of the quarter of H for the past *forty* years.

A Complete Solution:

$$Y = 0.93F_x + 1.86F_j \tag{43}$$

$$C = 0.51F_x + 1.02F_j + 0.322M - 8.16 \tag{44}$$

$$G = 0.1116F_x + 0.2232F_j - 0.0061\bar{G} - 2.32 \tag{45}$$

$$H = 0.237F_x + 0.474F_j - 0.0142\bar{H} - 3.57 \tag{46}$$

$$J = 0.14F_j - 0.93F_x \tag{47}$$

$$X = 1.86F_x + 1.72F_j \tag{48}$$

J represents cumulated values of J (taken from the 1929 base point approximately determined by Kuznets) at the beginning of the quarter in question.

J' represents the difference between J and a downward trend line (which trend line is believed to represent the decreasing need for stocks owing to quicker communications).

M (Modigliani factor) represents the highest *previous* value of Y attained a year or more previously. (Rising income is assumed to take about a year to affect a lasting change in consumption habits.)

Computation of Values of Variables.

A solution for Y, obtained from equations 38, 39, and 40, is:

$$Y = 0.93F_x + 1.86F_j \tag{49}$$

The values of the predetermined variables F_x and F_j are then computed for the beginning of our period, the first quarter of 1921. Upon getting a value for Y for this period, the values of the other variables for this same first quarter of 1921 are obtained. We may then move on to compute the values for the second quarter of 1921, and so on through the whole period 1921–1933.

Comments on the Clark Model.

The same set of equations, with different parameters, are used for the period 1934–1941. It is interesting to note that, if a dependence matrix were drawn up, the derivative (slope) of Y with respect to P (which is included in F_x) is 0.93. The derivative of X with respect to P is 1.86; the derivative of C' with respect to P is 0.51.

EXERCISES

1. Remove the condition of a positive slope for the supply relation in model I ($\delta > 0$), and establish an alternative set of conditions for a plausible economic model; i.e., price and quantity are both to be positive. Note also that the intercept of the supply line might be negative.

2. Check the solution of model IA. Note the difference in the solution if $\delta = 2$.

3. Examine the nature of the sign of each of the quantities of the matrix on page 26, and compare these signs with those of the matrix on page 25.

4. Given two equations:

$$2x - 3y = 5$$

and

$$x + 2y = 4$$

a third can be derived from these two by multiplying the second by 2 and adding it to the first, getting $4x + y = 13$. Now examine the solution. Plot the three lines.

5. Given the following equations:

$$2x - 3y = 5$$
$$2x - 3y = 7$$
$$4x - 6y = 10$$

plot and examine.

6. Test models I and II for the three conditions mentioned on page 28.

7. Solve:

$$x + y + z = 1$$
$$x + 2y + 3z = 2$$
$$2x - 3y + z = 4$$

8. Examine the constants in the matrix on page 31 for sign.

9. Given the following model:

$$d = \alpha + \beta p + \zeta t$$
$$s = \gamma + \delta p + \epsilon r$$
$$d = s$$

where t is an exogenous variable measuring time in years from some base period, and r is exogenous, measuring rainfall, obtain the reduced form, and set up a dependence matrix.

10. In model IV, assume that $\alpha = 20$ (billion dollars per annum); $\beta = \frac{3}{4}$; $I = 20$ (billion dollars per annum); $G = 20$ (billion per annum); calculate the

national income. Alternatively, for a national income of 250 billion, calculate the necessary government deficit if α, β, and I are assumed as above. Construct a diagram showing the relationship between G and Y.

11. From model V construct a dependence matrix.

12. Consider the linear relation $y = 3x - 2$ as an approximation to the expression $y = x^2$ between the values of $x = 1$ and $x = 2$. Measure the error in y at the points where $x = 1\frac{1}{4}$, $1\frac{1}{2}$, $1\frac{3}{4}$, 1.63. Notice how large the error is when $x = 3$. Draw a chart of the two functions.

13. Devise a suitable linear approximation to $y = \log x$ between the values of $x = 5$ and $x = 10$, and find the error when $x = 7\frac{1}{2}$.

READINGS

1. J. Tinbergen, *Statistical Testing of Business Cycle Theories* (League of Nations, 1939). A classic work in model construction.
2. C. Clark, "A System of Equations Explaining the United States Trade Cycle, 1921 to 1941," *Econometrica*, *17*: 93–124. Clark offers a system of 6 linear equations in 6 endogenous and 5 exogenous variables fitted to quarterly data over twenty-one years.
3. J. Marschak, *Introduction to Econometrics*, mimeographed notes on lectures given at the University of Buffalo, 1948.
    ———, *Income, Employment and the Price Level*, notes on lectures given at the University of Chicago, Autumn, 1948 and 1949 (New York, Kelly, 1951).
4. Ta-Chung Liu and Ching-Gwan Chang, "United States Consumption and Investment Propensities: Prewar and Postwar," *American Economic Review*, September 1950.
5. T. C. Schelling, *National Income Behavior; an Introduction to Algebraic Analysis* (New York, McGraw-Hill, 1951). An excellent presentation for the nonmathematician. It offers a very thorough development of macro models.

The Concept of a Derivative

I LINEAR RELATIONS

Consider the function $y = 10 + 2x$ which may be charted as a straight line, and is called a linear function in two variables. We are very often interested in the way in which y changes when x changes. Clearly,

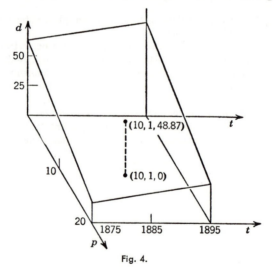

Fig. 4.

when x increases by 1, y increases by 2 because the coefficient of x is 2. This is what we have called the slope in the x direction, and may be expressed as

$$\frac{\Delta y}{\Delta x} = \frac{y_1 - y_0}{x_1 - x_0} = \frac{(10 + 2x_1) - (10 + 2x_0)}{x_1 - x_0}$$

$$= \frac{2x_1 - 2x_0}{x_1 - x_0} = \frac{2(x_1 - x_0)}{x_1 - x_0} = 2$$

Consider now our old friend, the Schultz demand relation:

$$d = 70.62 - 2.259p + 0.837t$$

Here we have two independent variables, p and t; and d may change as a result of a change in either one of them, or of both together. This function is illustrated in Fig. 4. Let us choose a base point where $p = 10$ and $t = +1$, giving a value of $d = 48.87$. We may indicate this point on the surface as (10, 1, 48.87). Now, if we hold t constant and increase p, we move in a southerly direction. As p increases by one unit, and t does not change at all, d decreases by 2.259. This slope in the p direction, t being constant, may be indicated by

$$\left.\frac{\Delta d}{\Delta p}\right)_t = -2.259$$

Similarly, if we increase t while keeping p constant, the slope in an easterly direction may be indicated by

$$\left.\frac{\Delta d}{\Delta t}\right)_p = +0.837$$

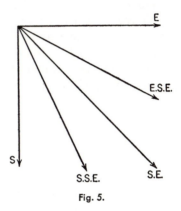

Fig. 5.

It is, of course, possible to move in a southeasterly direction by increasing both p and t at the same rate, or to increase them in the direction technically known as South South East (S.S.E.), but we do not have special terminology to indicate these movements. See Fig. 5. The student may find it interesting to compute the slope of the function as we move in a S.E. direction thus: Increasing p by one unit, d decreases by 2.259 units; but, as t increases by one unit, d increases by 0.837 units, leaving a resultant of -1.422. Hence the slope in the S.E. direction is -1.422. Similarly, the slope in the S.S.E. direction is $(1 \times -2.259) + (\frac{1}{2} \times 0.837) = -1.840$.

All of this is quite simple for a linear function with only two independent variables, but, as we increase the number of independent variables, rather than writing the symbol

$$\left.\frac{\Delta d}{\Delta p}\right)_{t,r,s,\cdots}$$

where $t,r,p\cdots$ are independent variables, we prefer to write simply: $\partial d/\partial p$.

Now let us turn to the expression found for the solution of p on page 20:

$$p = \frac{\alpha - \gamma}{\delta - \beta}$$

which may be written as

$$p = \left(\frac{1}{\delta - \beta}\right)\alpha + \left(\frac{-1}{\delta - \beta}\right)\gamma$$

or as

$$p = a\alpha + b\gamma$$

where $a = 1/(\delta - \beta)$ and $b = -a$.

We regard p here as a function of the parameters, so that, if any one of the parameters were to be changed, the equilibrium value of p would change accordingly. In order to find how this value of p would change for a unit change in any of the parameters, keeping all the other parameters unchanged, we may write:

$$\frac{\partial p}{\partial \alpha} = \frac{1}{\delta - \beta}$$

$$\frac{\partial p}{\partial \gamma} = \frac{-1}{\delta - \beta}$$

That is, an increase in α of one unit will imply that p increases by $1/(\delta - \beta)$; or, how much p will change depends upon the values of δ and β in such a way that, the smaller the value of δ, the more will a change in α affect the equilibrium value of p. The student should study carefully Fig. 1 to check the meaning of this in geometrical terms.

This discussion has been limited to linear relations, and it will be noted that the relationship between p and δ is not linear. This can be seen if we insert the following values:
$\alpha = 10, \gamma = 2, \beta = -1$, to get

$$p = \frac{8}{\delta + 1}$$

If the student will now take for δ the successive values of $0, 1, 2, 3, 4, 5, \cdots$ and compute the values of p and plot the function, he will see that it is not a straight line. The slopes of nonlinear relations will be considered in section II of this appendix.

II NONLINEAR RELATIONS

The concept of a derivative, which is essential to the study of calculus, is not really very difficult to understand. It may be defined as the slope of a curve at a point.   Consider the function $y = x^2$, which has been plotted in Fig. 6.   At any point on this curve, a tangent can be drawn and the slope of this tangent can be computed.   That slope would be the rate at which y is increasing at that point, as x increases.   But the

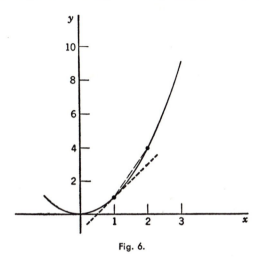

Fig. 6.

slope varies all along the curve.   How can we measure the slope at a particular point?   We proceed as follows.

The curve passes through the point $(1, 1)$, which can be shown by substituting these values into the equation and finding that they satisfy it.   Let us take this point as a base, and use the method of successive approximations.   As x moves from 1 to 2, y goes from 1 to 4, so that the average rate of increase over this range is $(4 - 1)/(2 - 1) = 3$. That is, y increases three times as fast as x; or, in other words, for a unit increase in x, y increases by 3 on the average.   The slope of a line joining the two points $(1, 1)$ and $(2, 4)$ is $+3$.   But this is not the slope of the tangent to the line at the former point.   A closer approximation to this latter slope is obtained if we choose another point on the curve, say where $x = 1.5$ and $y = 2.25$.   The slope of the line joining the points $(1, 1)$ and $(1.5, 2.25)$ is $(2.25 - 1)/(1.5 - 1) = 1.25/0.5 = 2.5$. Now a third and closer approximation to the slope of the tangent can be obtained by taking a closer point, say where $x = 1.25$ and $y = 1\frac{9}{16}$. The slope over this range is

$$\frac{1\frac{9}{16} - 1}{1\frac{1}{4} - 1} = \frac{\frac{9}{16}}{\frac{1}{4}} = \frac{9}{16} \times \frac{4}{1} = \frac{9}{4} = 2\frac{1}{4}$$

Continuing with a fourth approximation, we choose the point where

$x = 1\frac{1}{8}$ and $y = 1\frac{17}{64}$, and obtain an average slope of

$$\frac{1\frac{17}{64} - 1}{1\frac{1}{8} - 1} = \frac{17}{64} \times \frac{8}{1} = 2\frac{1}{8}$$

Now the successive approximations to the slope, $3, 2\frac{1}{2}, 2\frac{1}{4}, 2\frac{1}{8}, \cdots$, may be charted according to their x values, as in Fig. 7. It seems quite clear

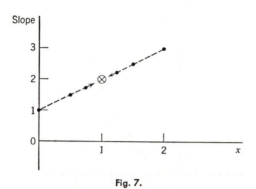

Fig. 7.

that by continuing to take closer and closer approximations we should approach ever closer to the value of 2. It looks, therefore, as if the value of the tangent to the function $y = x^2$ at the point $(1, 1)$ is 2. This can indeed be verified by approaching the point $(1, 1)$ from the opposite direction. The first approximation can be obtained by using the two points $(0, 0)$ and $(1, 1)$, getting an average slope of $(1 - 0)/(1 - 0) = 1$. The second approximation could be obtained from the points $(\frac{1}{2}, \frac{1}{4})$ and $(1, 1)$, getting

$$\frac{1 - \frac{1}{4}}{1 - \frac{1}{2}} = \frac{3}{4} \times \frac{2}{1} = 1\frac{1}{2}$$

The third approximation, from $(\frac{3}{4}, \frac{9}{16})$ and $(1, 1)$, is

$$\frac{1 - \frac{9}{16}}{1 - \frac{3}{4}} = \frac{7}{16} \times \frac{4}{1} = 1\frac{3}{4}$$

Clearly we are approaching the value 2.

This process of successive approximations could be applied to any of the simple functions that we are likely to use. The student should amuse himself by estimating the slope of the function $y = 10 - \frac{1}{2}x + x^2$ at the point where $x = 0$. (*Ans.* $-\frac{1}{2}$.) Then he might obtain further practice by computing the slopes of this function at the points where $x = 1, 2, 3, \cdots$.

These results can be obtained more directly and easily for these simple functions. Consider again the function $y = x^2$.

We may establish a base point (x_1, y_1) at which the slope is to be computed. Then we add a little bit to x, say Δx, called "delta x." The corresponding value for y must then be

$$y_2 = (x_1 + \Delta x)^2 = x_1{}^2 + 2(\Delta x)x_1 + (\Delta x)^2$$

Thus the increase in y is

$$\Delta y = y_2 - y_1 = x_1{}^2 + 2(\Delta x)x_1 + (\Delta x)^2 - x_1{}^2 = 2(\Delta x)x_1 + (\Delta x)^2$$

The slope between the two points (x_1, y_1) and (x_2, y_2) is

$$\frac{\Delta y}{\Delta x} = \frac{2(\Delta x)x_1 + (\Delta x)^2}{\Delta x} = 2x_1 + \Delta x$$

We have learned that the approximation is improved as we move the points closer together, i.e., as $\Delta x \to 0$. Of course, $\Delta y \to 0$ also, but the ratio $\Delta y / \Delta x$ need not approach zero. For the particular function that is being considered above, it approaches $2x_1$. But x_1 is any point, and so we may substitute any value of x, and so call it simply x. We may now define the concept, that of a derivative, as follows:

$$\frac{dy}{dx} \equiv \lim. \left(\frac{\Delta y}{\Delta x}\right)_{\Delta x \to 0}$$

That is, dy/dx is the limit of the ratio $\Delta y / \Delta x$ as Δx (and necessarily Δy also) approaches zero. We have found that for the function $y = x^2$, $dy/dx = 2x$. Then, when $x = 1$ and $y = 1$, the slope is $2x = 2$, which is what we found above by the method of successive approximations.

By using this symbolic approach for the general power function $y = x^n$, we should find that the derivative is

$$\frac{dy}{dx} = nx^{n-1}$$

so that, when $y = x^3$, $dy/dx = 3x^2$. And, when $y = ax^4$, $dy/dx = 4ax^3$. The derivative of a constant is zero

$$\frac{dc}{dx} = 0$$

Now take the function $y = 10 - \frac{1}{2}x + x^2$. We can compute the general formula for the slope as:

$$\frac{dy}{dx} = 0 - \frac{1}{2} + 2x = 2x - \frac{1}{2}$$

Thus, if we wish to know the value of the slope of the function, where $x = 0$, it can now be found directly by substituting the value of x into the formula for the derivative:

$$\left.\frac{dy}{dx}\right)_{x=0} = -\tfrac{1}{2}$$

When $x = 1, 2, 3, \cdots$, the slopes are, respectively, $1\tfrac{1}{2}, 3\tfrac{1}{2}, 5\tfrac{1}{2}, \cdots$. The student should plot the function and check these values.

We have worked out the derivative only for simple power functions which, when added together, form what are called polynomials:

$$y = \alpha_0 + \alpha_1 x + \alpha_2 x^2 + \cdots + \alpha_{n-1} x^{n-1} + \alpha_n x^n$$

It is somewhat more difficult to work out general formulas for other functions; but some of these functions can be expressed in power form. Consider now the expression for the equilibrium value of p in a simple market model (page 20):

$$p = \frac{\alpha - \gamma}{\delta - \beta}$$

Let $\alpha - \gamma = a$ and $\delta - \beta = b$. Then

$$p = \frac{a}{b} = ab^{-1}$$

$$\frac{\partial p}{\partial b} = \left.\frac{dp}{db}\right)_{a \text{ const.}} = (-1)ab^{-2} = \frac{-a}{b^2}$$

Now it can be shown that

$$\frac{dp}{d\delta} = \frac{dp}{db} \times \frac{db}{d\delta}$$

when $b = f_1(\delta)$, i.e., b is some function of δ, and $p = f_2(b)$, i.e., p is some function of b. Thus

$$\frac{\partial p}{\partial \delta} = \frac{-a}{b^2} \cdot \frac{\partial b}{\partial \delta} = \frac{-a}{b^2} (1) = \frac{-a}{b^2} = -\frac{(\alpha - \gamma)}{(\delta - \beta)^2}$$

Similarly,

$$\frac{\partial p}{\partial \beta} = a(-1)b^{-2} \frac{\partial b}{\partial \beta}$$

$$= a(-1)b^{-2}(-1) = \frac{a}{b^2} = \frac{\alpha - \gamma}{(\delta - \beta)^2}$$

The derivatives of p with respect to α and γ were found above in the first part of this appendix. The student should now study these functions by trying illustrative values for the parameters. For the treatment of other functions, the student is referred to the regular textbooks on calculus; but in any case he can try the method of successive approximations.

CHAPTER 4

Nonlinear Models

A model is designated as linear if *all* the equations composing it are linear. If but one of the equations is nonlinear, then the model is designated as nonlinear because the solution of the model entails the solution of a nonlinear equation. The presence of a second nonlinear equation need not make the solution more complicated than the presence of one alone.

There are many types of nonlinear relations. We shall begin with one of the simplest types, a quadratic equation, such as equation 1 in model VII.

$$d = \alpha_0 + \alpha_1 p + \alpha_2 p^2 \qquad (1)$$

$$s = \beta_0 + \beta_1 p \qquad (2) \text{ VII}$$

$$s = d \qquad (3)$$

A NUMERICAL EXAMPLE

It will be simpler, and adequate for our purposes, to insert numerical values for the parameters, and to deal with a specific structure:

$$d = 100 - 20p + p^2 \qquad (4)$$

$$s = 5 + p \qquad (5) \text{ VIIA}$$

$$d = s \qquad (6)$$

The demand relation (equation 4) requires some examination. It will be recalled that the Schultz demand curve for sugar (equation 8, Chap. 2) was applicable only for a limited range of values of p and d. In model I, the values of p and q were not restricted beyond requiring that they both be positive and finite, though they could have been restricted further. Now we must consider further restrictions. A plotting[1] of equation 4 will reveal the fact that, when p is greater than 10, the slope of the curve is positive. This part of the curve can be excluded from our consideration by requiring $0 \le p \le 10$.

We may now solve our equations. First combine (5) and (6), eliminating variable s. Then combine this result with (4), getting a quadratic in p, which gives us two solutions. One of these solutions is ruled out by

[1] The student should look into some very elementary book on analytical geometry and practice the plotting of nonlinear functions.

We give an example: Consider the area of a rectangle whose length is l inches, and width w inches. Therefore the area of the rectangle is $w \times l$ square inches, and its perimeter is $2(w + l)$. Now suppose that for some reason we wish to keep the perimeter fixed:

$$2(w + l) = k$$

where k is some fixed numerical number, like 10. The area will be seen to vary as a function of the lengths of the sides, thus:

$$a = w \times l$$

But from the first equation above, we can derive:

$$w = \frac{k}{2} - l$$

and by substituting this into the second equation:

$$a = \left(\frac{k}{2} - l\right) l = \frac{k}{2} l - l^2$$

which expresses the area as a function of the length of one side. This function, plotted as in Fig. 1, is seen to be a parabola. The area becomes zero at two places:

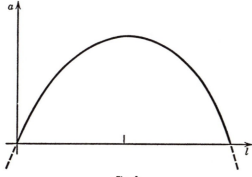

Fig. 1.

(1) where l becomes zero, and (2) where l becomes $k/2$. Half way between, i.e., where $l = k/4$, the area is a maximum value of $k^2/16$. The student should verify these computations by giving k the value of 10, working them all out, and plotting them.

Now it should be noted that the parabolic function itself does not stop at the l axis, but continues downward. This part of the function does not interest us, because the variable a represents the area of a rectangle that is conceived only in positive

our requirement that $p \leq 10$. A glance at Fig. 2 shows the part of the parabola (4) excluded, and the excluded intersection point. The valid solution of model VA thus becomes[2]

$$p = \frac{21 - \sqrt{61}}{2}$$

$$s = d = \frac{31 - \sqrt{61}}{2}$$

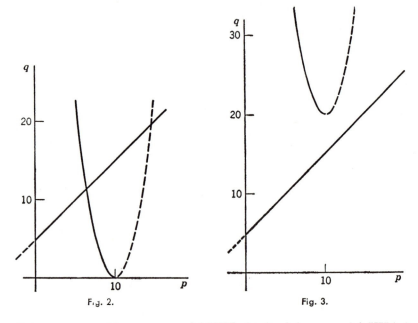

Fig. 2.   Fig. 3.

Let us now consider a new model VIII obtained from model VIIA by replacing the demand curve with the following:

$$d = 120 - 20p + p^2 \qquad (7) \quad \text{VIII}$$

There is now no real number that satisfies the equations of our model simultaneously. Geometrically the supply and demand curves do not meet. (See Fig. 3.)

---

units. Hence negative values for a are not allowed, and we might have written $a \geq 0$. From the diagram we can see that this implies that $0 \leq l \leq k/2$. Within these ranges the function serves us perfectly; outside these ranges the function is useless for the present problem.

[2] The student should not be frightened by a quantity such as $\sqrt{61}$ to which he cannot attach a simple integer. He can approach as closely as he wishes to it, such as 7.8, or 7.81, or 7.810, or 7.8102, etc. Technically, this is called an irrational number.

In such situations, when there is no real solution, mathematicians have resorted to a fiction: they assume that there is some kind of "number" that will give a "solution." By applying the usual formula for the solution of a quadratic equation, we get:

$$p = \frac{-b \pm (b^2 - 4ac)^{1/2}}{2a}$$

where $a = 1$, $b = -21$, $c = 115$. Therefore

$$p = \frac{21 \pm (441 - 460)^{1/2}}{2} = \frac{21 \pm \sqrt{-19}}{2}$$

We now face the difficulty that every real number, when squared, is a positive number. Hence there is no real number that can have a negative number like -19 for a square. Here is where the fiction enters. Let us suppose that there is some "number" which, when squared, gives us a negative number. In particular, let us define a number, which we may dub "imaginary,"

$$i = \sqrt{-1}$$

then

$$-19 = \sqrt{(-1)(19)} = \sqrt{-1} \cdot \sqrt{19} = i\sqrt{19}$$

and the "solution" becomes

$$p = \frac{21 \pm i\sqrt{19}}{2}$$

We thus have two solutions,

$$p_1 = \frac{21 + i\sqrt{19}}{2}$$

and

$$p_2 = \frac{21 - i\sqrt{19}}{2}$$

These are called complex numbers, because they have a real part, $21/2$, and an imaginary part $i\sqrt{19}/2$. We shall find, in a subsequent chapter, that the invention of an imaginary number, so as to give us some kind of "solution," will be of considerable benefit.

THE PROBLEM OF SOLUTIONS

Thus the introduction of nonlinearities into the model gives rise again to the two problems that we managed to control in the case of completely linear models: multiple solutions, on the one hand, and the lack of any real solution, on the other. They arise here for a very different reason—nonlinearity.

Let us be clear as to the significance of a solution. In terms of economics, the solved values form a set of equilibrium values of the variables. If a group of equations have no real solution, or a multiplicity of solutions, that is of very considerable importance.

If there were no real solution for a given economic model, it would imply either (a) the relations inadequately portray actual relations with the real world, or (b) the particular quantities and prices that exist in the real world must be the result of other causal factors not encompassed in the model; that is, sociological factors, such as the custom of "fair prices" which cause prices to remain relatively fixed, while institutional factors assist in the performance of the price functions of rationing and allocating the commodity. In either case the implications for economic theory are serious.

The implications of multiple solutions are not so serious. Multiple solutions have been illustrated by theorists on many occasions.[3] Some of the solutions can be ruled out because of the inappropriateness of the relations at those points, producing instability.[4] We might expect to have more than one respectable equilibrium point left; but this fits in quite well with some economic theories. It is possible that a substantial change in economic conditions might cause a shift from one equilibrium point to another. But the existence of many equilibrium points does not seem to be often envisaged by economic theorists.

We shall therefore search for equilibrium points that are real, plausible, and stable—and not too numerous.

MONOTONIC RELATIONS

Certain kinds of nonlinear relations give rise to single solutions. They are the single-valued functions, such as logarithms and reciprocals. These functions have not been given their due in economic theory, although logarithms have been much used in demand theory.[5] In fact, the usefulness of linear relations can be very much expanded if variables can be transformed so as to result in a set of completely linear relations.

[3] Leon Walras, *Elements of Pure Economics*, translated by William Jaffe (Homewood, Illinois, Irwin, 1954), Lesson 7.

[4] See below, page 55.

[5] H. Wold, *Demand Analysis*, p. 17, and R. Stone, *The Measurement of Consumers' Expenditure and Behavior in the United Kingdom, 1920–38* (Cambridge: At the University Press, 1954).

For example, if a variable X enters a set of relations always in the same way, as in logarithmic form, a new variable can be created by the following transformation:

$$X' = \log X \qquad (8)$$

so that the relations are linear in X'.

Let us consider the following nonlinear model:

$$d = \alpha_0 + \alpha_1 \log p \qquad (9)$$
$$s = \beta_0 + \beta_1 \log p \qquad (10) \qquad \text{IX}$$
$$d = s$$

which can be transformed to a linear model:

$$d = \alpha_0 + \alpha_1 p' \qquad (11)$$
$$s = \beta_0 + \beta_1 p' \qquad (12) \qquad \text{IXA}$$
$$d = s$$

Such a model, with proper values for the parameters, would appear somewhat as in Fig. 4.

It will be noted that these monotonic functions have slopes that never change sign. That is, if the slope is positive at any point, it remains positive throughout its length, and never becomes negative; if, on the other hand, it has a negative slope at any point, it has a negative slope throughout. Such functions do not turn back on themselves, as parabolas do.

If we had a logarithmic expression and a straight line, they could, of course, meet at two different places; but we were careful to state above that the variable in question, like the variable p above, *always* appears in the model in logarithmic form, and in no other way.

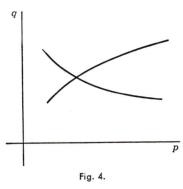

Fig. 4.

By a transformation we can then get rid of the logarithm, obtain a linear model, and apply the theory worked out above.

APPROXIMATIONS

A warning should be issued in regard to the use of approximations. When it is suspected that a relation is nonlinear, and, because of lack of adequate data and theoretical support, a linear relation is used as an approximation, care must be taken to assess the nature of the approximation in the area of interest.

For example, in macro models, the fact that the income figures in the nineteen-fifties have been extremely high implies that the upper reaches of some of the relations have been the relevant areas. Yet a linear approximation may "not fit well" in this extreme area, as seen in Fig. 5; and the greater the possible curvature in the "real" relationship, the greater the danger of error.

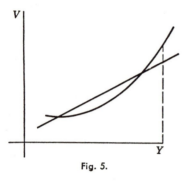

Fig. 5.

STABILITY

Some further attention must be given to the nature of equilibrium points. An equilibrium may be defined as a condition in which all the forces are in balance, and hence there is no tendency to move from that point. But such an equilibrium point may be stable or not, depending on the forces in the neighborhood of that point. Thus, a marble lying at the bottom of a hemispherical bowl is in *stable equilibrium* because, if it should be jarred a bit, it will tend to return to the same point of rest. It may not move directly, because it may overshoot the point, and then come back again, but the distances from the equilibrium point grow smaller and smaller until it comes to rest. Now, if the bowl is turned upside down and the marble placed on top, it might be possible to balance it so that it stays there; but a slight jar would send it rolling ever faster away from that equilibrium point. While balanced on top, it is in equilibrium, but it is an *unstable equilibrium*. Finally, a piece of chalk lying on a desk, if it is rolled a bit one way or the other, will tend to rest where it stops. It is in *neutral equilibrium*.

These physical concepts may be applied to our models. Consider a market with a demand curve of negative slope and a supply curve of positive slope. We say that an equilibrium exists where the quantity demanded equals the quantity supplied. Moreover, it is a stable equilibrium because, if we were to suppose a price p_1, higher than equilibrium price p_0, the amount supplied would tend to be greater than the amount demanded at that price, and the bidding in the market would tend to force the price down. Conversely, if we were to have a price p_2, less than p_0, the amount demanded would tend to exceed the amount supplied, and the price would be bid up (see Fig. 6).

Now consider a supply curve of negative slope, as in Fig. 8. An analysis similar to that just undertaken would show that the equilibrium point in this case is also stable. But, when the supply curve has a negative slope that is steeper[6] than the demand curve, we find that the point of equilibrium is an unstable one. We are inclined to conclude that the situation illustrated in Fig. 9 is most unusual.

These conclusions regarding the stability and instability of the equilibrium points are dependent upon the equilibrating process, and an alternative process has been proposed. It has been suggested that an

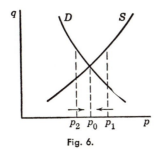

Fig. 6.

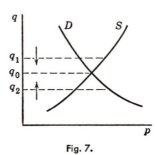

Fig. 7.

equilibrium exists when the demand price equals the supply price. According to this theory, if the demand price is greater than the supply price, there will be an expansion in output. If the demand price is less than the supply price, there will be a contraction in output. Applying

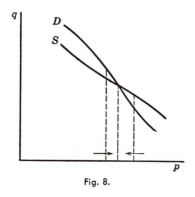

Fig. 8.

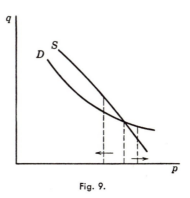

Fig. 9.

this theory to the "normal" Marshallian cross, we find that the equilibrium point is a stable one (see Fig. 7). However, applying it to the situations illustrated in Figs. 8 and 9, we find that the conclusions obtained previously are reversed. That is, in Fig. 8, where the demand

[6] With respect to the price axis.

curve is steeper[7] than the supply curve, the equilibrium point is found to be unstable; and in Fig. 9, where the demand curve is flatter[8] than the supply curve, the equilibrium point is found to be stable.

These apparently conflicting results have caused some economic theorists concern. However, it may be noted that price changes can be thought of as short-run changes, whereas changes in output require more time to accomplish, and hence each equilibrating theory is appropriate in its proper place.[9] An equilibrating price which equates amount demanded to amount supplied is appropriate to short-run markets. An equilibrating quantity that equates demand price and supply price is appropriate only for long-run supply and demand curves.

This discussion of the concept of stability illustrates the point that any separation of statics and dynamics is arbitrary, since any static model implies certain assumptions about adjustments, which is essentially a dynamic process. In the next chapter we consider dynamic models.

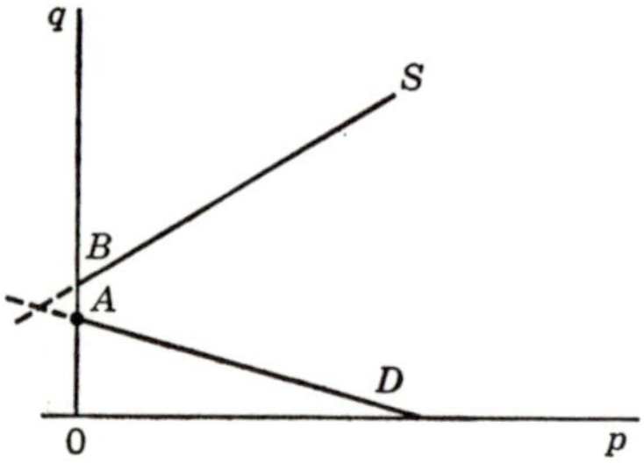

Fig. 10.

It is sometimes possible to have an equilibrium point in economic terms when there appears to be none in the mathematical terms just used. Consider the case illustrated in Fig. 10. In limiting ourselves to the first quadrant, there is no meeting point for the two straight lines. But this diagram can be thought of as illustrating the case of a free good. The real equilibrium point is at A. Hence the supply curve should be thought of as consisting of parts of two straight lines: a vertical line from the origin to B, and then the part of the line rising from B.

AN APPROACH TO KEYNESIAN THEORY

Hicks did a great service when he translated Keynes's model developed in *The General Theory of Employment, Interest and Money* into mathematical terms and contrasted it with other models.[10] His version is a

---

[7] With respect to the price axis.

[8] With respect to the price axis.

[9] E. F. Beach, "Market Theory of Walras and Marshall," *Jahrbücher für National-ökonomie und Statistik, 165:* 279–284.

[10] J. R. Hicks, "Mr. Keynes and the 'Classics': A Suggested Interpretation," *Econometrica, 5:* 147.

simple one in that only three equations are used, but the beginner may be puzzled because he uses a general expression for functional relations. In order to clarify the ideas, we begin by inserting parabolic (i.e., quadratic) functions as follows:

$$M = \kappa Y \tag{13}$$

$$I = \alpha_0 + \alpha_1 i + \alpha_2 i^2 \tag{14} \text{ X}$$

$$I = \beta_0 + \beta_1 i + \beta_2 i^2 + \gamma_1 Y + \gamma_2 Y^2 \tag{15}$$

Endogenous variables $\begin{cases} Y: & \text{Total income} \\ I: & \text{Investment} \\ i: & \text{Rate of interest} \end{cases}$

Exogenous variable $M:$ Quantity of money

The first equation (13) is a very simple one, showing M and Y to be proportional, κ being the factor of proportionality. The second equation (14) shows I as a quadratic function of i, somewhat like that illustrated in Fig. 11. This is the demand for capital. The third equation (15) shows the supply of capital for investment to be a function of two variables, i and Y, the relation being quadratic in each as in Fig. 12.

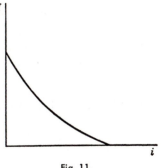

Fig. 11.

The nature of the relations in this model makes the problem of solving a relatively simple one. We can give a particular value to the exogenous variable M, and from equation 13 derive a value for Y which can be inserted in equation 15. We are thus left with two unknowns in two equations of no great difficulty; thus: Let M take on the specific value M_0. Then

$$Y = \frac{1}{\kappa} M_0$$

and from (15), we get

$$I = \beta_2 i^2 + \beta_1 i + \omega \tag{16}$$

where

$$\omega = \beta_0 + \frac{\gamma_1}{\kappa} M_0 + \frac{\gamma_2}{\kappa^2} M_0^2 \tag{17}$$

Combining this equation with (14), we eliminate I, getting a quadratic in i which has two roots. One of these roots is obviously inappropriate if the parts of the curves that interest us are those illustrated in the

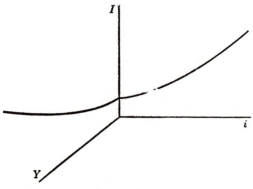

Fig. 12.

charts. The student should practice by substituting reasonable numerical values for the parameters and working out the solution. Hicks did not wish to be confined to a particular type of function such as a quadratic, and expressed the model in terms of general functions, as:

HICKS'S CLASSICAL MODEL

$$M = \kappa Y \tag{18}$$

$$I = C(i) \tag{19} \quad \text{XI}$$

$$I = S(i, Y) \tag{20}$$

The variables are as in model X. The first equation is identical with the corresponding one in model X. Equation 19 gives I as some function of (i) without specifying the nature other than indicating what general shape he expected it to have.[11] Equation 20 gives I as a general function of two variables, i and Y. Thus the supply of capital varies not only with i but also with Y, whereas the demand for capital depends only on i, and not on Y. This classical model is then contrasted with Hicks's version of Keynesian theory in the following section.

[11] See his charts on p. 153.

HICKS'S KEYNESIAN MODEL

$$M = L(i, Y) \tag{21}$$

$$I = C(i) \tag{19} \quad \text{XII}$$

$$I = S(Y) \tag{22}$$

The second equation of this model is the same as the corresponding equation in the classical model, but the other two are different. In equation 21 the supply of money is shown to be related to both i and Y through the "liquidity function." In the third equation (22), savings are seen to depend on Y alone, i playing no part. In this way Hicks points up sharply Keynes's contributions. Once the theory has been set up in this fashion, a more general model suggested itself to Hicks, as follows:

HICKS'S GENERAL MODEL

$$M = L(i, Y) \tag{21}$$

$$I = C(i, Y) \tag{23} \quad \text{XIII}$$

$$I = S(i, Y) \tag{20}$$

Here the variables i and Y are involved in each of the equations. When the theory has been set up in this more general fashion, the question then naturally arises: Why should there be the restrictions indicated by the two more limited models? Theorists are thus moved to examine the nature of those special theories. But we are not here primarily interested in economic theory as such, and this discussion of Hicks's models is concluded with the remark that any one of these models could be expanded to include four more equations in four more endogenous variables, and one more exogenous variable, as Hicks suggests:

$$I = wx \left(\frac{dN_x}{dx} \right) \tag{24}$$

$$Y = wx \left(\frac{dN_x}{dx} \right) + wy \left(\frac{dN_y}{dy} \right) \tag{25}$$

$$\text{XIV}$$

$$x = f_x(N_x) \tag{26}$$

$$y = f_y(N_y) \tag{27}$$

$$\text{Endogenous variables} \begin{cases} x: & \text{Output of investment goods} \\ y: & \text{Output of consumption goods} \\ N_x: & \text{Number of men producing investment} \\ & \text{goods} \\ N_y: & \text{Number of men producing consumption} \\ & \text{goods} \end{cases}$$

Exogenous variable w: Rate of money wages per head

Equation 26 states that x is some given function of N_x, the function, whether quadratic, logarithmic, or some other, indicated by f_x. Similarly, equation 27 states that f_y is some function of N_y. In equation 24, dN_x/dx is the derivative of the variable N_x with respect to x, and hence is the number of workmen required for an additional unit of output. Multiplying this by the wage rate, we get $w(dN_x/dx)$, the marginal cost of a unit of output of investment goods. When this marginal cost is multiplied by the number of units of investment goods x, we get, of course, total investment I. Equation 25 is derived similarly.

A number of economic theorists have attempted to devise models of the whole economy. J. E. Meade has set up one of ten equations and six exogenous variables.[12] He is, however, not quite clear about some of these, and he has little interest in a solution. A. C. Pigou has set up a model of eight equations and one exogenous variable, which he proceeds to condense to a four-equation model.[13] Pigou's models are, however, unsatisfactory for reasons additional to those discussed by Tsiang.[14] A study of these models by Meade and Pigou suggests that students would be assisted very much, and authors would be protected against vagueness and even mistakes, if they were more careful to lay out models in specific terms.

MODIGLIANI MODEL

One of the finest illustrations of good model building and using is that of F. Modigliani.[15] The following equations are laid out:

---

[12] *Review of Economic Studies*, Vol. 4 (1936), and *The New Economics*, S. E. Harris, ed. (New York, Knopf, 1947), Chap. XLII.

[13] *Employment and Equilibrium* (London, Macmillan, 1941).

[14] Sho-Chien Tsiang, *The Variations of Real Wages and Profit Margins in Relation to the Trade Cycle* (London, Pitman, 1947).

[15] "Liquidity Preference and the Theory of Interest and Money," *Econometrica*, *12*: 45–88.

$$M = L(r, y) \qquad (28)$$

Endogenous variables

$$M = kY \qquad (29)$$

Y: Money income

$$I = I(r, Y) \qquad (30)$$

r: Rate of interest

$$S = S(r, Y) \qquad (31)$$

S: Saving

$$S = I \qquad (32)$$

I: Investment

$$Y \equiv PX \qquad (33)$$

P: Price level

$$X = X(N) \qquad (34)$$

N: Aggregate employment

$$W = X'(N)P \qquad (35)$$

W: Money wage rate

$$C \equiv Y - I \qquad (36)$$

X: An index of physical output

$$N = F\left(\frac{W}{P}\right) \qquad (37)$$

C: Consumption

Exogenous variable

$$W = \alpha W_0 + \beta F^{-1}(N) \cdot P \qquad (38)$$

M: Quantity of money in system

$$\alpha = 1, \quad \beta = 0 \quad \text{for} \quad N \leqq N_0$$

$$\alpha = 0, \quad \beta = 1 \quad \text{for} \quad N > N_0$$

where N_0 is said to be "full employment."

F^{-1} is the inverse of function F in (37).[16]

From these equations Modigliani sets up three different models:

Model XV, a Keynesian system, consisting of equations 28 to 38, excluding equations 29 and 37.

Model XVI, a "crude classical" system, consisting of equations 29 instead of 28 and 37 instead of 38.

Model XVII, a "generalized classical" system, omitting equations 29 and 38, but including equations 28 and 37.

In each model there are nine equations in nine endogenous variables and one exogenous variable. Under proper conditions it can be assumed that there is a single solution. It may be noted that equations 28, 30, 31, and 32 contain only four endogenous variables, and thus form a determinate system. This subset is indeed the same as Hicks's generalized model.

The remaining equations should be compared carefully with the four supplementary equations added to the Hicks's models. The

---

[16] I.e., if $N = F(W/P)$, then $W/P = F^{-1}(N)$, as, for example, if $y = x^2$, then $x = \sqrt{y}$.

Modigliani models are more truly macro models with the price level appearing explicitly.

It should be noted that we have differentiated between an equation (=) and an identity(≡).[17] Equation 36 in the Modigliani model is an identity. That is, C is always equal to $Y - I$ by definition, and no inequality can be envisaged. Equation 35, on the other hand, is an equality assumed to hold under certain conditions of competition. Equation 32 can be considered an equilibrium condition for the model. Equation 33 is an identity, or better, a definition of P, and might be written as

$$P \equiv \frac{Y}{X} \tag{39}$$

But there is another problem of units in connection with this equation (33). Y is presumably measured in billions of dollars. P and X are indexes. It would seem to be preferable to write the equation

$$Y \equiv \gamma PX \tag{40}$$

with γ a constant inserted to make the units come out right.

Another question arises as a result of the fact that P and X are index numbers. Quite apart from the impossibility of having completely accurate index measurements with the vast variety of commodities, there is the question of the base of the index numbers. Apparently the base of the quantity index number X is fixed in the function of equation 34. If equation 33 is now seen to be the definition of P, the base of this index number will then be the same as that for X.

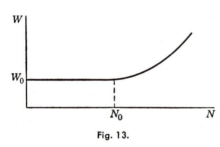

Fig. 13.

Finally the peculiar nature of equation 38 may be noted. It is illustrated in Fig. 13 for a fixed value of P. It is essentially two equations, as follows: For $N \leq N_0$,

$$W = W_0$$

For $N > N_0$,

$$W = F^{-1}(N) \cdot P$$

or

$$\frac{W}{P} = F^{-1}(N)$$

[17] J. Marschak, "Identity and Stability in Economics: A Survey," *Econometrica*, *10:* 61–74.

COMMENTS

It will be noticed that the authors quoted here are not very much interested in solutions of their models. They are usually careful to see that the number of equations just equals the number of endogenous variables, and their relations are monotonic, so that a single solution is generally assured. These authors are much more interested in the nature of the relationships—which variables are directly related, and what are the approximate shapes of the functions. In other words, it is the nature of the model that is their prime concern. Much work remains to be done in establishing proper relationships.

EXERCISES

1. Write out the general algebraic solution for model **VII**.
2. Suppose the supply equation in model **VIIA** is replaced by $s = \frac{1}{2}p^2$. Find the solution, and plot the curves.
3. In model **IX**, let

$$\alpha_0 = 3, \qquad \beta_0 = 0$$
$$\alpha_1 = -2, \qquad \beta_1 = 3$$

Solve and chart.

4. Consider the following model:

$$d_1 = \alpha_0 + \alpha_1 p_1' + \alpha_2 p_2'$$
$$d_2 = \beta_0 + \beta_1 p_1' + \beta_2 p_2'$$
$$s_1 = \gamma_0 + \gamma_1 p_1' + \gamma_2 p_2'$$
$$s_2 = \delta_0 + \delta_1 p_1' + \delta_2 p_2'$$
$$s_1 = d_1$$
$$s_2 = d_2$$

where $p_1' = \log p_1$ and $p_2' = +\sqrt{p_2}$. Solve in general, assign plausible values to the parameters, and chart.

5. Construct an appropriate model from Hans Neisser, "The New Economics of Spending: A Theoretical Analysis," *Econometrica*, 1944, pp. 237–255.

READINGS

1. J. R. Hicks, "Mr. Keynes and the 'Classics'; A Suggested Interpretation," *Econometrica*, April 1937.
2. Franco Modigliani, "Liquidity Preference and the Theory of Interest and Money," *Econometrica*, January 1944.

3. J. E. Meade, "A Simplified Model of the Keynes' System," *Review of Economic Studies*, Vol. 4 (1936).

4. O. Lange, "The Rate of Interest and the Optimum Propensity to Consume," *Economica*, New series, Vol. 5 (1938).

5. L. R. Klein, *The Keynesian Revolution* (New York, Macmillan, 1947).

6. L. R. Klein, "Theories of Effective Demand and Employment," *Journal of Political Economy*, Vol. 55 (1947).

7. G. Lutfalla, "La querelle des classiques et modernes," *Revue d'économique politique*, Vol. 57 (1947).

8. G. Tintner, "Static Macro-economic Models and Their Econometric Verifications," *Metroeconomica*, Vol. 1 (1949).

9. S. E. Harris, ed., *The New Economics* (New York, Knopf, 1948).

10. A. C. Pigou, "Real and Money Wage Rates in Relation to Unemployment," *Economic Journal*, September 1937.

11. A. C. Pigou, *Employment and Equilibrium* (London, Macmillan, 1941).

12. Sho-Chien Tsiang, "Professor Pigou on the Relative Movements of Real Wages and Employment," *Economic Journal*, December 1944.

13. Sho-Chien Tsiang, *The Variations of Real Wages and Profit Margins in Relation to the Trade Cycle* (London, Pitman, 1947).

14. A. C. Harberger, "Pitfalls in Mathematical Model Building," *American Economic Review*, December 1952.

CHAPTER 5

Continuous Dynamic Models

The models so far considered are static; that is, time plays no explicit part.[1] We must now consider dynamic models in which time enters explicitly. Other definitions of dynamic models have been given elsewhere,[2] but the simple one given here is adequate for our purposes, and in accordance with most lay discussions. We proceed to two different kinds of dynamic models, those involving differential equations, which we consider in this chapter, and those involving difference equations, which will be considered in the next chapter. To a large extent, these two approaches are alternatives. In the former case, the variables are thought of as changing continuously through time, with observations being taken at *certain points of time.* The mathematical techniques used here are borrowed from the realm of physics, where they have been of very great use. In the second case, we have finite difference equations. We deal in this second case with quantities that are relevant to certain *time periods.* By shortening the time periods, we can, of course, approach the situation of the continuous variables. Economic data are presented in a form more suitable to the second method, yet no other discipline has made great use of this technique.[3] Actuaries have developed some complicated formulas for smoothing series; but they are less interested than we in solving the corresponding equations.

[1] Time may enter implicitly as an assumed period relevant to the quantities considered. See, for example, A. C. Pigou, *Employment and Equilibrium* (London, Macmillan, 1941), Part I, Chap. IV, "The Meaning of Flow Equilibrium."

[2] J. R. Hicks, *The Trade Cycle* (Oxford: At the Clarendon Press, 1950), and W. J. Baumol, *Economic Dynamics* (New York, Macmillan, 1951), especially the Introduction.

[3] Samuelson found it necessary to compile a summary treatment himself. See his *Foundations of Economic Analysis* (Cambridge, Harvard University Press, 1947).

SOME SIMPLE MODELS

It is assumed here that the reader is familiar with the concept of a derivative or slope, but, to refresh his memory, some simple examples are taken from economic theory. First, consider a total revenue function:

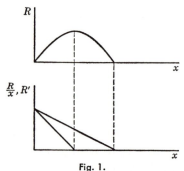

Fig. 1.

$$R = \alpha x^2 + \beta x \qquad (1)$$

where x represents the quantity of the commodity sold, and R the total revenue. Then the marginal revenue is

$$R' = \frac{dR}{dx} = 2\alpha x + \beta \qquad (2)$$

$$\alpha < 0, \qquad \beta > 0$$

Now, if we were given the marginal revenue function, the total revenue curve could be ascertained. Note that this is not simply a matter of using integration, which would give us

$$\int R' \, dx = \int (2\alpha x + \beta) \, dx = \alpha x^2 + \beta x + \gamma \qquad (3)$$

It is necessary to keep in mind the further condition that the total revenue curve passes through the origin; i.e., that, when x is zero, R is zero, and therefore $\gamma = 0$.

Equation 2 is called a "differential equation" of a very simple type, and its solution is equation 3.

As another example of a simple differential equation, consider the marginal cost function:

$$C' = \alpha x^2 + \beta x + \gamma \qquad (4).$$

Integration gives us

$$C = \frac{\alpha}{3} x^3 + \frac{\beta}{2} x^2 + \gamma x + \delta \qquad (5)$$

If we do not have any additional information about fixed costs, we cannot determine a specific value for δ. In a long-run cost function or "planning" cost function, of course, $\delta = 0$.[4]

---

[4] E. F. Beach, "The Use of Polynomials to Represent Cost Functions," *Review of Economic Studies*, XVI (3), No. 41: 158–169.

A SIMPLE DYNAMIC MODEL

In the two examples just discussed, the independent variable was quantity or output. We wish now to use time as the independent variable, and thus derive differential coefficients with respect to time. Since this time differential lies at the heart of our present concept of dynamics, it is wise to explore the concept thoroughly. It will help us if we use a very simple example from physics.

Let s be the distance traveled by a particle from some starting point. Then velocity is defined by ds/dt or the rate of change of distance with respect to time. Acceleration is defined as the rate of change of velocity with respect to time. Thus

$$v \equiv \frac{ds}{dt} \tag{6}$$

$$a \equiv \frac{dv}{dt} = \frac{d^2s}{dt^2} \tag{7}$$

where d^2s/dt^2 is the second derivative of s with respect to time. Let us suppose now that a particle is subject to a constant acceleration g. This would be the situation of a particle falling through space under the influence of the gravity of the earth.[5] Thus

$$\frac{d^2s}{dt^2} = g \tag{8}$$

Integrating, we find

$$\frac{ds}{dt} = \int g \, dt + c_1 = gt + c_1 \tag{9}$$

Integrating again, we find

$$\begin{aligned} s &= \int gt \, dt + \int c_1 \, dt + c_2 \\ &= \tfrac{1}{2}gt^2 + c_1 t + c_2 \end{aligned} \tag{10}$$

Thus, under the assumption that the acceleration of a particle is constant, the distance traveled is found to be a function of time, involving two arbitrary constants, c_1 and c_2. These constants are called arbitrary because they can have any constant value, and this function will satisfy the original condition that acceleration is constant.

If we care to specify the original conditions further, specific values can be assigned to these constants.[6] Let us assume that the particle

[5] H. B. Phillips, *Calculus* (New York, Wiley, 1927), Chap. IV.
[6] These are called "initial conditions."

started from rest at time $t = 0$. When $s = 0$, then $v = 0$. But

$$v = \frac{ds}{dt} = gt + c_1$$

so that

$$v(0) = 0 + c_1$$

Thus,

$$c_1 = 0$$

Similarly,

$$s(0) = \tfrac{1}{2}(0) + 0 + c_2$$

so that

$$c_2 = 0$$

From these conditions, which might be written:

$$a = g, \quad v_0 = 0, \quad s_0 = 0 \tag{11}$$

we find that

$$s = \tfrac{1}{2}gt^2$$

which is the solution of the problem.

A SCHULTZ MODEL

A simple dynamic model in economics is obtained when a trend factor is added to an otherwise static relation. Henry Schultz found trend factors in his demand relations. Consider the following model, using one of his demand formulas:

$$d = \alpha_0 + \alpha_1 p + \alpha_2 t \tag{12}$$

$$s = \beta_0 + \beta_1 p + \beta_2 r \tag{13} \text{ XVIII}$$

$$d = s \tag{14}$$

where t and r are exogenous variables.

The equilibrium values are found to be functions of time, as

$$p = \frac{\beta_0 - \alpha_0}{\alpha_1 - \beta_1} + \frac{\beta_2}{\alpha_1 - \beta_1} r - \frac{\alpha_2}{\alpha_1 - \beta_1} t \tag{15}$$

$$d = s = \frac{\alpha_1 \beta_0 - \alpha_0 \beta_1}{\alpha_1 - \beta_1} + \frac{\alpha_1 \beta_2}{\alpha_1 - \beta_1} r - \frac{\alpha_2 \beta_1}{\alpha_1 - \beta_1} t \tag{16}$$

In this simple model, the time variable t is treated like any other exogenous variable in the models previously considered. Hence the equilibrium value of each of the endogenous variables will be expressed as a function of time. In this particular model, all of them are linear functions of time. It is necessary for us to indicate some time origin at which $t = 0$ (for the Schultz demand relations considered above, the origin was July 1, 1885) and to indicate whether t is expressed in years, months, or some other unit.

DYNAMIC MODELS

We turn now to models in which the time variable t plays a rather different part. All the endogenous variables vary over time, and are thus expressed as functions of time. Here time is an independent variable of special importance. In drawing up the model, these functions are expressed in general terms, and our task is that of finding the specific functions, i.e., finding out precisely how they vary over time. The equations of the model express relationships among the variables. From the equations we find a differential equation in a single variable and its derivative, which must be solved. Many of these differential equations are quite simple, and the solving of them presents no great problems. Special procedures have been developed and can be found in any textbook on differential equations. With a little practice the beginner can handle the simpler equations. But some of these differential equations are very difficult to handle, and special training in mathematics is required. The problem is to find an expression that will satisfy the differential equation in hand; and frequently the procedure is simply to try something that one feels might work.

DOMAR MACRO MODEL

Consider the model

$$S(t) = \alpha Y(t) \qquad (17)$$

$$I(t) = \beta Y'(t) \qquad (18) \quad \text{XIX}$$

$$S(t) = I(t) \qquad (19)$$

$$\alpha > 0, \qquad \beta > 0$$

where S is saving, I is investment, and Y is income. Y' is, of course, dY/dt. All variables are functions of time; they are so indicated in the model, but, for brevity, the t will be omitted frequently in the discussion. The fact that these variables are functions of time implies that time is a special variable here. The endogenous variables S, I, and Y are rates of flow, not necessarily different from the variables of the previous chapter, except that we are interested in the particular way in which they vary continuously with time. Clearly time has become a more essential part of the model.

The first equation states that saving is a fixed proportion of income; the second states that investment varies as the rate of change of income over time.

Because of the rates of change involved here, the full solution of the model is a much more complicated affair than it was in ordinary equations. We proceed in three steps, the first of which is to combine (i.e., solve) the three equations to get

$$Y' - \frac{\alpha}{\beta} Y = 0 \qquad (20)$$

This is a first-order homogeneous differential equation with a constant coefficient. It is a differential equation merely because it involves a derivative, Y'; it is homogeneous because there is no constant term; it is of the first order because the highest order of any derivative appearing in it is 1; and the coefficient $(-\alpha/\beta)$ is a constant value. In dealing with linear equations in previous models, an equation in one unknown was the end product, called the solution for that variable. Here it is not so. Actually, we have two equations in two unknowns.[7]

$$X - \lambda Y = 0 \qquad (21)$$

$$X - Y' = 0 \qquad (22)$$

The solution is therefore not yet complete. The next step requires the methods of calculus. It is known[8] from elementary calculus that

$$\frac{d}{dt} ae^{bt} = bae^{bt} \qquad (23)$$

Hence it is reasonable to try the substitution[9] $Y = ae^{bt}$, which implies

$$Y' = bae^{bt} \qquad (24)$$

---

[7] And thus, the original model consisted of four equations in four unknowns.

[8] The constant e is a very important one in mathematics. The function $y = e^x$ is unique in that it is its own derivative. When $x = 0$, $y = 1$. As x increases in the positive direction, y increases ever more rapidly. As x moves in the negative direction, y approaches zero.

[9] As an alternative, we might try $Y = e^{bt}$, involving only one extra constant, b. Differentiating, we find $Y' = be^{bt}$. Substituting in our differential equation, we get $be^{bt} - (\alpha/\beta)e^{bt} = 0$. Hence $Y = e^{bt}$ is suitable if $b = \alpha/\beta$; i.e., $Y = \exp\left(\frac{\alpha}{\beta} t\right)$ is a solution. But a little thought suggests that we might get a more general solution by using $Y = ae^{bt}$, as above, since the solution we have obtained here, $Y = \exp\left(\frac{\alpha}{\beta} t\right)$, requires Y_0 to be equal to 1.

getting

$$bae^{bt} - \frac{\alpha}{\beta} ae^{bt} = 0 \qquad (25)$$

$$\left(b - \frac{\alpha}{\beta}\right) ae^{bt} = 0 \qquad (26)$$

Assuming that a is a constant, not zero, this implies that

$$b - \frac{\alpha}{\beta} = 0, \quad b = \frac{\alpha}{\beta} \qquad (27)$$

Thus it is found that

$$Y = a \exp\left(\frac{\alpha}{\beta} t\right) \qquad (28)$$

is consistent with our differential solution, and hence is a solution of it.[10]
Testing this solution, we substitute this value for Y into (20)

$$\frac{\alpha}{\beta} a \exp\left(\frac{\alpha}{\beta} t\right) - \frac{\alpha}{\beta} Y = 0 \qquad (29)$$

which is correct. Hence it is certain that (28) is a solution. A further knowledge of calculus would tell us that there is no other solution. But an extra constant, a, has been introduced into the picture. This is an "arbitrary" constant, that is, one that can be given any numerical value that we wish, and the system will conform to the equation originally set down, i.e. (17), (18), and (19). We may, however, specify a particular value for a if we introduce another condition, called an initial condition, in stating a specific value for Y, say Y_0, at some point

---

[10] Some may prefer the following approach: the differential equation $Y' - (\alpha/\beta)Y = 0$ may be written as

$$\frac{1}{Y} \frac{dY}{dt} = \frac{\alpha}{\beta}$$

Integrating both sides, we find

$$\int \frac{dY}{Y} = \int \frac{\alpha}{\beta} dt$$

$$\log Y = \frac{\alpha}{\beta} t + c$$

$$Y = a \exp\left(\frac{\alpha}{\beta} t\right)$$

where

$$a = \log c$$

of time called zero time.   Then

$$Y_0 = ae^0 = a \qquad (30)$$

The final solution thus becomes

$$Y = Y_0 \exp\left(\frac{\alpha}{\beta} t\right) \qquad (31)$$

It should be noted that this solution is not a fixed value, as in static models.   It is a certain path over time specified by the constants originally introduced into the model.   Here both constants are positive, so that the path is a curved line with positive slope, increasing ever more rapidly from the initial starting point.   The rapidity of the increase will depend on the value of the ratio α/β.

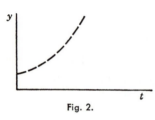

Fig. 2.

Reviewing the procedure for solving a dynamic model involving rates of change, we recall that there are three steps:

(1) Solving the original set of equations to get a differential equation, that is, an equation involving a single variable and its derivatives.

(2) Solving the differential equation to obtain an expression for the variable in terms of t.   This expression will usually involve some arbitrary constants, which we should particularize in the third step by

(3) Introducing some initial conditions, that is, stated values of some of the variables at a certain point of time.   These initial conditions could have been stated as part of the original model, so that all the necessary information is contained in the equations of the model.[11]   This procedure will be adopted in the next example.

In the meantime, solutions should be found for the remaining variables of the model.   In the present case, it is very simple:

$$I(t) = S(t) = \alpha Y(t) = \alpha Y_0 \exp\left(\frac{\alpha}{\beta} t\right)$$

DOMAR DEBT MODELS

Domar uses a set of models somewhat like the one just examined in order to explore the relations between national income and national debt.

[11] It may be noted that these initial conditions are somewhat like exogenous variables.

Consider the model

$$D'(t) = \alpha Y(t) \qquad (32)$$

$$Y'(t) = \beta \qquad (33)$$

$$Y(0) = Y_0 \qquad (34) \qquad \text{XX}$$

$$D(0) = D_0 \qquad (35)$$

$$\alpha > 0, \qquad \beta > 0$$

In this model the national income increases at a constant rate β per unit of time and the rate of increase of the national debt D' is a fixed proportion of the national income. The third and fourth equations give initial conditions.

Step 1. Differentiating the first equation with respect to time, and substituting from the second equation, we get

$$D''(t) - \alpha\beta = 0 \qquad (36)$$

This is a second-order nonhomogeneous differential equation with constant coefficients. It is nonhomogeneous because there is a constant term $\alpha\beta$ involving no variable. This equation happens to be a very simple one, and can be solved directly by integrating twice.

Step 2.

$$D'(t) = \int \alpha\beta \, dt + a = \alpha\beta t + a \qquad (37)$$

$$D(t) = \int \alpha\beta t \, dt + \int a \, dt + b \qquad (38)$$

$$= \tfrac{1}{2}\alpha\beta t^2 + at + b \qquad (39)$$

Step 3. Introducing the initial condition that, at time zero, the national debt was D_0,

$$D(0) = \tfrac{1}{2}\alpha\beta(0) + a(0) + b \qquad (40)$$

so that

$$D_0 = b \qquad (41)$$

and

$$D(t) = \tfrac{1}{2}\alpha\beta t^2 + at + D_0 \qquad (42)$$

Now, from equations 32 and 34 we find that

$$D'(0) = \alpha Y_0 \qquad (43)$$

But from (42):

$$D'(0) = \alpha\beta(0) + a \qquad (44)$$

Therefore

$$a = \alpha Y_0 \qquad (45)$$

and the final solution for D is

$$D(t) = \tfrac{1}{2}\alpha\beta t^2 + \alpha Y_0 t + D_0 \qquad (46)$$

The final solution for Y is obtained directly by integrating and inserting the initial condition (34), getting

$$Y(t) = \beta t + Y_0 \tag{47}$$

The model is now completely solved, and the nature of the time paths of these variables can be explored. But Domar was interested in the ratio of debt to income

$$\frac{D(t)}{Y(t)} = \frac{\frac{1}{2}\alpha\beta t^2 + \alpha Y_0 t + D_0}{\beta t + Y_0} \tag{48}$$

$$= \frac{D_0}{\beta t + Y_0} + \frac{\alpha Y_0 t}{\beta t + Y_0} + \frac{\frac{1}{2}\alpha\beta t^2}{\beta t + Y_0} \tag{49}$$

As t increases without limit, the first fraction tends toward zero, the second fraction tends to approach a constant, and the third fraction increases without limit (i.e., tends toward $+\infty$). These results can be seen by dividing both numerator and denominator by t, which leaves the value of each respective fraction unchanged. We find therefore that the ratio of debt to income in this particular model tends over time to increase without limit.

A SECOND DOMAR DEBT MODEL

Consider now another version of the Domar debt model obtained by modifying the second equation so that income may increase by a constant percentage:

$$D'(t) = \alpha Y(t) \tag{50}$$

$$Y'(t) = \beta Y(t) \tag{51}$$

$$Y(0) = Y_0 \tag{52} \quad \textbf{XXI}$$

$$D(0) = D_0 \tag{53}$$

$$\alpha > 0, \qquad \beta > 0 \tag{54}$$

The solving of this model is a somewhat difficult matter, but the relations are essentially simple, and we shall apply simple procedures, combining steps 1 and 2. Considering the second equation alone, its nature suggests that we try substituting the following value for $Y(t)$: $Y(t) = ae^{bt}$, so that

$$Y'(t) = bae^{bt} \tag{55}$$

Substituting these values in (51), we find that

$$b = \beta \tag{56}$$

and therefore

$$Y(t) = ae^{\beta t} \tag{57}$$

is suitable. Now, using (52), we find that

$$a = Y_0$$

and hence

$$Y(t) = Y_0 e^{\beta t} \tag{58}$$

This is a solution for $Y(t)$. Now solve for $D(t)$. Substituting this in (50), we get

$$D'(t) = \alpha Y_0 e^{\beta t} \tag{59}$$

Integrating, we find

$$D(t) = \frac{\alpha}{\beta} Y_0 e^{\beta t} + c \tag{60}$$

Introducing (53):

$$D_0 = \frac{\alpha}{\beta} Y_0 + c \tag{61}$$

so that

$$c = D_0 - \frac{\alpha}{\beta} Y_0 \tag{62}$$

Hence the final solution for $D(t)$ is:

$$D(t) = D_0 - \frac{\alpha}{\beta} Y_0 + \frac{\alpha}{\beta} Y_0 e^{\beta t} \tag{63}$$

$$= D_0 + \frac{\alpha}{\beta} Y_0 (e^{\beta t} - 1) \tag{64}$$

And, considering the ratio of debt to income:

$$\frac{D(t)}{Y(t)} = \frac{D_0}{Y_0 e^{\beta t}} + \frac{\alpha}{\beta} \left(1 - \frac{1}{e^{\beta t}} \right) \tag{65}$$

As t increases, the first fraction tends to vanish, and the second approaches a limit α/β. Thus, as Domar found, when the debt increases as a constant proportion of income, if the ratio of debt to income is not to increase indefinitely (as in the previous model), income must increase geometrically.

EVANS PRICE ADJUSTMENT MODEL[12]

$$d = \alpha_0 + \alpha_1 p \qquad (66)$$

$$s = \beta_0 + \beta_1 p \qquad (67) \quad \text{XXII}$$

$$\frac{dp}{dt} = \gamma(d - s) \qquad (68)$$

$$\alpha_1 < 0, \qquad \beta_1 > 0, \qquad \gamma > 0$$

where d, s, and p are functions of time.

This is a model of a particular market for some commodity. The demand and supply equations are the same as those that we have used above in model I. The innovation here is equation 68, which states that the rate of change of price over time is proportional to the excess demand $(d - s)$. The factor of proportionality γ being positive implies that a positive excess demand causes a rise in price, and a negative excess causes a fall.

Substituting from the first two equations into the third, we find

$$\frac{dp}{dt} = \gamma\{\alpha_0 - \beta_0 + (\alpha_1 - \beta_1)p\} \qquad (69)$$

$$= \gamma(\alpha_1 - \beta_1)(p - p_e) = \lambda(p - p_e) \qquad (70)$$

where $p_e = (\alpha_0 - \beta_0)/(\beta_1 - \alpha_1)$ the equilibrium price in the model, and $\lambda = \gamma(\alpha_1 - \beta_1)$.

This is a nonhomogeneous differential equation, and will be discussed in more detail below; but its simplicity lends itself to a useful trick used by Allen:[13] Introduce a new variable

$$v(t) = p(t) - p_e \qquad (71)$$

Then, differentiating, we find

$$v'(t) = p'(t) = \lambda\{p(t) - p_e\} \qquad (72)$$

and

$$\frac{v'(t)}{v(t)} = \frac{\lambda\{p(t) - p_e\}}{p(t) - p_e} = \lambda$$

[12] G. C. Evans, *Mathematical Introduction to Economics* (New York, McGraw-Hill, 1930), p. 48.

[13] R. G. D. Allen, *Mathematical Analysis for Economists* (London, Macmillan, 1947), p. 436.

Now we have the differential equation

$$\frac{1}{v(t)} \frac{dv(t)}{dt} = \lambda \tag{73}$$

and, proceeding as in the previous models, the integral is found to be $v(t) = Ae^{\lambda t}$ and thus $p(t) = p_e + Ae^{\lambda t}$. Now, at time $t = 0$, where $p(0) = p_0$, it is found that

$$A = p_0 - p_e$$

so that

$$p(t) = p_e + (p_0 - p_e)e^{\lambda t} \tag{74}$$

where p_e and λ are as above.

In this case, $\lambda < 0$, so that the price tends over time to approach its equilibrium value.[14]

MARKET STABILITY

The short-run market model I may be re-written as follows:

$$q_D = \alpha_0 + \alpha_1 p \tag{75}$$

$$q_S = \beta_0 + \beta_1 p \tag{76} \text{ model I}'$$

$$q_D = q_S \tag{77}$$

The equilibrium values of the variables are found to be:

$$p_e = \frac{\alpha_0 - \beta_0}{\beta_1 - \alpha_1} ; \qquad q_e = \frac{\beta_1 \alpha_0 - \alpha_1 \beta_0}{\beta_1 - \alpha_1} \tag{78}$$

This model does not tell us how this equilibrium point is attained, and hence has limited usefulness. Model XXII now fills this gap. Equation 68 represents an equilibrating force tending to move price towards the equilibrium price if λ is negative, which is true when $\gamma > 0$, $\alpha_1 < 0$, and $\beta_1 > 0$. This may be called the normal case; but other conditions should be considered. Economic theory allows the possibility of a positive-sloped demand curve under some circum-

---

[14] A more general formulation of this adjustment process for nonlinear supply and demand relations is given by Samuelson (*Foundations*, p. 263) as follows:

$$p(t) = p_e + (p_0 - p_e) \exp \theta (D_p{}^e - S_p{}^e)t$$

where $D_p{}^e$ is the slope of the demand curve with respect to the p axis at the equilibrium point, $S_p{}^e$ is the slope of the supply curve at the equilibrium point, and θ is a positive constant, indicating the first derivative, at the equilibrium point, of the adjusting function H in $dp/dt = H(d - s)$. For our linear demand and supply equations, $D_p{}^e = \alpha$, $S_p{}^e = \beta$, and $\theta = \gamma$.

stances, as in the case of an inferior good, so that α_1 might be positive. The model is still stable so long as the numerical value of α_1 is less than the numerical value of β_1, because then λ is still negative. Thus the model remains stable if the demand line is flatter (with respect to the p axis) than the supply line. But the model is unstable if the supply line is the flatter one (with respect to the p axis), because then $\lambda > 0$ and the price tends to move away from the equilibrium price.

We should also consider the situation when both lines have negative slopes, since economic theory allows this possibility as well. The supply curve of a factor of production may bend backward. The details are left to the student to work out. The result is that the model is stable if the supply line is the flatter one (with respect to the p axis) and unstable in the reverse case.

In summary, we find therefore, that the short-run market will be unstable, if equation 68 is an adequate approximation of the bidding processes in a short-run market, only in three cases: (a) when both lines have negative slopes and the demand curve is flatter than the supply curve with respect to the p axis; (b) when both lines have positive slopes and the supply line is flatter with respect to the p axis; and (c) when the supply line has a negative slope and the demand line has a positive slope. The student should consider the realities of these three cases by thinking out their probabilities (which we think are small) and the results (the price is driven to another point of equilibrium which may exist when the lines are not straight throughout their lengths; sometimes that price is zero; sometimes the industry is wiped out).

Equation 68 expresses a short-run equilibrating force. This force might be expressed in other ways, but essentially it should depend upon the excess demand $(q_D - q_S)$, and hence it should be some function of this quantity. Long-run forces, however, are not to be described in these terms. Consider the following model:

$$p_D = \alpha_0 + \alpha_1 q \qquad (79)$$

$$p_S = \beta_0 + \beta_1 q \qquad (80) \ \text{I}''$$

$$p_D = p_S \qquad (81)$$

Here equation 79 expresses the variable "demand price" as a function of quantity marketed, and equation 80 expresses "supply price" as a function of the quantity marketed. These are Marshall's long-run demand and supply relations. The equilibrium values are

$$q_e = \frac{\alpha_0 - \beta_0}{\beta_1 - \alpha_1} \quad \text{and} \quad p_e = \frac{\beta_1 \alpha_0 - \alpha_1 \beta_0}{\beta_1 - \alpha_1} \qquad (82)$$

It will be noticed that these formulas are similar to those for the equilibrium values in the previous model, but it must be remembered that the constants have different meanings here, with q as the independent variable. Thus α_0 is the intercept of the demand line on the p axis, and α_1 is the slope with respect to the q axis.

This static model can be changed to a dynamic one by replacing the static equilibration equation $p_D = p_S$ by a dynamic equilibrating equation suggested by Marshall:[15]

$$\frac{dq}{dt} = \gamma(p_D - p_S) \tag{83}$$

We take γ to be a positive constant, so that, if the demand price for a particular quantity exceeds the supply price for that quantity, the quantity will tend to expand. The student should return to model XXII and work out the implications of this new model. He will find another λ which must be negative if the model is to be stable, and such stability will be found to characterize the normal case in which the demand line has a negative slope and the supply line has a positive slope. But he should then explore the situation when both lines have negative slopes, which is quite possible under long-run conditions, and also the situation when both lines have positive slopes, which is somewhat less usual. He will find that the results will be formally similar to those discovered for the short-run market; but, when he recalls that the slopes are now the inverses of what they were before, since q is now the independent variable, he concludes that the stability conditions are really quite different; that is, the stability conditions for long-run conditions are very different from those for short-run conditions.

ALLEN SPECULATIVE MODEL[16]

$$d(t) = \alpha_0 + \alpha_1 p(t) + \alpha_2 p'(t) \tag{84}$$

$$s(t) = \beta_0 + \beta_1 p(t) + \beta_2 p'(t) \tag{85}$$

$$d(t) = s(t) \tag{86}$$

$$d(0) = d_0, \quad p(0) = p_0 \tag{87}$$

XXIII

$$\alpha_0 > 0, \qquad \alpha_1 < 0, \qquad \alpha_2 > 0$$

$$\beta_0 > 0, \qquad \beta_1 > 0, \qquad \beta_2 < 0$$

---

[15] *Principles of Economics* (London, Macmillan, 1930, 8th ed.), p. 374.
[16] Allen, *op. cit.*, and Evans, *op. cit.*

where $p'(t)$ indicates the rate of change of price with respect to time; i.e., $p'(t) = dp(t)/dt$.

Since $\alpha_2 > 0$, the amount demanded increases when price is increasing, whereas $\beta_2 < 0$ indicates that the amount supplied decreases when price is increasing. These two parameters express the effect of speculation. The other signs have been discussed above (Chap. 3). Solving for $p'(t)$, we get

$$p'(t) = \frac{\alpha_0 - \beta_0}{\beta_2 - \alpha_2} + \frac{\alpha_1 - \beta_1}{\beta_2 - \alpha_2} p(t) \tag{88}$$

Referring to model I'', it is seen that, without speculative elements in the demand and supply equations, the equilibrium price is[17]

$$p_e = \frac{\alpha_0 - \beta_0}{\beta_1 - \alpha_1} \tag{89}$$

Introducing this constant p_e, we get

$$p'(t) = \frac{\alpha_1 - \beta_1}{\beta_2 - \alpha_2} \{p(t) - p_e\} \tag{90}$$

Writing $(\alpha_1 - \beta_1)/(\beta_2 - \alpha_2) = \lambda$ and

$$p(t) - p_e = v(t)$$

so that

$$v'(t) = p'(t)$$

we have a simple differential equation:

$$v'(t) = \lambda v(t), \quad \text{or} \quad \frac{1}{v(t)} \frac{dv(t)}{dt} = \lambda \tag{91}$$

whose integral is $v(t) = Ae^{\lambda t}$. Thus

$$p(t) = p_e + Ae^{\lambda t} \tag{92}$$

At time $t = 0$, let there be some price p_0. Then $A = p_0 - p_e$. The movement of this price over time is therefore along the path described by:

$$p(t) = p_e + (p_0 - p_e)e^{\lambda t} \tag{93}$$

where p_0 is the initial price,

$$p_e = \frac{\alpha_0 - \beta_0}{\beta_1 - \alpha_1} \quad \text{and} \quad \lambda = \frac{\alpha_1 - \beta_1}{\beta_2 - \alpha_2}$$

This expression deserves careful study. The path will start at the initial price, but its subsequent movement will depend upon the value

[17] At equilibrium, $p'(t) = 0$, giving us model I.

of λ. It has been assumed that $\alpha_1 - \beta_1$ is negative, as is also $\beta_2 - \alpha_2$. Hence λ is positive, and therefore $e^{\lambda t}$ becomes larger and larger as time goes on. If the initial price is above the equilibrium price, this $p(t)$ increases without limit and with increasing speed. If the initial price is below the equilibrium price, then the price falls in a similar fashion. This speculative model is unstable, moving ever farther from the equilibrium price.

Suppose that we had made the assumption that $\beta_2 > 0$, i.e., the amount supplied increased with a positive rate of change of price. This would imply that suppliers did not respond in a speculative fashion. If the response of suppliers to price changes over time was still less than the responses of the demanders (i.e., $\beta_2 < \alpha_2$), the resulting path is essentially the same as before. But, if $\beta_2 > \alpha_2$, then $\beta_2 - \alpha_2$ is positive and λ is negative. The value of $e^{\lambda t}$ then becomes less and less as time passes. This implies that the second factor of (93) dwindles away:

$$(p_0 - p_e)e^{\lambda t} \rightarrow 0 \qquad \text{as } t \rightarrow \infty \qquad (94)$$

If the initial price is above the equilibrium price, then $p(t)$ gradually falls to p_e. If the initial price is below the equilibrium price, then the price will gradually rise to the equilibrium price. It may be noted that, if $(p_0 - p_e) = 0$, so that $p_0 = p_e$, there is no tendency to change from this value regardless of the value of λ.

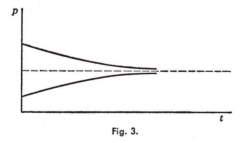

Fig. 3.

Once the path for $p(t)$ has been ascertained, the movement over time of the other variables can be derived. Returning to equation 84, we get

$$d(t) = \alpha_0 + \alpha_1\{p_e + (p_0 - p_e)e^{\lambda t}\} + \alpha_2\lambda(p_0 - p_e)e^{\lambda t} \qquad (95)$$

$$= \alpha_0 + \alpha_1 p_e + (\alpha_1 + \alpha_2\lambda)(p_0 - p_e)e^{\lambda t} \qquad (96)$$

Now, referring again to model I, it is seen that without the speculative elements, i.e., when $p'(t) = 0$ in the demand and supply equations, the equilibrium quantity is

$$d_e = \alpha_0 + \alpha_1 p_e \tag{97}$$

Thus

$$d(t) = d_e + (\alpha_1 + \alpha_2 \lambda)(p_0 - p_e)e^{\lambda t} \tag{98}$$

and the initial amount demanded is

$$d_0 = d_e + (\alpha_1 + \alpha_2 \lambda)(p_0 - p_e) \tag{99}$$

Again it is clear that, when λ is positive, the value of d moves farther and farther away from its starting value. If $(\alpha_1 + \alpha_2 \lambda)(p_0 - p_e)$ is positive, d increases without limit. If λ is negative, this second factor approaches zero, and d approaches d_e.

THE SOLUTION OF MODELS

Upon reviewing the nature of the first-order differential equations and their solutions,[18] it will be seen that they can be classified into three groups:

I. The derivative is a constant: $y' = a$. The solution gives y as a linear function of time $y = l(t)$.

Ia. The derivative is a linear function of time: $y' = l(t)$. The solution gives y as a parabolic function of time: $y = l(t^2, t)$.

II. The derivative is proportional to the variable itself: $y' = ay$. The solution entails the constant e: $y = Ae^{at}$. In this case the differential equation is homogeneous; i.e., there is no constant term, and there is no equilibrium value.

III. The derivative is a linear function of y with a constant term: $y' = ay + b$. In this case the differential equation is nonhomogeneous, and the solution consists of two parts, one of which is a stationary or equilibrium value, and the other is a dynamic element.[19]

One method of solving this kind of equation has been given above. The equilibrium value is found, and the dynamic part is expressed as a function of the difference between the equilibrium value and the initial value. The straightforward mathematical solution will now be illustrated for the Evans price adjustment model. The relevant differential equation is

$$p'(t) = Ap(t) + B$$

[18] For an excellent introduction to the solution of differential equations, see Baumol, *op. cit.*, Chapter 12.

[19] Cf. Samuelson's designations of "steady-state" and "transient" parts, respectively. *A Survey of Contemporary Economics*, ed. H. S. Ellis (Philadelphia, Blakiston, 1948), pp. 367–377.

Step I. Solve the homogeneous part[20] of the equation, which is

$$p'(t) = Ap(t)$$

getting

$$p(t) = ae^{At}$$

Step II. Substitute in the original nonhomogeneous equation for p some constant value, b:

$$0 = Ab + B$$

thus finding that[21]

$$b = \frac{-B}{A}$$

Step III. Add these two part solutions together to get the general solution, thus:

$$p(t) = ae^{At} - \frac{B}{A}$$

Step IV. Introduce the initial condition that, at time

$$t = 0, \quad p(0) = p_0$$

and find that

$$a = p_0 + \frac{B}{A}$$

This gives the solution

$$p(t) = \left(p_0 + \frac{B}{A}\right)e^{At} - \frac{B}{A}$$

Now, referring to the Evans price adjustment model, we note that, in the original differential equation $p'(t) = Ap(t) + B$,

$$A = \gamma(\alpha_1 - \beta_1) \quad \text{and} \quad B = -\gamma(\alpha_1 - \beta_1)p_e = -\gamma(\beta_0 - \alpha_0)$$

The final solution may thus be written

$$p(t) = (p_0 - p_e)e^{\gamma(\alpha_1 - \beta_1)t} + p_e \tag{100}$$

which is identical with that found above on page 77.

SECOND–ORDER EQUATIONS

A general approach to second-order differential equations can be developed in somewhat the same manner. It may be noted that two initial conditions will be needed. Again, there are three classes:

[20] A homogeneous equation is one without a constant term. In this case the "homogeneous part" is obtained by dropping the constant term B.

[21] Assuming $A \neq 0$.

I. The second derivative is a constant: $y'' = A$. The solution gives y as a parabolic function of time: $y = l(t^2, t)$.

Ia. The second derivative is a linear function of time: $y'' = l(t)$. The solution gives y as a cubic function of time: $y = l(t^3, t^2, t)$.

II. The second derivative is a linear function of the first derivative: $y'' = Ay' + B$. Introduce a new variable $x = y'$, and get a first-order equation in x which can be solved as shown previously.

III. The general second-order linear differential equation with constant coefficients:[22] $y'' = Ay' + By + C$.

Step I. Solve the homogeneous part of the equation

$$y'' = Ay' + By$$

by substituting $y = ae^{bt}$, and its derivatives $y' = bae^{bt}$ and $y'' = b^2 ae^{bt}$, getting

$$b^2 - Ab - B = 0$$

This is the "characteristic equation" and its roots are

$$\frac{A \pm (A^2 + 4B)^{1/2}}{2}$$

Thus there are two values that b can have. Call them

$$b_1 = \frac{A + (A^2 + 4B)^{1/2}}{2}$$

$$b_2 = \frac{A - (A^2 + 4B)^{1/2}}{2}$$

Thus, clearly, one solution is $y = a_1 e^{b_1 t}$, and another solution is $y = a_2 e^{b_2 t}$. The reader should test each one. He should then test the more general solution

$$y = a_1 e^{b_1 t} + a_2 e^{b_2 t} \tag{101}$$

and he will find that this also is a solution for any numerical values that he wishes to choose for a_1 and a_2, which are known as the arbitrary constants.

A warning should be issued here that as long as b_1 and b_2 are real roots and not equal, there is no trouble. But, if the quantity under the square root sign $(A^2 + 4B)$ happens to be zero or negative, then the procedure is modified as shown in the next model discussed.

---

[22] The method can be applied to higher-order linear equations. For example, a third-order equation leads to a third-degree characteristic equation. The coefficients may be functions of time.

Step II. Substitute $y = c$, where c is a constant, in the original differential equation[23]

$$0 = 0 + Bc + C$$

finding

$$c = -\frac{C}{B}$$

Step III. Add these two partial solutions to get the general solution, thus

$$y = a_1 e^{b_1 t} + a_2 e^{b_2 t} - \frac{C}{B} \tag{102}$$

Step IV. Use the two initial conditions to find the values of the arbitrary constants a_1 and a_2. These initial conditions are (1) the value of y at $t = 0$, and (2) the value of y' at $t = 0$.

$$y_0 = a_1 + a_2 - \frac{C}{B} \tag{103}$$

$$y_0' = a_1 b_1 + a_2 b_2 \tag{104}$$

Here we have two equations which can be solved for the two unknowns a_1 and a_2 in terms of the other letters which are all constants. Thus a_1 and a_2 can be expressed in terms of y_0, y_0', A, B, and C.

SAMUELSON'S INVESTMENT MODEL[24]

The solution of a second-order differential equation can be illustrated from a model devised by Samuelson such that a deficiency of capital below a certain equilibrium level leads to an acceleration of the rate of investment, and a surplus of capital to a deceleration of the rate of investment.

$$k(t) = K(t) - K_e \tag{105}$$

$$\frac{dk(t)}{dt} = I(t) \tag{106} \quad \textbf{XXIV}$$

$$\frac{dI(t)}{dt} = -mk(t) \tag{107}$$

$$m > 0$$

---

[23] If $B = 0$, substitute $y = ct$; if $B = A = 0$, substitute $y = ct^2$.

[24] *A Survey of Contemporary Economics*, ed. H. S. Ellis (Philadelphia, Blakiston, 1948), p. 363.

Initial Conditions	*Variables*
$k(0) = k_0$	$K(t)$: amount of capital
$I(0) = I_0$	$k(t)$: excess of capital over equilibrium amount (K_e)
	$I(t)$: investment
	K_e: exogenous

Differentiating (106) and substituting from (107), we get

$$\frac{d^2k(t)}{dt^2} = -mk(t) \tag{108}$$

In solving this second-order differential equation, we follow the steps of page 83:

Step I: Substitute $k(t) = ae^{At}$ in the homogeneous part, getting the characteristic equation

$$A^2 = -m \tag{109}$$

This is a very simple equation, but, since m is positive, the roots of the equation are imaginary numbers.

$$b_1 = +\sqrt{-m} \tag{110}$$

$$b_2 = -\sqrt{-m} \tag{111}$$

The general solution, however, is as usual

$$k(t) = a_1 e^{b_1 t} + a_2 e^{b_2 t} \tag{112}$$

Since there is no constant term in our differential equation, steps II and III are eliminated. We now re-write the expression, before the initial conditions are introduced, in step IV.

The following well-known relations can be found in the mathematical treatises:

$$e^{it} = \cos t + i \sin t; \qquad e^{-it} = \cos t - i \sin t \tag{113}$$

where $i = \sqrt{-1}$. Thus

$$a_1 e^{b_1 t} = a_1 e^{i\sqrt{m}t} = a_1 (\cos \sqrt{m}t + i \sin \sqrt{m}t) \tag{114}$$

and

$$a_2 e^{b_2 t} = a_2 e^{-i\sqrt{m}t} = a_2 (\cos \sqrt{m}t - i \sin \sqrt{m}t) \tag{115}$$

Therefore

$$k(t) = (a_1 + a_2) \cos \sqrt{m}t + (a_1 - a_2)(i \sin \sqrt{m}t) \tag{116}$$

Now, introduce the initial conditions (step IV), finding that:

$$k_0 = (a_1 + a_2) \tag{117}$$

and

$$I_0 = (a_1 - a_2)i\sqrt{m} \tag{118}$$

Therefore

$$k(t) = k_0 \cos \sqrt{m}t + (I_0/\sqrt{m}) \cdot \sin \sqrt{m}t \tag{119}$$

It will be observed with pleasure that all the imaginary numbers have been canceled out and the path of $k(t)$ through time can now be plotted.[25] Clearly the path will be an oscillating one, the amplitude of the variations depending on the initial values of k and I, and the periodicity depending on the phase constant m. These variations in K continue ad infinitum, with no tendency to increase or die away.

Consider now a modification of this model. Suppose that the rate of change of investment is influenced in two ways: (1) as before, the rate of investment is slowed up by excess capital; and in addition (2) the rate of investment is slowed up by a high investment level, as through a shortage of investment goods. This model is really a combination of two separate models suggested by Samuelson. Thus

$$\frac{d^2k(t)}{dt^2} = -gk(t) \quad \text{and} \quad \frac{dk(t)}{dt} = -hk(t) \tag{120}$$

Now setting up a single equation containing these concepts:

$$\frac{d^2k(t)}{dt^2} + n\frac{dk(t)}{dt} + mk(t) = 0 \tag{121}$$

This differential equation may be solved by following the regular steps suggested above.

Step I. The characteristic equation is found to be

$$b^2 + nb + m = 0 \tag{122}$$

and its roots are

$$b = \frac{-n \pm (n^2 - 4m)^{\frac{1}{2}}}{2} \tag{123}$$

These roots will be

(a) real if $n^2 - 4m > 0$

(b) complex if $n^2 - 4m < 0$

(c) real and equal if $n^2 - 4m = 0$

Consider the *first case* (a). Assume $n^2 - 4m > 0$. Then b_1 and b_2

[25] It should be remembered that t is measured in radians, i.e., in units equal to $360°/2\pi \approx 57.29°$.

are two real numbers, and

$$k(t) = a_1 e^{b_1 t} + a_2 e^{b_2 t} \tag{124}$$

The value of the constants a_1 and a_2 can be found by introducing two initial conditions.

The time path of $k(t)$ is a little complicated because of the two factors. But, if b_1 and b_2 are both negative, k will eventually approach zero. If one of these roots is positive and the other negative, the positive root will eventually be the predominating factor as time increases, even if its a coefficient is very small, and the net result will be unstable. If both roots are positive, then k will be the more explosive. Various values of m and n and initial conditions k_0 and I_0 may be tried to illustrate these results.

Consider now the *case (b)*, when the roots are complex (i.e., contain imaginary elements). It may be noted that imaginary elements appear in pairs, so that, if one of the roots has an imaginary element, the other must also (if we assume that m and n are real numbers, or functions of time whose coefficients are real numbers). The solution of $k(t)$ can then be written in the forms of sines and cosines, and the imaginary elements will then drop out. Let the roots be written as follows:

$$b_1 = u + iv, \quad b_2 = u - iv \tag{125}$$

where $i = \sqrt{-1}$. Then

$$a_1 e^{b_1 t} = a_1 e^{(u+iv)t} = a_1 e^{ut} (\cos vt + i \sin vt) \tag{126}$$

and

$$a_2 e^{b_2 t} = a_2 e^{(u-iv)t} = a_2 e^{ut} (\cos vt - i \sin vt) \tag{127}$$

Then

$$k(t) = (a_1 + a_2) e^{ut} \cos vt + (a_1 - a_2) e^{ut} i \sin vt \tag{128}$$

Introducing the initial conditions:

$$k_0 = (a_1 + a_2) \tag{129}$$

$$I_0 = u k_0 + iv (a_1 - a_2) \tag{130}$$

Therefore

$$k(t) = e^{ut} \{ k_0 \cos vt + \frac{I_0 - u k_0}{v} \sin vt \} \tag{131}$$

This solution for $k(t)$ contains a new factor, e^{ut}, which will tend to explode or to disappear, depending on whether u is positive or negative. If u is zero, there is but one factor as in the previous example and we have oscillations in perpetuity.

Consider finally the *third case* (*c*), when the roots are equal. In this case, $n^2 = 4m$ and $b_1 = b_2 = -n/2$. The solution is then written as

$$k(t) = a_1 e^{bt} + a_2 t e^{bt} \qquad (132)$$

where $b = -n/2$, and the constants a_1 and a_2 are now to be found by introducing the initial conditions as in case (*a*).

$$k(0) = a_1 e^{b0} + a_2 0 e^{b0} \qquad (133)$$

Therefore

$$k_0 = a_1$$

$$I_0 = \frac{dk(0)}{dt} = a_1 b e^{b0} + a_2 e^{b0} + a_2 0 b e^{b0} \qquad (134)$$

Therefore

$$I_0 = a_1 b + a_2 \qquad (135)$$

Thus

$$a_1 = k_0 \qquad (136)$$

$$a_2 = I_0 - k_0 b = I_0 + k_0 \frac{n}{2} \qquad (137)$$

and the final solution may be written:

$$k(t) = k_0 \exp\left(-\frac{n}{2}t\right) + \left(I_0 + k_0 \frac{n}{2}\right) t \exp\left(-\frac{n}{2}t\right) \qquad (138)$$

$$= \left\{k_0 + t\left(I_0 + k_0 \frac{n}{2}\right)\right\} \exp\left(-\frac{n}{2}t\right) \qquad (139)$$

Clearly the determining factor in the ultimate stability or instability of the movement of k is n (which is equal to $\sqrt{4m}$). If n is negative (which is unlikely), then k eventually increases without limit. If n is positive, k eventually approaches zero. If, however, n is small enough, and I_0 large enough, the factor tI_0 may cause some early increase in k. As an example, try $n = 1$, $I_0 = 10$, and $k_0 = 100$.

THE LITTLER MODEL[26]

Equations		Variables
$N = A + B$	(140)	N: National income
$S = B + \lambda(\alpha_0 - \alpha)$	(141)	A: Expenditure on consumption goods XXV
$\alpha(0) = \alpha_0$	(142)	B: Investment
$\nu(0) = \nu_0$	(143)	S: Saving

$$\alpha = \frac{dA}{dt} \qquad \nu = \frac{dN}{dt} \qquad \beta = \frac{dB}{dt} \qquad \phi = \frac{dS}{dN}$$

[26] H. G. Littler, "Pure Theory of Money," *Canadian Journal of Economics and*

The unusual nature of the variables must be noted. The α, β, and ν are flows over time, and the A, B, and N are integrals from some point of time. Another notable aspect of the Littler model is his definition of saving which he derives by a most interesting application of mathematical principles. It differs from the Keynesian definition, being rather reminiscent of the Robertson definition.[27] With it, he develops some useful multiplier theory among other things.

We proceed by differentiating each of the two main equations with respect to time, then differentiate the first one a second time, and substitute from the other, getting

$$\frac{d^2N}{dt^2} = \frac{d^2B}{dt^2} + \frac{1}{\lambda}\left(\frac{dB}{dt} - \frac{dS}{dt}\right) \tag{144}$$

This equation cannot be solved in the general sense, but we introduce some restrictions which are usually imposed in the theory of the multiplier:

$$\frac{dB}{dt} = \beta \quad \text{(constant)}$$

$$\frac{dS}{dN} = \phi \quad \text{(constant)}$$

Thus we get

$$\frac{d^2N}{dt^2} + \frac{\phi}{\lambda} \cdot \frac{dN}{dt} = \frac{\beta}{\lambda} \tag{145}$$

This is a second-order differential equation with constant coefficients. Re-writing it in terms of ν gives

$$\frac{d\nu}{dt} + \frac{\phi}{\lambda}\nu = \frac{\beta}{\lambda} \tag{146}$$

from which the solution obtained is

$$\nu = \frac{\beta}{\phi} + \left(\nu_0 - \frac{\beta}{\phi}\right)\exp\left(-\frac{\phi}{\lambda}t\right) \tag{147}$$

Integrating again, we find

$$N = \int \frac{\beta}{\phi}\,dt + \int\left(\nu_0 - \frac{\beta}{\phi}\right)\exp\left(-\frac{\phi}{\lambda}t\right)dt + c \tag{148}$$

Political Science, November 1944. Littler's symbols are unusual in that Greek letters are used for variables.

[27] "Saving and Hoarding," *Economic Journal*, XLIII: 399–413.

At time $t = 0$, $N = 0$, and this gives us

$$N = \frac{\beta}{\phi} t + \frac{\lambda(\phi \nu_0 - \beta)}{\phi^2} \left[1 - \exp\left(-\frac{\phi}{\lambda} t \right) \right] \tag{149}$$

Thus we have N as a composite of two parts, one increasing steadily with time, and the other tending toward zero. This is an unusually interesting model, especially in the way in which the original equations were derived. It can be studied with profit.

This concludes the discussion of the use of differential equations in working out the implications of continuous dynamic models. The presentation here has not been a complete discussion of differential equations—the reader is encouraged to follow a mathematician's orderly presentation of the subject, and, with this introduction, he should be able to do so. The intention has been merely to analyze the implications of some of the illustrative types of models being discussed in economic theory.

EXERCISES

1. In the gravity example discussion on page 67, assume the following initial conditions: $v_0 = 1$, $s_0 = 1$. Find the values of the arbitrary constants c_1 and c_2.

2. In the Domar debt model, take the following income equations as alternative to (33)

(a) $Y = \beta$
(b) $Y = \beta + \gamma t$

and find the tendency of the ratio of debt to income in each case.

3. Solve the differential equation involved in the Allen speculative model by the method explained on page 83.

READINGS

1. N. J. Silberling, *The Dynamics of Business* (New York, McGraw-Hill, 1943). An excellent source book for factual material; though rapidly getting out of date as such books do, its series cover the United States economy for quite long periods.

2. W. J. Baumol, *Economic Dynamics* (New York, Macmillan, 1951). A very fine presentation of the mathematical techniques for handling differential equations though we are offered more than enough to handle the rather simple illustrative economic models. His approach allows a comparison between continuous and discrete models.

3. P. A. Samuelson, "Dynamic Process Analysis," Chapter 10 of *A Survey of Con-*

temporary Economics (Philadelphia, Blakiston, 1948), especially pp. 359–363 and pp. 384–387.

4. E. Domar, "The 'Burden of Debt' and the National Income," *American Economic Review, XXXIV:* 798–827 (December 1944).

5. R. Frisch, "Propagation Problems and Impulse Problems in Dynamic Economics," *Economic Essays in Honour of Gustav Cassel* (London, Allen, 1933), pp. 171–205. This article is a landmark in the development of economists' ideas on dynamic models. The first four pages should be read by all. Much of the rest can be understood with little mathematical training.

CHAPTER 6

Sequence Models

In the previous chapter, time derivatives were used, making the model dynamic. The variables were thought of as changing continuously through time. The solution of the model entailed the solution of a differential equation, and the result was a definite time path for each endogenous variable.

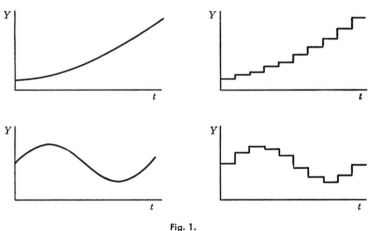

Fig. 1.

In the present chapter, time is cut up into periods, and the variables move in jumps from one period to the next. Such variations are said to be discontinuous, or discrete. Actually, by making the time periods smaller and smaller, we can approach as closely as we like to the continuous course. Corresponding to the time derivative of the continuous curve, there is a difference, called ΔY:

$$\Delta Y = Y_i - Y_{i-1} \tag{1}$$

93

This correspondence is seen clearly when the difference is divided by the time difference

$$\frac{\Delta Y}{\Delta t} = \frac{Y_t - Y_{t-1}}{t - (t - 1)} \tag{2}$$

Equations involving these finite differences are of great importance in economics because a great many economic data are presented in the form of quantities relevant to a period rather than to a point of time. For example, the gross national product is given for a year, or profits for a quarter. This is particularly true of quantities bought or sold, though prices frequently appear as at points of time. Consider now a simple difference model.

THE HARROD MODEL[1]

Equations		*Variables*	
$S(t) = \alpha Y(t)$	(3)	$S:$ Savings	
$I(t) = \beta[Y(t) - Y(t - 1)]$	(4)	$Y:$ Income	XXVI
$S(t) = I(t)$	(5)	$I:$ Investment	

Parametric Conditions	*Initial Condition*
$\alpha > 0, \quad \beta > 0$	$Y(0) = Y_0$

Combining these three equations, we get[2]

$$\alpha Y(t) = \beta Y(t) - \beta Y(t - 1) \tag{6}$$

or

$$Y(t) = \left(\frac{\beta}{\beta - \alpha}\right) Y(t - 1) \tag{7}$$

Obviously, we can also write

$$Y(t - 1) = \left(\frac{\beta}{\beta - \alpha}\right) Y(t - 2) \tag{8}$$

and

$$Y(t - 2) = \left(\frac{\beta}{\beta - \alpha}\right) Y(t - 3) \tag{9}$$

[1] R. F. Harrod, "An Essay in Dynamic Theory," *Economic Journal, XLIX:* 14–33.

[2] Equation 4 is called a "difference" equation although we do not here express it in terms of the difference. The reader should verify that equation 4 can be written as follows:

$$\Delta Y = \frac{\alpha}{\beta} Y(t)$$

and so on. Thus

$$Y(t) = \left(\frac{\beta}{\beta - \alpha}\right)^t Y_0 \tag{10}$$

This equation is the solution of the difference equation (7) since it expresses $Y(t)$ in terms of the parameters and the initial value of Y. It gives the path of $Y(t)$ through time. This path clearly depends on the value of the constant.

$$A = \frac{\beta}{\beta - \alpha} \tag{11}$$

Consider the various possible paths, according to the values of A, as illustrated in Fig. 2.

The borderline cases, when $A = 1, 0$, or -1, are left to the reader to work out. In the present model the variable Y represents income, and therefore cannot be negative. Hence the first two charts of Fig. 2 are not applicable. We must require that $\beta/(\beta - \alpha) > 0$.

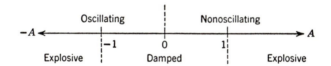

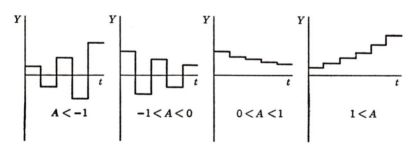

Fig. 2.

But in the original model both α and β were specified as positive. Hence we find that $\beta > 0$. We may note also that $\beta/(\beta - \alpha)$ cannot be less than 1 unless $\alpha < 0$, which has been ruled out. We therefore conclude that for this model $\beta/(\beta - \alpha) > 1$, and only the fourth case applies. $Y(t)$ increases without limit.

Returning to equations 3 and 5 of the model, we can easily derive the final solutions for I and for S:

$$I(t) = S(t) = \alpha \left(\frac{\beta}{\beta - \alpha}\right)^t Y_0 \tag{12}$$

The reader should work out this time path.

One final observation may be made on this model. There is no fixed equilibrium value for any of the variables. If there were an equilibrium value Y_e, it should satisfy the difference equation (7):

$$Y_e = \frac{\beta}{\beta - \alpha} Y_e \tag{13}$$

which requires that $\alpha = 0$, which is ruled out in the conditions of the model.

Now consider the following example of the Harrod model. Given:

$\alpha = 0.05$ (14) $Y_0 = 300$ (billion)

$\beta = 0.55$ (15)

then

$$\frac{\beta}{\beta - \alpha} = \frac{0.55}{0.50} = 1.01 \tag{16}$$

The model is:

$$S(t) = 0.05\, Y(t) \tag{17}$$

$$I(t) = 0.55\,[Y(t) - Y(t - 1)] \tag{18}$$

$$S(t) = I(t)$$

and the solution is

$$Y(t) = (1.01)^t (300) \tag{19}$$

t	$Y(t)$
0	300.00
1	303.00
2	306.03
3	309.09
4	312.18
..	.....

THE COBWEB MODEL[3]

As a second introductory model, the famous Cobweb problem will be explored. This problem has been thoroughly discussed in the literature

[3] M. Ezekiel, "The Cobweb Theorem," *Quarterly Journal of Economics*, 1938, and P. A. Samuelson, *A Survey of Contemporary Economics*, ed. H. S. Ellis (Philadelphia, Blakiston, 1948).

and lends itself well to graphics. We shall first use numerical coefficients. Let p be the price in dollars per bushel, and q the quantity in millions of bushels, of some perishable farm crop:

Supply relation:
$$q_t = \tfrac{3}{2}p_{t-1} - 3 \qquad\qquad (20)$$

Demand relation:
$$p_t = 17 - \tfrac{1}{3}q_t \qquad\qquad (21)\ \text{XXVIIA}$$

The subscripts refer to time periods. The demand relation shows the price in period t to be a function of the quantity produced in that period. The supply relation shows the quantity produced in any period to be a function of the price in the previous period.

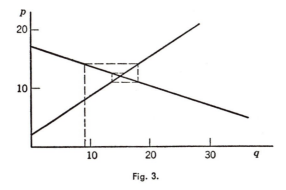

Fig. 3.

These two relations are shown in Fig. 3, and the time sequence can be computed by taking some initial crop, such as 9 million bushels. With a crop of this size, the demand relation informs us that the price will be $14.00. With the price of $14.00 ruling in period one, the crop produced in the next period (aside from droughts, frost, etc.) will be 18 million bushels, as seen from the supply relation. The appropriate price for this large crop will be $11.00, and so on.

t	q	p
0	9	14
1	18	11
2	$13\tfrac{1}{2}$	$12\tfrac{1}{2}$
3	$15\tfrac{3}{4}$	.
4	.	.
.	.	
.		
∞	15	12

In this particular numerical example, the quantity sequence approaches 15 and the price sequence approaches 12. This point (15, 12) is obtained by solving the two equations as if all variables referred to the same point of time. Such a point (15, 12) is a point of *equilibrium* because, once there, no tendency exists to move elsewhere, as long as the demand and supply curves are fixed. These equilibrium values satisfy both equations at the same time. In the present example, the equilibrium point is a point of stable equilibrium because, wherever we start, we tend to approach this equilibrium point.

From the chart, it can be seen that this stability in the model results from the fact that the supply line is steeper with reference to the quantity axis ($\frac{2}{3}$) than is the demand line ($\frac{1}{3}$). If the demand relation were the steeper, the model would have been an explosive one; and, if the slopes were the same, price and quantity would continue to oscillate between the two fixed values.[4] It may be noted in passing that it is the slopes and not the elasticities that are the relevant aspects of the curves.

Samuelson[5] presents an interesting variation by introducing a bend in the supply curve. His model is unstable near the point of intersection of the demand and supply curves, but there is a region of stability, resulting from the greater steepness in the supply curve, causing the variations in quantity and price to approach (from both directions) the "equilibrium cycle." His presentation is excellent and readable.

THE GENERAL COBWEB MODEL

The problem may be treated in more generality by introducing algebra:

Supply: $q_t = \alpha + \beta p_{t-1}$ (22)

Demand: $p_t = \gamma + \delta q_t$ (23)

XXVII

Initial condition: $q(0) = q_0$

where α is the intercept on the q axis;
    β is the slope with respect to the p axis;
    γ is the intercept on the p axis;
    δ is the slope with respect to the q axis.

By combining the first two equations, eliminating p:

$$q_t = \alpha + \beta\gamma + \beta\delta q_{t-1} \qquad (24)$$

This is a difference equation expressing q in terms of its value in the

[4] See Ezekiel, *op. cit.*, for various models of this kind.

[5] *A Survey of Contemporary Economics*, ed. H. S. Ellis (Philadelphia, Blakiston, 1948), pp. 368–373, and also his *Foundations*, p. 323 *et passim*.

previous period. If, now, there is an equilibrium value of q, it must also satisfy this equation, because the q value remains the same in consecutive periods:

$$q_e = \alpha + \beta\gamma + \beta\delta q_e \tag{25}$$

from which we find

$$q_e = \frac{\alpha + \beta\gamma}{1 - \beta\delta} \tag{26}$$

Now, subtracting (25) from (24):

$$q_t - q_e = \beta\delta(q_{t-1} - q_e) \tag{27}$$

Obviously,

$$q_t - q_e = (\beta\delta)^2(q_{t-2} - q_e)$$
$$= (\beta\delta)^3(q_{t-3} - q_e) \tag{28}$$

or

$$q_t = q_e + (\beta\delta)^t(q_0 - q_e) \tag{29}$$

where q_0 is some initial value of q. This model is clearly stable if $|\beta\delta| < 1$. But β is the slope with respect to the *price* axis, so that the stability condition may be expressed as $|\delta/\beta'| < 1$, where $\beta' = 1/\beta =$ the slope of the supply curve with respect to the *quantity* axis. Thus the model is stable if the numerical value of the slope of the demand curve is less than the numerical value of the slope of the supply curve. Since the demand curve has a negative slope, the approach to equilibrium will be oscillatory, giving rise to cycles which are called endogenous since they result from the given set of parameters, the positive slope of the supply curve β against the negative slope of the demand curve δ.

THE SOLUTION OF SEQUENCE MODELS

The difference equation involved in the Harrod model

$$Y(t) = AY(t - 1)$$

where $A = \beta/(\beta - \alpha)$, is a first-order linear homogeneous difference equation with a constant coefficient. It is comparable to the differential equation (20) involved in the Domar macro model of the previous chapter.

The difference equation involved in the Cobweb model

$$q(t) = Aq(t - 1) + B \tag{30}$$

where $A = \beta\delta$ and $B = \alpha + \beta\gamma$, is a first-order linear difference equation with constant coefficients, but is nonhomogeneous because of the constant term B. Second- and higher-order difference equations will be discussed below, but in this book we shall consider only equations with constant coefficients. It is intended to give only an outline of methods of solution, so that a student who wishes more details should go next to the mathematical textbooks.

Comparable to the convenient classification of first-order differential equations of the previous chapter, the following is a classification of first-order difference equations. The similarities may be noted.

I. The difference is a constant:

$$Y(t) - Y(t-1) = \alpha \tag{31}$$

or, re-written:

$$Y(t) = \alpha + Y(t-1) \tag{32}$$

The solution of this difference equation is

$$Y(t) = t\alpha + Y_0 \tag{33}$$

II. The difference is proportional to the variable:

$$Y(t) - Y(t-1) = \alpha Y(t) \tag{34}$$

or, re-written:

$$(1-\alpha)Y(t) = Y(t-1) \tag{35}$$

$$Y(t) = \frac{1}{1-\alpha} Y(t-1) \tag{36}$$

As has been found in the Harrod model, the solution of this equation is

$$Y(t) = \left(\frac{1}{1-\alpha}\right)^t Y_0 \tag{37}$$

III. The difference is a linear function of the variable:

$$Y(t) - Y(t-1) = \alpha Y(t) + \beta \tag{38}$$

or, re-written:

$$Y(t) = AY(t-1) + B$$

where

$$A = \frac{1}{1-\alpha} \quad \text{and} \quad B = \frac{\beta}{1-\alpha} \tag{39}$$

This is the type of equation involved in the Cobweb theorem, and must now be solved. As in the case of the differential equations, there are two different approaches. This equation was solved above by finding an equilibrium value, and then computing the dynamic factor. We now give the straightforward mathematical approach.[6] And again, the

---

[6] T. C. Schelling, *National Income Behavior* (New York, McGraw-Hill, 1951), Appendix.

steps are similar to those for the solution of a differential equation (see page 83). We note four steps in solving the general equation:

$$Y(t) - AY(t - 1) - B = 0 \qquad (40)$$

Step I. Solve the homogeneous part of the equation[7]

$$Y(t) - AY(t - 1) = 0 \qquad (41)$$

by substituting

$$Y(t) = ax^t \qquad (42)$$

We first note that

$$Y(t - 1) = ax^{t-1} \qquad (43)$$

Then

$$ax^t - Aax^{t-1} = 0 \qquad (44)$$

$$ax^{t-1}(x - A) = 0 \qquad (45)$$

Thus we find that $Y(t) = ax^t$ is a solution if $x = A$, i.e., if

$$Y(t) = aA^t \qquad (46)$$

Step II. Find a "particular solution" of the complete nonhomogeneous equation. Substitute in the original nonhomogeneous equation the simplest form of a solution: $Y = c$, where c is some constant.

$$c = Ac + B \qquad (47)$$

or

$$c = \frac{B}{1 - A} \qquad (48)$$

We may note that $1 - A \neq 0$.

Step III. Add these two part solutions together to get the general solution, thus:

$$Y(t) = aA^t + \frac{B}{1 - A} \qquad (49)$$

Step IV. Now introduce the initial condition that $Y(0) = Y_0$

$$Y_0 = aA^0 + \frac{B}{1 - A} = a + \frac{B}{1 - A} \qquad (50)$$

Therefore

$$a = Y_0 - \frac{B}{1 - A} \qquad (51)$$

---

[7] Notice that x^t plays the important role in solving difference equations that e^x plays in solving differential equations.

Hence the final solution is

$$Y(t) = A^t \left(Y_0 - \frac{B}{1-A} \right) + \frac{B}{1-A} \tag{52}$$

Upon substituting in the values of A and B, this solution will be seen to be identical with that previously found on page 99.

SAMUELSON'S INTERACTION MODEL[8]

Second-order difference equations may be solved in much the same way as the general first-order equations. The similarity to differential equations should also be noted. Such a solution will be illustrated by Samuelson's interaction model:

$Y(t) = C(t) + I(t)$	(53)	$Y(t)$:	Income
$C(t) = \alpha Y(t-1)$	(54)	$C(t)$:	Consumption
$I(t) = \beta[C(t) - C(t-1)]$	(55)	$I(t)$:	Investment
$Y(0) = Y_0$		$\alpha > 0$	XXVIII
$Y(1) = Y_1$		$\beta > 0$	

Step I. From the model, derive the appropriate difference equation. This may be done by substituting the second and third equations into the first, getting

$$Y(t) - \alpha(1+\beta)Y(t-1) + \alpha\beta Y(t-2) = 0 \tag{56}$$

Step II. Solve this homogeneous second-order difference equation by substituting

$$Y(t) = ax^t \tag{57}$$

and getting

$$x^t - \alpha(1+\beta)x^{t-1} + \alpha\beta x^{t-2} = 0 \tag{58}$$

$$x^{t-2}[x^2 - \alpha(1+\beta)x + \alpha\beta] = 0 \tag{59}$$

Thus $Y(t) = ax^t$ is a solution if

$$x^2 - \alpha(1+\beta)x + \alpha\beta = 0 \tag{60}$$

i.e., if

$$x = \frac{\alpha(1+\beta) \pm [\alpha^2(1+\beta)^2 - 4\alpha\beta]^{1/2}}{2} \tag{61}$$

[8] P. A. Samuelson, "Interaction between the Multiplier Analysis and the Principles of Acceleration," *Review of Economic Statistics*, 1939. Our formulation is a slight modification of his.

There are here two possible values for x:

$$x_1 = \frac{\alpha(1 + \beta) + [\alpha^2(1 + \beta)^2 - 4\alpha\beta]^{\frac{1}{2}}}{2}$$

and

$$x_2 = \frac{\alpha(1 + \beta) - [\alpha^2(1 + \beta)^2 - 4\alpha\beta]^{\frac{1}{2}}}{2} \tag{62}$$

both of which will satisfy the characteristic equation. We thus have two solutions:

$$Y(t) = a_1 x_1{}^t \quad \text{and} \quad Y(t) = a_2 x_2{}^t \tag{63}$$

When there are two such possible solutions, a more general solution would be the sum of the two:

$$Y(t) = a_1 x_1{}^t + a_2 x_2{}^t \tag{64}$$

where a_1 and a_2 are arbitrary constants.

This general solution will now be handled differently, depending on the nature of the roots x_1 and x_2 of the quadratic equation. There are three possible cases:

(i) The roots are real and unequal.

(ii) The roots are real and equal.

(iii) The roots are complex; i.e., they involve imaginary numbers.

In case (i), we proceed directly to step III:

Step III. Introduce the two initial conditions so as to specify the arbitrary constants a_1 and a_2:

$$Y_0 = Y(0) = a_1 x_1{}^0 + a_2 x_2{}^0 = a_1 + a_2 \tag{65}$$

$$Y_1 = Y(1) = a_1 x_1 + a_2 x_2 \tag{66}$$

Solving these two equations for a_1 and a_2, we get

$$a_1 = \frac{Y_1 - Y_0 x_2}{x_1 - x_2} \tag{67}$$

$$a_2 = \frac{Y_1 - Y_0 x_1}{x_2 - x_1} \tag{68}$$

The general solution thus becomes

$$Y(t) = \left(\frac{Y_1 - Y_0 x_2}{x_1 - x_2}\right) x_1{}^t + \left(\frac{Y_1 - Y_0 x_1}{x_2 - x_1}\right) x_2{}^t \tag{69}$$

where x_1 and x_2 are given above in terms of α and β. Now the various possible time paths can be explored.

The method used above, on page 95, can be used, but the present situation is complicated by the presence of the two parts of the solution. The time path may be oscillating or not, and damped or explosive, depending on the values of x_1 and x_2. It may be noted that the larger numerical root will eventually predominate, though the smaller numerical root may predominate early, if its a value is large.

In case (ii), when the roots of the auxiliary equation are real and equal, the form of the solution is a little different:

$$Y(t) = a_1 x^t + a_2 t x^t \qquad (70)$$

where

$$x = \frac{\alpha}{2}(1 + \beta) \qquad (71)$$

Now proceed to

Step IV. Introduce the initial conditions:

$$Y_0 = a_1 \qquad (72)$$

$$Y_1 = a_1 x + a_2 x \qquad (73)$$

Therefore

$$a_1 = Y_0 \qquad (74)$$

$$a_2 = \frac{Y_1 - Y_0 x}{x} \qquad (75)$$

and the final solution may be written:

$$Y(t) = Y_0 x^t + \frac{Y_1 - Y_0 x}{x} t x^t \qquad (76)$$

This solution can be re-written as

$$Y(t) = [Y_0(1 - t)x + Y_1 t] x^{t-1} \qquad (77)$$

In case (iii), the roots of the auxiliary equations are complex, that is, they involve the imaginary number $\sqrt{-1}$, which we shall designate as i. That is,[9] $i = \sqrt{-1}$. The general solution,

$$Y(t) = a_1 x_1{}^t + a_2 x_2{}^t \qquad (78)$$

may now be re-written. First let the complex numbers be

$$x_1 = c + di \quad \text{where } c = \tfrac{1}{2}\alpha(1 + \beta) \qquad (79)$$

$$x_2 = c - di \quad \text{and} \quad d = \tfrac{1}{2}[4\alpha\beta - \alpha^2(1 + \beta)^2]^{1/2} \qquad (80)$$

[9] See A. N. Whitehead, *Introduction to Mathematics*, Home University Library of Modern Knowledge, Oxford, 1948.

These can be expressed in trigonometric form as:[10]

$$c + di = (c^2 + d^2)^{\frac{1}{2}}(\cos B + i \sin B) \tag{81}$$

$$c - di = (c^2 + d^2)^{\frac{1}{2}}(\cos B - i \sin B) \tag{82}$$

where B is some angle such that

$$\cos B = \frac{c}{\sqrt{c^2 + d^2}} \quad \text{and} \quad \sin B = \frac{d}{\sqrt{c^2 + d^2}} \tag{83}$$

Now, by De Moivre's theorem,[11]

$$x_1{}^t = (c + di)^t = (c^2 + d^2)^{t/2}(\cos B + i \sin B)^t$$
$$= (c^2 + d^2)^{t/2}(\cos tB + i \sin tB) \tag{84}$$

$$x_2{}^t = (c - di)^t = (c^2 + d^2)^{t/2}(\cos B - i \sin B)^t$$
$$= (c^2 + d^2)^{t/2}(\cos tB - i \sin tB) \tag{85}$$

Thus

$$Y(t) = a_1 x_1{}^t + a_2 x_2{}^t \tag{86}$$
$$= (c^2 + d^2)^{t/2}[(a_1 + a_2)\cos tB + (a_1 - a_2)i \sin tB] \tag{87}$$

It may be noted that the complex numbers always[12] appear in pairs that are called conjugate, as $c + di$ and $c - di$, so that this method of procedure is general. The numbers a_1 and a_2 are quite arbitrary, so that we can put in whatever numbers we wish, and still satisfy the original equation.

It is now expedient (as we shall see) to write

$$a_1 + a_2 = g \tag{88}$$

$$(a_1 - a_2)i = h \tag{89}$$

where g and h are real numbers. This implies that $a_1 - a_2$ is imaginary; but there is no reason that such a number cannot be chosen.

[10] When a complete number is expressed as $c + di$, where c and d are real numbers and $i = \sqrt{-1}$, it can be pictured as a pointer on a diagram, the value of c being measured horizontally, and the value of d measured vertically. Clearly B is the angle shown, whose sine is $\dfrac{d}{(c^2 + d^2)^{\frac{1}{2}}}$ and whose cosine is $\dfrac{c}{(c^2 + d^2)^{\frac{1}{2}}}$.
Therefore

$$c + di = (c^2 + d^2)^{\frac{1}{2}}\left[\frac{c}{(c^2 + d^2)^{\frac{1}{2}}} + \frac{d}{(c^2 + d^2)^{\frac{1}{2}}}i\right]$$
$$= (c^2 + d^2)^{\frac{1}{2}}(\cos B + i \sin B)$$

[11] See L. Dickson, *First Course in the Theory of Equations* (New York, Wiley, 1922).
[12] When the coefficients of the original equation are real numbers.

The final solution thus becomes

$$Y(t) = A^t(g \cos tB + h \sin tB) \tag{90}$$

Now

$$c = \frac{\alpha(1 + \beta)}{2} \quad \text{and} \quad d = \left[\frac{4\alpha\beta - \alpha^2(1 + \beta)^2}{4}\right]^{\frac{1}{2}} \tag{91}$$

and

$$A = (c^2 + d^2)^{\frac{1}{2}} = \left[\frac{\alpha^2(1 + \beta)^2}{4} + \frac{4\alpha\beta - \alpha^2(1 + \beta)^2}{4}\right]^{\frac{1}{2}} = \sqrt{\alpha\beta} \tag{92}$$

Angle B is such that

$$\cos B = \frac{c}{\sqrt{c^2 + d^2}} = \frac{\alpha(1 + \beta)}{2\sqrt{\alpha\beta}} \tag{93}$$

and

$$\sin B = \frac{d}{\sqrt{c^2 + d^2}} = \left[\frac{4\alpha\beta - \alpha^2(1 + \beta)^2}{4\alpha\beta}\right]^{\frac{1}{2}} = \left[1 - \frac{\alpha(1 + \beta)^2}{4\beta}\right]^{\frac{1}{2}} \tag{94}$$

The arbitrary constants g and h are now to be determined by the introduction of the initial conditions:

$$Y(t) = (\alpha\beta)^{t/2}(g \cos tB + h \sin tB) \tag{95}$$

At time $t = 0$,

$$Y_0 = g \cos 0 + h \sin 0 \tag{96}$$

Thus $g = Y_0$. At time $t = 1$,

$$Y_1 = \sqrt{\alpha\beta}(g \cos B + h \sin B)$$
$$= \sqrt{\alpha\beta}(Y_0 \cos B + h \sin B) \tag{97}$$

Solving for h, we get

$$h = \frac{Y_1 - \sqrt{\alpha\beta}Y_0 \cos B}{\sqrt{\alpha\beta} \sin B} = \frac{2Y_1 - Y_0\alpha(1 + \beta)}{[4\alpha\beta - \alpha^2(1 + \beta)^2]^{\frac{1}{2}}} \tag{98}$$

Thus the final solution for Y is:

$$Y(t) = (\alpha\beta)^{t/2}\left\{Y_0 \cos tB + \left(\frac{2Y_1 - Y_0\alpha(1 + \beta)}{[4\alpha\beta - \alpha^2(1 + \beta)^2]^{\frac{1}{2}}}\right) \sin tB\right\} \tag{99}$$

The possible time path will be comparable to those discussed above (page 88) except that now t can take on only whole number values, one for each time period, and the functions proceed in steps.

Again it may be noted that there is in general no equilibrium other than zero possible for the homogeneous equation. There are some cases but they are of negligible importance.[13]

SAMUELSON'S SECOND INTERACTION MODEL

An interaction model in which there is a possible equilibrium[14] is one in which a constant term appears in the characteristic equation of the model, making it nonhomogeneous.

The following is such a model:

$$Y(t) = C(t) + I(t) \qquad (100)$$ $Y(t)$: Income

$$C(t) = \alpha Y(t - 1) \qquad (101)$$ $C(t)$: Consumption

$$I(t) = \beta\{C(t) - C(t - 1)\} + \gamma \qquad (102)$$ $I(t)$: Investment

$$Y(0) = Y_0 \qquad (103)$$

$$Y(1) = Y_1 \qquad (104) \qquad \qquad \text{XXIX}$$

The investment is now a function of two parts: one, the acceleration part, depends upon previous income, and the other is independent of consumption—it may be constant, as here, or a function of time.[15]

The solution of such a system will be only slightly different from that of the previous one, and will be treated more briefly:

Step I. From the model, derive the characteristic equation by combining the equations of the model:

$$Y(t) - \alpha(1 + \beta)Y(t - 1) + \alpha\beta Y(t - 2) - \gamma = 0 \qquad (105)$$

Step II. Solve the homogeneous part of the equation (i.e., assuming that $\gamma = 0$), deriving, as before, the three types of solution, depending on the nature of the roots of the auxiliary equation:

Case (i), roots real and unequal:

$$Y(t) = a_1 x_1{}^t + a_2 x_2{}^t \qquad (106)$$

Case (ii), roots real and equal:

$$Y(t) = a_1 x^t + a_2 t x^t \qquad (107)$$

Case (iii), roots complex:

$$Y(t) = A^t(g \cos tB + h \sin tB) \qquad (108)$$

---

[13] In case (i), one root may be unity, and the other less than 1. In case (iii), $A = 1$ gives an equilibrium cycle.

[14] The equilibrium values may be negative, as in Baumol's capital and interest model; see *Economic Dynamics*, pp. 171–172.

[15] P. A. Samuelson, *Foundations*, p. 341, where this element is a periodic function of time.

Step IIa. Find a "particular solution" of the complete nonhomogeneous equation by trying: $Y = b$ (constant)

$$b - \alpha(1 + \beta)b + \alpha\beta b - \gamma = 0 \tag{109}$$

$$b = \frac{\gamma}{1 - \alpha} \tag{110}$$

In this model, $1 - \alpha \neq 0$, so that the particular solution is acceptable. If $1 - \alpha = 0$, then we should try substituting $Y(t) = bt$, where b is a constant.

The three types of general solutions are therefore:

(i) $\quad Y(t) = a_1 x_1{}^t + a_2 x_2{}^t + \dfrac{\gamma}{1 - \alpha}$ \hfill (111)

(ii) $\quad Y(t) = a_1 x^t + a_2 t x^t + \dfrac{\gamma}{1 - \alpha}$ \hfill (112)

(iii) $\quad Y(t) = A^t(g \cos tB + h \sin tB) + \dfrac{\gamma}{1 - \alpha}$ \hfill (113)

We are now ready for the introduction of initial conditions in step III, to particularize the arbitrary constants. This is left to the student.

Clearly it is now possible to have an equilibrium solution whenever the first parts tend to zero.

The solution of third- (and higher-) order equations follows this same pattern. The auxiliary equations will be cubics (and higher powers) whose solution will require some knowledge of equation theory, but the steps outlined above will be the same. Naturally the number of arbitrary constants and the number of initial conditions will each equal the order of the difference equation involved.

EXERCISES

1. In the Harrod model, chart time paths of $Y(t)$ in each of the following cases:

	α	β	Y_0
(a)	$\frac{1}{5}$	2	100
(b)	$-\frac{1}{5}$	2	100
(c)	-4	2	100
(d)	$\frac{1}{5}$	2	-100

2. In the previous problem, comment on the plausibility of each of the four cases, explaining why. Devise other sets of values for the parameters so as to

illustrate each possible type of movement (some of which will not be plausible for the present model).

3. In the Cobweb model, suppose that the supply curve has a negative slope. Find the conditions for stability.

4. In the cyclical case of the interaction model (page 106), introduce the initial conditions, and find the values of the arbitrary constants g and h.

5. Derive the complete solution of the Kahn model:[16]

$$C(t) = \alpha Y(t-1) + \beta \qquad \begin{aligned} C(t)&: \quad \text{Consumption} \\ Y(t) &= C(t) + I \qquad Y(t)&: \quad \text{Income} \qquad \text{XXX} \\ I&: \quad \text{Investment} \end{aligned}$$

READINGS

1. W. J. Baumol, *Economic Dynamics* (New York, Macmillan, 1951). Provides an excellent introduction to the solving of difference equations, with many numerical examples. In the footnotes he proves the necessity of the steps shown in this chapter without proof.
2. P. A. Samuelson, "Dynamic Process Analysis," Chapter 10 in H. S. Ellis (ed.) *A Survey of Contemporary Economics* (Philadelphia, Blakiston, 1948).
3. P. A. Samuelson, *Foundations of Economic Analysis* (Harvard, 1947). Many examples of difference equations are offered throughout the book, but the "Mathematical Appendix B" gives very thorough treatment of this subject which is so often given little attention in mathematical texts.
4. J. Tinbergen, *Statistical Testing of Business Cycle Theories* (Geneva, League of Nations, 1939). A pioneering work in the use of difference equations in economics, including a rather simple explanation of the solving of simple equations.
5. J. Tinbergen, "Econometric Business Cycle Research," *The Review of Economic Studies, VII:* 73–90 (1940). A simple explanation of the meaning and use of difference equations.
6. J. R. Hicks, *A Contribution to the Theory of the Trade Cycle* (Oxford: At the Clarendon Press, 1950). Mathematical Appendix. This appendix can now be read with profit. Hicks calls this approach "period analysis," and explains why he prefers it to the use of differential equations.
7. T. C. Schelling, *National Income Behavior, An Introduction to Algebraic Analysis* (New York, McGraw-Hill, 1951). See especially his Appendix, pp. 275–284.

[16] Adapted from J. R. Hicks, *The Trade Cycle*, p. 170. See Kahn's original article in the *Economic Journal, XLI:* 173–198.

PART II

ECONOMETRIC MODELS

INTRODUCTION

The mathematical theory of models has been developed in Part I. The abstract models that were discussed there are very useful, even necessary tools in exploring the consistency and implications of economic theory. Yet many theorists, like Pigou, Knight, and Hicks, content themselves with the use of bits of statistical evidence to check certain aspects of their theory.[1] Some investigators have been making more complete use of statistical data to assess the over-all fit of their models. Alternatively, they develop models to attempt to explain the interaction of sets of data. These further applications of models require an understanding of the elements of statistical theory, and in particular the theory of regression and correlation. The next few chapters are devoted to this phase of the problem. It will be advisable for students to acquaint themselves with such tools as the frequency distribution, averages and measures of dispersion and the concepts of random variable, and probability distribution, but the essential framework of concepts will be reviewed here. The general level of difficulty is somewhat higher than in Part I.

---

[1] This is what Stone calls casual empiricism; Richard Stone, *The Measurement of Consumers' Expenditure and Behaviour in the United Kingdom, 1920–1938* (Cambridge: At the University Press, 1954), p. XXIX.

CHAPTER 7

The Elements of Statistical Theory

THE CONCEPT OF PROBABILITY

Statisticians have tried to give the word "probability" a precise meaning. First of all, it is important to distinguish between "probability" and "possibility." An event that cannot possibly happen has no probability of happening; but, if an event is possible, its probability may be great or small. For example, if a person playing bridge with three other honest players is dealt a hand from a pack that has been well shuffled, it is possible that he may be dealt a hand of thirteen spades. The probability of such an event, however, is very, very small.

It has become the custom to assign positive numerical quantities to events to measure their probability in such a way that the total of all the probabilities is 1. Let us take an example.

THE PROBABILITY DISTRIBUTION

Consider the tossing of a coin which is just as likely to turn up heads as tails, and no other possibilities are allowed. Here we have two events whose probabilities are equal, and since their sum must equal 1, which we can call certainty, then the probability of each event is 1/2. We may write these probabilities as:

$$P(\text{H}) = 1/2$$
$$P(\text{T}) = 1/2$$

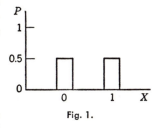

Fig. 1.

This is a simple probability distribution, illustrated in Fig. 1 with the number of heads indicated along the X axis and the probability along the vertical axis. Here we have only two events indicated by $X = 0$ in the case of tails, and $X = 1$ in the case of heads.

We say that X is a *random variable*. In our present example of the tossing of a single coin, there are only two possible values for X. In any particular toss, only one of the events can happen; one of them must happen but which it will be cannot be predicted. If the operation is repeated a large number of times—say a thousand times—then the result can be predicted with great accuracy: it will be found that the number of heads will be very nearly equal to the number of tails. Table 1

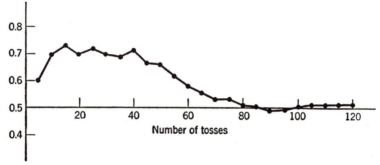

Fig. 2.   Relative frequency of heads.

illustrates an actual case, with the relative frequencies of heads plotted in Fig. 2. In the early stages of such an experiment, the relative frequency can vary considerably from the value of the limit, but, as the

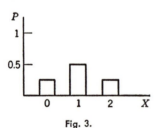

Fig. 3.

number of tosses increases, it moves quite close to the limit line. The reader should try such an experiment himself.

A different probability distribution can be obtained if we consider the tossing of two coins at once. The four possibilities are listed in Table 2, and the relevant probability distribution is shown in Fig. 3.

The probability of each of the events in Table 2 is 1/4 since they are all equally likely and they exhaust the possibilities. These probabilities are presented in two different ways in Table 3.

The first column of the table shows the probabilities of the various events in detail. However, we seldom distinguish between the coins; we are more interested in the number of heads or the number of tails that turn up at any toss. Hence we combine the second and third events to make an event of twice the probability of each of the others. These probabilities are shown in the second column of Table 3 and in Fig. 3. As an exercise, the reader should now construct a probability distribution for the tossing of three coins. He should try his hand at

Table 1

Numbers of Tosses	Number of Heads	Number of Tails	Relative Frequency of Heads
5	3	2	0.60
10	7	3	0.70
15	11	4	0.73
20	14	6	0.70
25	18	7	0.72
30	21	9	0.70
35	24	11	0.69
40	29	11	0.72
45	30	15	0.67
50	33	17	0.66
55	34	21	0.62
60	35	25	0.58
65	36	29	0.56
70	37	33	0.53
75	40	35	0.53
80	41	39	0.51
85	43	42	0.506
90	44	46	0.489
95	47	48	0.495
100	50	50	0.500
105	53	52	0.505
110	56	54	0.508
115	59	56	0.513
120	62	58	0.516

Table 2

Event	Coin A	Coin B	X
1	H	H	2
2	H	T	1
3	T	H	1
4	T	T	0

Table 3

$P(\text{HH})$	1/4	$P(X = 0)$	1/4
$P(\text{HT})$	1/4	$P(X = 1)$	1/2
$P(\text{TH})$	1/4	$P(X = 2)$	1/4
$P(\text{TT})$	1/4		

the probability distribution of the faces of a die, of which there are six, and all equally likely if the die is a true one. The probability distribution for the rolling of two dice is a little more complicated, but not beyond the reach of an alert intellect.

The probability distributions illustrated by the tossing of coins, the rolling of dice, or the dealing of cards are discontinuous or "discrete" distributions, because there is only a limited number of values that the random variable X can possibly take. In the tossing of a single coin, for example, it is not possible to obtain a value of $X = \frac{1}{2}$. For many problems it is more convenient to use a continuous distribution, that is, one for which X may take on any real value within a certain range. Such a probability distribution is illustrated in the next example.

CONTINUOUS PROBABILITY DISTRIBUTIONS

Suppose that each member of a class of one hundred students were asked to measure the length of the classroom with a given yard stick, and the results were tabulated as in Table 4 and charted in Fig. 4.

Table 4

Length (to the nearest inch)	Number of Measurements
39′ 6″	1
39′ 7″	0
39′ 8″	2
39′ 9″	4
39′ 10″	9
39′ 11″	20
40′ 0″	23
40′ 1″	19
40′ 2″	14
40′ 3″	6
40′ 4″	1
40′ 5″	1
	100

Limited only by the precision of measurement, any value of X in the neighborhood of the true length, 40 feet, is possible. By increasing the number of measurements and decreasing the width of the bars, we can get as close as we like to a continuous curve, and it is indeed convenient to use such a curve. In this particular example, the continuous curve which we should approach is one of exceptional importance in statistical theory, the *normal curve*. Since there is apparently no reason for bias in the results, negative errors are as likely as positive errors, and the curve can be expected to be symmetrical about the true value (40 feet). Furthermore, small errors are likely to be considerably more numerous than large errors, and very large errors are very unlikely. The factors affecting any particular measurement are many, as in the tossing of a coin, and they are conflicting in their tendencies to affect the result. We shall assume that no one of these factors, such as the unevenness of the floor, has a predominating importance in the result.

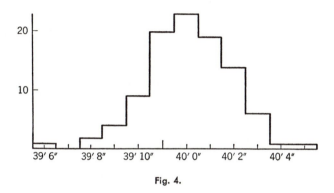

Fig. 4.

In view of the importance of the normal probability distribution, it will be examined with some care. It has the following formula:

$$f = Ae^{-\frac{1}{2}x^2}$$

This formula may at first be a bit frightening, but a little study is reassuring. It is a relation between two variables, f and x; all the remaining symbols are constants. The constant e has been found to be very strategic in the study of logarithms. Its value is 2.7182818+. Its value can be computed to any degree of accuracy that is desired, but, as we continue to compute, the numbers keep on coming, and never stop. This is characteristic of irrational numbers. In a sense we can never know its value exactly in the same way in which we can state the value of $2\frac{1}{2}$ as 2.5000 ⋯ or $\frac{3}{4}$ as 0.75000 ⋯ .

Another famous constant that is an irrational number is π, the ratio of the circumference of any circle to the diameter of that circle. The value of π turns out to be 3.1415926+. It happens to appear in the formula for the normal curve, soon to be discussed.

The second constant in our equation is A, and we find it convenient to give it a value such that the area under the curve equals 1, since this area is the sum of all the probabilities.

Now let us return to the equation. We recognize A and e as two constants, and hence, for any value of x, the abscissa, we can compute a value of f, the ordinate. It will be noted that x is squared, and this implies that the curve will always be positive, i.e., above the x axis, and will be symmetrical about the y axis because for each positive value of x there will be a negative value of x (numerically equal, like $\frac{1}{2}$ and $-\frac{1}{2}$) which will give the same value of f.

In the continuous probability distribution, or, as it is sometimes called, continuous probability density function, the probability is not located at certain points, as it is for the discrete probability distribution, but is spread out as indicated by the area between the curve and the x axis. For any range of the x variable, such as the range from 0 to $\frac{1}{2}$, the area under the curve from 0 to $\frac{1}{2}$ gives the probability of a value of x falling in the range. There is a curious anomaly that, since a single point has no width, the area above a point is zero, and hence the probability of a particular single value is zero. But this is necessary, since there is an infinity of points along the x axis; indeed, there is an infinity of points within the range from 0 to $\frac{1}{2}$, and, if we assigned some positive value to each of these points, the area under the curve would have to be infinite. Thus we consider probabilities only for ranges and can say, for example, that the fact that the arithmetic mean of the distribution, at zero, divides the area in half implies that negative values are as probable as positive ones.

The normal curve is generally set up as a function of two characteristics of the distribution, the arithmetic mean (μ) and the standard deviation[1] (σ) with x measured from the mean thus:

$$ f = \frac{1}{\sigma\sqrt{2\pi}} \exp\left[-\frac{1}{2}\left(\frac{x-\mu}{\sigma}\right)^2 \right] $$

The function is illustrated in Fig. 5. The modal point is precisely at the mean. Within the range $\mu - \sigma$ and $\mu + \sigma$ the curve is concave downward and outside of that range the curvature is reversed, so that the function is concave upward. Beyond the range $\mu - 3\sigma$ and $\mu + 3\sigma$,

[1] The standard deviation, which is generally indicated by a small Greek sigma, σ, is the measure of the scatter or spread of the items away from the arithmetic mean. A group of university students might happen to have the same average age as a group of people chosen outside the university, but the range in the ages of the university students would probably be much smaller, varying from about 16 to 30, whereas in a group chosen more widely there might well be some infants, on the one hand, and some old people, on the other. The standard deviation of the university group would tend to be less than the standard deviation of the group containing infants and oldsters. It is defined specifically below, on page 125. The square of the standard deviation is generally known as the variance, indicated by σ^2.

the function approaches the base line so very closely that very little of the area of the curve (and hence very little probability) lies beyond this range.

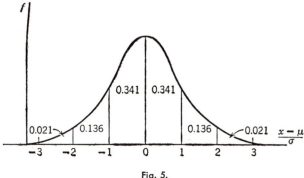

Fig. 5.

We are more interested in the areas under various portions of the curve than in the ordinates, since these areas give us the probabilities of the corresponding x values. Table 5 gives the areas between the mean and certain values of x. Since the curve is symmetrical, a doubling of the P values gives the areas on both sides of the mean.

Table 5

$\frac{x - \mu}{\sigma}$	P
0.0	0.0000
1.0	0.3413
2.0	0.4772
3.0	0.49865
4.0	0.4999683
5.0	0.4999997133

Let us take the value of $(x - \mu)/\sigma = 1$, where $P = 0.3413$. In this case, $x - \mu = \sigma$, i.e., $x = \mu + \sigma$. Thus the table tells us that the area under the curve between $x = \mu$ and $x = \mu + \sigma$ equals 0.3413. Doubling the probability gives us the area under the curve from $\mu - \sigma$ to $\mu + \sigma$ as 0.6826. Thus 68.26 per cent of the area of the curve lies within a range of σ on either side of the mean. As a rough check on distributions that appear to be about normal, we frequently notice whether there are about two-thirds of the points within one standard deviation on either side of the mean. Similarly it can be seen from the table that within a range of two standard deviations on either side of the mean there is a little over 95 per cent of the area; and within a range of three standard deviations on either side of the mean, 99.7 per cent of the area. Frequently we wish to know how far out we have to go in order to include the central 95 per cent of the curve; the answer is 1.96σ, since only 5 per cent of the area is beyond this range.

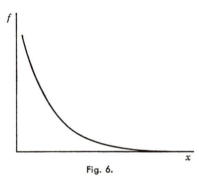

Fig. 6.

The normal curve was introduced as an example of a continuous probability distribution for a continuous random variable (X). Another example is the curve illustrated in Fig. 6, which shows very high probability for small values of x and very small probabilities for large values of x. A formula for this curve can be found in most textbooks on statistical theory. The x value might be the number of children born in a single delivery, as twins, triplets, or quadruplets. The probability distribution is said to be J-shaped.

There is an important difference between the examples that we have just been discussing, that is, the measuring of a distance, or the counting of births, and the earlier examples of tossing coins, rolling dice, or dealing cards. In the first simple examples of games, the conditions are known so precisely[2] that the probabilities can be computed from these conditions. In most applications we do not know the conditioning factors precisely, and hence we attempt to approximate the probabilities from observation data.

BIVARIATE DATA

All the examples so far have had a random variable, X, for which we have attempted to find probabilities or frequencies. Now let us consider two related variables, such as the heights and weights of individuals. Let the height be X and the weight be Y, and consider Fig. 7, in which the small circle represents an individual whose height is 70 inches, and whose weight is 180 pounds. Each dot on this *scatter chart* represents an individual. Clearly the dots are not scattered evenly over the chart, but tend to be concentrated along the diagonal of the chart. This is to be expected because taller men are normally heavier than shorter men. A person who is very tall and yet very light is unusual,

[2] At least we assume them to be. One experimenter actually threw dice 49,152 times and found them biased. See M. G. Kendall, *The Advanced Theory of Statistics*, Vol. I, p. 199 (London, Charles Griffin, 1948).

as is the short and very heavy man. Thus the dots should be found less frequently in the top left-hand corner and in the bottom right-hand

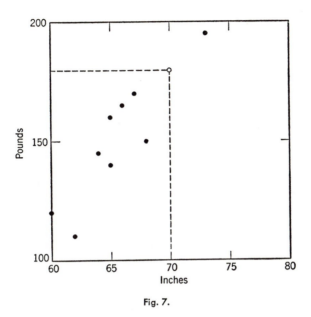

Fig. 7.

corner. If we were to draw a line of relationship through these dots, we could see how much weight tended to be added for each additional inch of height. This question will be studied further in the next chapter.

INTRODUCTION TO SAMPLING THEORY: SAMPLING MODEL I

The essential elements of sampling may be illustrated by a very simple example. Suppose that we have 55 pieces of paper of which 10 have the number 1 on them, 9 have the number 2, 8 have the number 3, and so on. These pieces of paper are put in a hat and thoroughly mixed up. One of the pieces is drawn without looking, the number noted, and the piece of paper returned to the hat.[3] Such a drawing is repeated 15 times so as to give us a sample of 15 numbers.

The original *population* or *universe* that is being sampled is illustrated in Fig. 8. The arithmetic mean is 4 and the standard deviation is the square root of 6. Some samples actually drawn are given in Table 6. The first sample of 15 items had a mean of 2.8 and a standard deviation

---

[3] To assure a random sample, good mixing is essential, and hence paper disks with metal edges are better than just pieces of paper, and a bowl is better than a hat.

Table 6

Number on Tag	Sample I	Sample II	Sample III	Sample I+II	Sample I+II+III	Sample IIIa	Sample IIIb	Sample IIIc
1	5	3	2	8	10	1	1	0
2	3	2	3	5	8	1	2	0
3	3	2	0	5	5	0	0	0
4	1	3	4	4	8	1	1	2
5	1	0	1	1	2	0	0	1
6	1	0	1	1	2	1	0	0
7	1	3	0	4	4	0	0	0
8	0	1	3	1	4	0	1	2
9	0	1	1	1	2	1	0	0
10	0	0	0	0	0	0	0	0
	15	15	15	30	45	5	5	5
$\bar{X}$	2.8	4.2	4.5	3.5	3.8	4.4	3.4	5.8
σ_s	1.9	2.6	2.7	2.4	2.6	2.9	2.5	1.8
$\hat{\sigma}$	1.9	2.7	2.8	2.4	2.6	3.2	2.8	2.0

of 1.9. In actual practice only one sample is drawn and inference is made from that sample about the original population. Let us see how it would work out in this case.

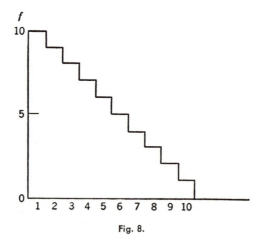

Fig. 8.

Suppose that we had drawn a sample of 30 with an arithmetic mean of 3.5.[4] The arithmetic mean of the population would then be estimated as 3.5. We happen to know that the population mean is 4.0, and hence that the estimate is in error by 0.5. It is to be expected that there will be errors in our estimates, but, if the sampling is truly random,

[4] We are here taking the sum of samples I and II in Table 3.

we can make some significant statements about the extent of the error, and hence about the reliability of the estimate.

Statistical theory has given us a formula for the "standard error of the mean":

$$\sigma_{\bar{x}} = \frac{\sigma}{\sqrt{N}}$$

where σ is the standard deviation of the population and N is the number of items in the sample. Clearly the sampling error in our estimate will vary directly with the standard deviation of the population and inversely as the square root of the number of items in the sample. A larger sample gives us more accuracy in estimation, but the accuracy will double (that is, the sampling error will fall to half) only when the sample is quadrupled.

In any actual problem we shall not know the standard deviation of the population—such variability is one of the characteristics of the population that we are seeking by our sampling process. But sampling theory tells us that we can use here the value of the standard deviation of the sample as an estimate of the standard deviation of the population. Hence we write

$$\sigma_{\bar{x}} = \frac{\sigma}{\sqrt{N}} \approx \frac{\sigma_s}{\sqrt{N}} = \frac{2.45}{\sqrt{30}} = 0.45$$

where the sign $\approx$ means "nearly equal to." We then make one of the following statements:

(a) The arithmetic mean of the population lies within the range $\bar{X}_s \pm \sigma_{\bar{x}} = 3.5 \pm 0.45 = 3.01$ to 3.95.

(b) The arithmetic mean of the population lies within the range $\bar{X}_s \pm 2\sigma_{\bar{x}} = 3.5 \pm 0.90 = 2.60$ to 4.40.

(c) The arithmetic mean of the population lies within the range $\bar{X}_s \pm 3\sigma_{\bar{x}} = 3.5 \pm 1.35 = 2.15$ to 4.85. If we consistently estimate the range in one of these ways, we shall find ourselves to be correct, respectively: (a) roughly two times out of three; (b) 95 times out of a hundred; (c) 997 times out of a thousand. We can use a small range or a wider one; but the smaller the range, the more often shall we be wrong, and the wider the range, the more often shall we be right. The amount of certainty required will depend upon circumstances. In estimating the amount of drug in a dose it is important to be precise, but in estimating the amount of sulphur in a batch of coke, we need not be so precise. In general, we may say that the mean of the population is likely to be within a range of two standard errors, and almost certainly to be within a range of three standard errors.

In the sample of 30 that we have drawn, it is to be noted that the first range just misses the true mean of 4.0, but the second range, that of two standard deviations, catches it easily. Taking a larger sample[5] of 45, the arithmetic mean of 3.8 was obtained, and the standard error of the mean was:

$$\sigma_{\bar{x}} = \frac{\sigma}{\sqrt{N}} \approx \frac{2.6}{\sqrt{45}} \approx 0.39$$

This larger sample does enclose the true mean within the first range of $3.8 \pm 0.39 = 3.41$ to 4.19.

This procedure in estimating the variability of the means of samples is based upon the theorem that the distribution of sample means approaches a normal distribution as the number of samples increases. This *central limit theorem* is perhaps the most important one in statistical theory, and its proof has exercised the talents of some of the first-rate mathematicians. It will be noted that it does not depend upon the shape of the original distribution, but the approach to normality will be more rapid for those populations that are nearly normal; and it will be assisted also by having larger samples rather than smaller ones.

Table 7

Class Limits	Frequency
2.5–2.99	1
3.0–3.49	4
3.5–3.99	6
4.0–4.49	9
4.5–4.99	3
5.0–5.49	2
	25

This distribution of sample means is a statistical distribution. Suppose that we had taken 25 samples of size 15 from the triangular population[6] given above. The distribution of the 25 means might have been as shown in Table 7. The arithmetic mean of this distribution works out at 4.05 and the standard deviation at 0.61. If we had taken a hundred samples, the distribution would have been very close to a

---

[5] Sample I + II + III.

[6] The fact that we might sample 375 items from a population of 55 should cause no concern. The original population would have been essentially the same if we had ten times as many items of each kind. Actually, the "population" being sampled is a very large number of samples of 15 from such a group of 55 pieces of paper. For example, it is possible to get a sample of nothing but 10's, and hence a mean of 10, but the probability of this is $(1/55)^{15}$, which is an extremely small figure.

normal distribution. These tendencies for sampling errors to vanish as samples are made larger is part of what is quite generally known as the *law of large numbers.*

SOME THEORY OF ESTIMATION

In actual sampling situations we estimate the parameters of the population from the characteristics of the sample. In particular, the mean of sample I (2.8) would be used as an estimate of the mean of the population. From the theory of variability already discussed, it is clear that a larger random sample will provide a better estimate, and our sample of 30 gives a mean of 3.5; the sample of 45 is still better (3.8).

In estimating the standard deviation of the population, let us assume that the mean of the population is known. Then, from the first three samples, we compute the following values:

Sample	$\hat{\sigma}$
I	2.22
II	2.65
III	2.68
I and II	2.44

$$\hat{\sigma} = \left[\frac{\sum f(X - \mu)^2}{N} \right]^{\frac{1}{2}}$$

However, we are generally in ignorance of the actual mean of the population, and must use the deviation about the mean of the sample, that is, the standard deviation of the sample. The standard deviations have been computed for our samples and are given in Table 6. It will be noted that they are all smaller than the above estimates of σ. This is necessarily so, because from its nature the standard deviation is less than the root-mean-square deviation around any other value. Thus, the use of the standard deviation of the sample as an estimate of the standard deviation of the population gives us estimates that are too low—that is, they are biased downward. Statistical theory supplies us with a correction factor $[N/(N - 1)]^{\frac{1}{2}}$ applied as follows:

$$\hat{\sigma} = \sigma_s \left(\frac{N}{N - 1} \right)^{\frac{1}{2}} = \left[\frac{\sum f(X - \bar{X})^2}{N - 1} \right]^{\frac{1}{2}}$$

The result of the correction factor, it may be noted, is that we divide the sum by $N - 1$ rather than by N. A justification might be attempted in terms of the concept of *degrees of freedom.* If we are free to choose any N items from a population, we have N degrees of freedom. But, if we must select these N items in such a way as to have a certain mean, then we have only $N - 1$ degrees of freedom, because the last item will already be determined once the first $N - 1$ have been chosen.

This is relevant to the present situation because we are estimating the standard deviation from a group of N items from which we have already estimated the arithmetic mean.

It may now be recalled that, in the formula for the standard error of the mean, the standard deviation of the population is first proposed; but in sampling an unknown population this value will not be known, and hence we use an estimate of it derived from the formula just presented:

$$\hat{\sigma}_{\bar{x}} = \frac{\hat{\sigma}}{\sqrt{N}} = \left[\frac{\sum f(X - \bar{X})^2}{N(N-1)} \right]^{\frac{1}{2}}$$

Now we are able to make more precise statements about variability. We assume that the shuffling of the pieces has been well done, so that our samples are random. Having drawn a sample of 30, we consider the distribution of means of many samples of size 30, which is likely to be very close to normal. The standard deviation of this distribution of sample means is the standard error of the mean, which is estimated from our sample to be:

$$\hat{\sigma}_{\bar{x}} = \frac{\hat{\sigma}}{\sqrt{N}} = \frac{2.4}{\sqrt{30}} \approx 0.5$$

We wish now to ascertain the probability of obtaining a deviation from the mean of the population of as much as 0.5 or more—this implies a positive or a negative deviation of that much or more. That is, we wish to find the shaded area under the curve shown in Fig. 9. From

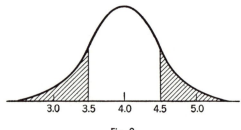

Fig. 9.

Table 5 this area is found to be 0.32. We should expect to find, therefore, because of random variation alone, deviations of as large as 0.5 or larger almost one-third of the time. We thus conclude that this sample might very well have come from the population with mean $\mu = 4$.

Suppose now that it is suspected that this sample of 30 might have been taken from a population with mean of 5. The standard deviation of the population is estimated as above, and the standard error of the mean. Then the question is asked whether there might arise a deviation as large as three times the standard deviation. Reference to Table 5 shows that a deviation as large as this, or larger, occurs by chance only three times in a thousand. This can be regarded as unlikely, and we conclude either that the sample was not random, or that it came from some other population.

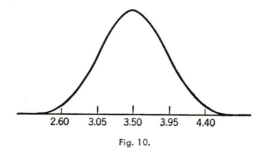

2.60   3.05   3.50   3.95   4.40

Fig. 10.

The question can be put a little differently. Our information comes from a sample of 30 with a mean of 3.5 and a standard deviation of 2.44. The standard error of the mean is computed as 0.45. It can be said that the true mean, or mean of the population, is likely to be within the range of 3.05 to 3.95, is very likely to be within the range of 2.60 to 4.40, and is almost certain to be within the range of 2.15 to 4.85. In this particular case we happen to know the true mean (4), and know that it lies within the second range.

SMALL SAMPLE THEORY

The sampling inference theory explained above is based on large samples. The statistical distribution of the means of random samples only approaches the normal distribution, and is sufficiently close to normal only if the samples are large. Thirty is a minimum number for such a sample, and 50 is much better. The greater variability in the means of smaller samples is seen in Table 6 where three samples of 5 are shown (these samples were added together to make sample III). The sampling distribution of means of these smaller samples follows a different law called the *t distribution*. This is a symmetrical distribution, so that positive deviations are as likely as negative ones, but the distribution is flatter in the center and spreads out more in the tails than the normal curve. Hence there is less concentration around the arithmetic mean.

Actually there is a family of t distributions depending on the size of the sample. That is, there is a different t distribution for each degree of freedom. The smaller the sample the flatter the curve, and the more it is spread out. The larger the sample the more it approaches the normal distribution, and for a sample of 30 items or more it is much like the normal curve. But even for a sample of 30 there is still a good deal more in the tails than for the normal curve.

Let us now follow the more correct procedure and test the sample of 30 with the t test. Suppose we have reason to believe that the mean of the population is 4. We then set up a hypothesis and level of significance:

Known: A sample of 30 items with $\bar{X} = 3.5$ and $s = 2.44$.

Hypothesis: Our sample is a random sample from a population with mean of 4.

Level of Significance: We shall reject the hypothesis if the probability of a deviation of 0.5 or more from $\mu = 4$ is less than 0.05, and accept it in all other cases.

Computation: The degrees of freedom: $n = N - 1 = 29$.

$$t = \frac{\bar{X} - 4}{\hat{\sigma}_{\bar{x}}} = \frac{3.5 - 4.0}{0.45} = -1.11$$

Table A, page 219, shows that, for $n = 29$, when $t = 1.055$,

$$P = 2 \times 0.15 = 0.3$$

when $t = 1.311$,

$$P = 2 \times 0.1 = 0.2$$

Conclusion: The hypothesis is accepted since the probability of a deviation of 0.5 or more from $\mu = 4$ is greater than 0.2. The difference between the means is not significant. The value of t would have to be as large as 2.045 before the hypothesis would be rejected on the basis of the level of significance which has been assumed above.[7]

TESTING STANDARD DEVIATIONS

The statistical distribution used in testing the standard deviation is a positively skewed distribution, illustrated in Fig. 11. For large samples it approaches the normal curve, and hence the normal probability distribution could be used for making tests in such cases. However, the tests for small samples are general, and will be illustrated here.

The distribution in question here is the χ^2 (Chi square) distribution,

[7] The figure 2.045 for t with 29 degrees of freedom at the 0.05 significance level may be compared with 1.96 for the normal distribution.

whose complicated formula we do not reproduce here. Its use in the present situation is based on the following theorem:

If s^2 is the variance[8] of a sample of N drawn from a normal population with variance σ^2, then Ns^2/σ^2 has a χ^2 distribution with $N - 1$ degrees of freedom.

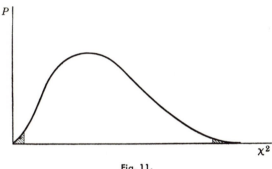

Fig. 11.

Like the t distribution, the χ^2 distribution is really a family of distributions, one curve for each number of degrees of freedom. Its use is illustrated from the sample drawn above.

Known: A sample of 30 items has been drawn with $\bar{X} = 3.5$ and $s^2 = 5.717$.

Hypothesis: Our sample is a random sample from a normal population with variance of 6.

Level of Significance: We shall reject the hypothesis if the probability of obtaining $s^2 = 5.717$, given $\sigma^2 = 6$, is less than 0.02, and accept it in all other cases.

Computation: The number of degrees of freedom is $n = 30 - 1 = 29$. From Table B, page 219, it is ascertained that

$$\chi^2_{0.99} = 14.256; \quad \chi^2_{0.01} = 49.588$$

Hence 98 per cent of the time $14.256 < \chi^2 < 49.588$. Assuming the original numbers to be normally distributed,

$$\chi^2 = \frac{Ns^2}{\sigma^2} = \frac{30(5.717)}{6} = 28.585$$

which is within the above range.

Conclusion: The hypothesis is accepted.

SUMMARY

From the brief treatment of statistical theory offered in this chapter it is seen that we are concerned with the behavior of a random variable, which is affected by the laws of chance and cannot be predicted. From

[8] The term "variance" means the square of the standard deviation.

our knowledge of the situation we can estimate probabilities from which we judge the likelihood of certain results.

Each situation requires careful study. Statisticians have shown the type of variation to be expected in a number of situations. The means of large samples are distributed as a normal distribution. Means of small samples are distributed as a t distribution. Sums of squares of a normal random variable follow a χ^2 distribution. These are only the most important statistical distributions; others have been developed for other circumstances.

Chance is defined here as the aggregation of a large number of causes, no one of which predominates. By randomness we mean the impossibility of prediction. When the conditions are precisely known, the probability distribution is known, but no more. The applicability of the theory of sampling to economics rests upon these concepts, and as the work develops in subsequent chapters these matters will be further explored.

EXERCISES

1. Set up a sampling model like that explained on page 121, and take 20 random samples (replacing the piece each time) of size 5, compute the 20 means, and draw up a frequency distribution. Group the samples into 10 samples of 10 each, compute the 10 means, and draw up a frequency distribution. Group these 10 samples into 5 samples of 20 items each, compute their means, and note the scatter of these means. Compute the arithmetic mean of all 100 items.

2. Repeat the sampling and computation procedures of Exercise 1 for a sampling model containing 50 items, each of the first 10 natural numbers being repeated 5 times. This is a "rectangular distribution."

3. From the sample data of the two previous exercises, estimate the means and standard deviations of the original populations, and the corresponding variabilities.

4. Toss two coins at once, and measure the relative frequencies as follows; plot the relative frequencies on a chart:

	Number of Heads			Relative Frequencies		
Tosses	None	One	Two	No Heads	One Head	Two Heads
5	1	2	2	1/5	2/5	2/5
10	2	5	3	2/10	5/10	3/10
etc.		etc.			etc.	

READINGS

1. S. S. Wilks, *Elementary Statistical Analysis* (Princeton, Princeton University Press, 1949). A fine introduction to statistical theory by an outstanding theo-

retical statistician. The student would need the elements of combinatorial algebra and calculus.

2. P. Hoel, *Introduction to Mathematical Statistics* (New York, Wiley, 2nd ed., 1954). This excellent textbook by a very able author follows a path that is somewhat different from the others, but a very rewarding path to follow.

3. E. B. Mode, *Elements of Statistics* (New York, Prentice-Hall, 1951). See especially Chap. IX.

4. J. E. Freund, *Modern Elementary Statistics* (New York, Prentice-Hall, 1952), especially Chapters 7 and 8.

5. F. E. Croxton and D. J. Cowden, *Applied General Statistics* (New York, Prentice-Hall, 1940). See especially Chapters XII and XIII. Most of this widely used textbook offers a more descriptive approach to statistics.

6. L. H. C. Tippett, *Statistics* (Home University Library of Modern Knowledge, Oxford University Press, 1949).

7. R. G. D. Allen, *Statistics for Economists* (London, Hutchinson's University Library, 1949).

CHAPTER 8

Simple Regression Theory

REGRESSION ANALYSIS

In Chapter 7 we were concerned with sampling of a single variable. This is known as univariate analysis. The next step is a study of two variables at the same time, known as bivariate analysis. A simple example of bivariate data, the heights and weights of a group of individuals, has already been introduced.[1] Suppose each of ten students is measured with respect to these two attributes, and the data, shown in Table 1, are plotted as the ten points shown in Fig. 1, called a *scatter chart.*

Table 1. Heights and Weights of Ten Students

Student	Height (inches)	Weight (pounds)
A	65	140
B	70	180
C	60	120
D	62	110
E	73	195
F	67	170
G	65	160
H	68	150
I	66	165
J	64	145

From the chart it is clear that an average line of relationship could be drawn through these points so that for any particular height an estimate of the weight could be given. Such an average line of relationship could be drawn freehand by holding a taut piece of string across the page as a guide. There should be about as many points

[1] See Chap. 7, p. 121.

above the line as below it, and they should be scattered well along the length of the line. As a check, the chart could be divided down the middle, so as to cut the base line in half, and the same test applied to each half of the chart separately; i.e., in the left-hand half of the chart there should be about as many points above the line as below it, and also in the right-hand half of the chart there should be about as many points above the line as there are below it. Such a line could be called a median line since it bears much the same relationship to these points as a median average does to its group of items.

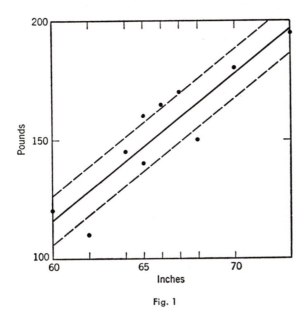

Fig. 1

A better line of average relationship can be computed mathematically in such a way as to minimize the sum of the squares of the deviations about it. This technique of "least squares" was used by the great mathematician Gauss to estimate the orbits of the planets. He knew that his measurements were not exact, and that he could not take all the factors into account, and he reasoned on the basis of the laws of probability that a line that was drawn so that the sum of the squares of the deviations from it was a minimum would give him the best result. Subsequent statistical theory has given further support to this device.

We proceed to compute a least squares line,[2] which in this case will

[2] It may be noted that the arithmetic mean is a least squares average since the sum of the squares of the deviations of the items from it is a minimum, which implies mathematically that the sum of the deviations about it will equal zero.

be the *line of regression* of Y on X. We shall be concerned with the deviations measured vertically from the line:

$$Y = a + bX$$

Our task is to find the values of a and b, that is, the intercept and the slope of this line. In order to do this,[3] we must compute certain sums which are then fitted into the two normal equations:

$$\sum(Y) = Na + b\sum(X)$$

$$\sum(XY) = a\sum(X) + b\sum(X^2)$$

The necessary sums are $\sum(X)$, $\sum(X^2)$, $\sum(Y)$, $\sum(XY)$, as computed in Table 2. Fitting these sums into the normal equations, we get:

$$1535 = 10a + 660b$$

$$102{,}115 = 660a + 43{,}688b$$

Solving,[4] we get

$$a = -261.64$$

$$b = +6.29$$

---

[3] With the aid of a little calculus, though Yule does without it (*Introduction to the Theory of Statistics*, London, Charles Griffin & Co., 1932, 10th ed., p. 231), the reason for these steps can be made clear. The deviations from the line can be written:

$$d = Y - Y_c = Y - a - bX$$

Then the sum of the squares is:

$$
\begin{aligned}
S = \sum(d^2) &= \sum[(Y - a - bX)^2] \\
&= \sum(Y^2 + a^2 + b^2X^2 - 2aY - 2bXY + 2abX) \\
&= \sum(Y^2) + Na^2 + b^2\sum(X^2) - 2a\sum Y - 2b\sum(XY) + 2ab\sum(X)
\end{aligned}
$$

This last step requires some familiarity with summation signs. This sum is now to be minimized with respect to a and b:

$$\frac{\partial S}{\partial a} = 2Na - 2\sum(Y) + 2b\sum(X)$$

$$\frac{\partial S}{\partial b} = 2b\sum(X^2) - 2\sum(XY) + 2a\sum(X)$$

Setting each of these partial derivatives equal to zero, we get the two normal equations as the conditions to be fulfilled for a minimum value of S. An examination of the nature of the function will show that it must be a minimum, and cannot be a maximum or other kind of "stationary" value.

[4] In order to solve the equations, multiply each element of the first equation by 66, getting

$$101{,}310 = 660a + 43{,}560b$$

Now subtract each element of this equation from the corresponding element of the

giving the regression equation $Y = -261.64 + 6.29X$. Now we may use the X value of each individual to compute what the Y value would be if he were an "average" individual. The ten values of Y computed in this way are listed in column Y_c of Table 2. The difference between the Y and the Y_c value is found for each individual, as shown in the next

Table 2.   Computation of Least Squares Straight Line

X	Y	X_2	XY	Y_c	$Y - Y_c$	$(Y - Y_c)^2$
65	140	4,225	9,100	147.2	−7.2	51.84
70	180	4,900	12,600	178.7	1.3	1.69
60	120	3,600	7,200	115.8	4.2	17.64
62	110	3,844	6,820	128.3	−18.3	334.89
73	195	5,329	14,235	197.5	−2.5	6.25
67	170	4,489	11,390	159.8	10.2	104.04
65	160	4,225	10,400	147.2	12.8	163.84
68	150	4,624	10,200	166.1	−16.1	259.21
66	165	4,356	10,890	153.5	11.5	132.25
64	145	4,096	9,280	140.9	4.1	16.81
660	1535	43,688	102,115	1535.0	0.0	1070.86

column headed $Y - Y_c$. The sum of the items in this column is theoretically zero, and actually it will be as close to zero as our rounding of numbers allows. This implies that the sum of the positive deviations just equals the sum of the negative deviations.[5] Finally these deviations are squared, and then summed in the last column. This sum is the value that was minimized; that is, it is less than the sum of squares of deviations measured vertically (i.e., in the Y direction) about any other straight line—whence the name of "least squares" line. The

second equation above, getting

$$805 = 0 + 128b$$

We see that the a has fallen out, and by dividing through both sides by 128 we get

$$b = \frac{805}{128} = 6.29$$

Now substituting this value for b into the first original equation, we get

$$1535 = 10a + (660)(6.29)$$

$$a = \frac{1535 - (660)(6.29)}{10} = -261.64$$

The positive b value indicates that the line slopes upward at a rate of 6.29 units of Y for each unit of X. The negative value of a tells merely that the intercept at the Y axis is 261.64 below the origin.

[5] In Fig. 1, it may be noted that there are 6 points above the line and 4 below it, but the lowest points are quite low.

square root of this sum of squares of deviations, divided by the number of points, is a kind of standard deviation around the line, and has been given the name of *standard error of estimate:*

$$\sigma_{Y \cdot X} = \left[\frac{\sum (Y - Y_c)^2}{N} \right]^{\frac{1}{2}} = \left[\frac{1070.86}{10} \right]^{\frac{1}{2}} = 10.3$$

The reason for this name becomes clear when its use is explained. Let the regression line be plotted on the scatter chart. Draw another straight line parallel to the regression line and a vertical distance of $\sigma_{Y \cdot X}$ above it. Draw another parallel straight line below the line of regression at a vertical distance of $\sigma_{Y \cdot X}$. The band between these two outside lines will be found to contain about two-thirds of the points; in Fig. 1 the number inside this band is found to be 6. On the assumption that the vertical deviations are normally distributed (if we had more of them a frequency distribution could be drawn up and examined), the standard error of estimate is the standard deviation of this distribution of deviations and can be used to estimate probabilities in much the same way as was done in the previous chapter.[6]

Suppose we have an individual not in the original group of students, whose height is 68 inches, and we wish to estimate his weight. The regression line gives an average weight of 166.1 pounds for people of such height, and we should expect that about 68 per cent of the individuals 68 inches in height will weigh between 155.8 pounds and 176.4 pounds. Naturally we should not expect our group of ten students to produce a regression line that was as generally useful as a regression line derived from a larger group that thoroughly covered the population in question.

CORRELATION

It is clear that, if all the points in the scatter chart were to lie on the regression line, then the standard error of estimate would be zero, and the estimate of Y from X could be made with perfect precision. At the opposite extreme, the least squares line would be perfectly horizontal, so that the average value of Y would be the same for all values of X. In this case, knowledge of X is of no assistance whatever in estimating Y. The standard error of estimate is then precisely equal to the standard deviation of the Y variable:

$$\sigma_{Y \cdot X} = \sigma_Y$$

[6] See page 119.

or

$$\left[\frac{\sum(Y - Y_c)^2}{N}\right]^{\frac{1}{2}} = \left[\frac{\sum(Y - \bar{Y})^2}{N}\right]^{\frac{1}{2}}$$

Therefore

$$\sum(Y - Y_c)^2 = \sum(Y - \bar{Y})^2$$

Thus the limits of variation of the standard error of estimate are:

$$0 \le \sigma_{Y \cdot X} \le \sigma_Y$$

Dividing each term by σ_Y and squaring, which does not affect the relationship, we get

$$0 \le \frac{\sigma_{Y \cdot X}^2}{\sigma_Y^2} \le 1$$

A measure of the closeness of the relationship between Y and X is thus $(\sigma_{Y \cdot X}/\sigma_Y)^2$ or better $[1 - (\sigma_{Y \cdot X}/\sigma_Y)^2]^{\frac{1}{2}}$, which gives the value of the Pearsonian *coefficient of correlation:*

$$r = \left[1 - \frac{\sigma_{Y \cdot X}^2}{\sigma_Y^2}\right]^{\frac{1}{2}}$$

A value of r that is nearly zero gives a line of regression that is nearly horizontal. A value of r that is nearly equal to 1 gives a line of regression that is very near the diagonal[7] with the points clustered closely

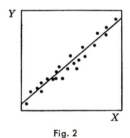

Fig. 2

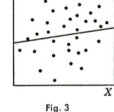

Fig. 3

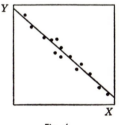

Fig. 4

around the line. If r has a negative value, then the slope of the line is negative. Thus a value of $r = -0.97$ means very high negative correlation, whereas $r = -0.14$ means very little correlation, though what there is implies that Y decreases as X increases.

ANALYSIS OF VARIANCE

It can be shown that

$$\sigma_Y^2 = \sigma_{Y \cdot X}^2 + \sigma_E^2$$

[7] Our scatter chart should be square.

where

$$\sigma_E^2 = \frac{\sum (Y_c - \bar{Y})^2}{N}$$

σ_Y^2 is the total variance of the Y variable, σ_E^2 is the "explained" variance, i.e., that part explained in terms of the line of regression; and $\sigma_{Y \cdot X}^2$ is the residual or "unexplained" variance.

To illustrate, take the particular point $X = 70$, $Y = 180$. The Y deviation from $\bar{Y}$ is in this case 26.5 pounds, of which 25.2 pounds is the expected deviation in view of the student's height, and 1.3 pounds is extra or above normal for individuals of that height. From the computations of Tables 2 and 3, we have

$$\sigma_Y^2 = \frac{\sum (\bar{Y} - Y)^2}{N} = 615.25$$

$$\sigma_E^2 = \frac{\sum (\bar{Y} - Y_c)^2}{N} = 506.40$$

$$\sigma_{Y \cdot X}^2 = \frac{\sum (Y - Y_c)^2}{N} = 107.09$$

Adding the last two, we get 613.49, which comes close enough to the first figure. If we had not rounded numbers in the computation, it

Table 3. Computation of Variances

X	Y	Y^2	Y_c	$\bar{Y} - Y_c$	$(\bar{Y} - Y_c)^2$
65	140	19,600	147.2	6.3	39.69
70	180	32,400	178.7	-25.2	635.04
60	120	14,400	115.8	37.7	1421.29
62	110	12,100	128.3	25.2	635.04
73	195	38,025	197.5	-44.0	1936.00
67	170	28,900	159.8	-6.3	39.69
65	160	25,600	147.2	6.3	39.69
68	150	22,500	166.1	-12.6	158.76
66	165	27,225	153.5	0	0.00
64	145	21,025	140.9	12.6	158.76
	1535	241,775	1535.0	0	5063.96

$$\sigma_Y^2 = \frac{\sum Y^2}{N} - \left(\frac{\sum Y}{N}\right)^2 = \frac{241,775}{10} - \left(\frac{1535}{10}\right)^2 = 615.25$$

would have been exact. We find therefore that the explained variance is 82 per cent of the total, leaving 18 per cent unexplained. The square roots may be taken, to give us $\sigma_Y = 24.8$; $\sigma_E = 22.5$; and $\sigma_{Y \cdot X} = 10.3$.

ALTERNATIVE REGRESSION OF X ON Y

It may be that we wish to estimate heights from weights rather than the other way around, as above. In that event, X is taken as the dependent variable, and Y as the independent variable. The regression equation is

$$X = a' + b'Y$$

The appropriate normal equations are:

$$\sum(X) = Na' + b'\sum(Y)$$
$$\sum(XY) = a'\sum(Y) + b'\sum(Y^2)$$

A standard error of estimate would be computed:

$$\sigma_{X \cdot Y} = \left[\frac{\sum(X - X_c)^2}{N} \right]^{1/2}$$

And the corresponding analysis of variance could be carried out. It should be emphasized that the deviations that are now minimized are measured in the X direction,[8] i.e., horizontal in Fig. 1.

The two regression lines are related rather closely. If the correlation is perfect, the two regression lines coincide. If the correlation is zero, the lines are at right angles. Any measure of correlation should therefore involve the slopes of these lines, as will be seen when the variables are measured from their respective means.

VARIABLES MEASURED FROM MEANS

It is sometimes better to express the variables in terms of deviations from their respective means:

$$x = X - \bar{X}; \quad y = Y - \bar{Y}$$

An interesting change takes place in the normal equations when this is done, for then $\sum x = 0$ and $\sum y = 0$. The normal equations for

---

[8] When the deviations are measured in the direction of one of the variables, the regression is called "elementary." Alternatively, the deviations minimized could be measured at right angles to the regression line, but this leads to rather more complicated procedures and for our present purposes has no advantage over the two discussed, in which the distinction between dependent and independent is important. Schultz assumed that both variables were subject to error, and assigned weights to the deviations related inversely to the amount of error suspected in the variables. This "weighted regression" has much to commend it. See below. See P. A. Samuelson, "A Note on Alternative Regressions," *Econometrica, 10:* 80–83.

the regression of y on x then reduce to

$$a = 0$$

$$\sum (xy) = b \sum (x^2)$$

and from the second equation:

$$b = \frac{\sum (xy)}{\sum (x^2)}$$

The corresponding slope for the regression of x on y becomes

$$b' = \frac{\sum (xy)}{\sum (y^2)}$$

Thus

$$bb' = \frac{\{\sum (xy)\}^2}{\sum (x^2) \cdot \sum (y^2)} = r^2$$

The square of the Pearsonian coefficient of correlation is therefore equal to the product of the slopes of the two regression lines. As the value of b' approaches the value of b they must both approach the value of 1 (or -1); i.e., they approach the diagonal of a square scatter chart. It must be noted, however, that the slope b is measured with respect to the X axis, whereas the slope b' is measured with respect to the Y axis. Therefore, as the angle between the regression lines increases, each slope approaches zero, and so also must r.

There is another important conclusion to be drawn from these equations. When the variables are measured from their respective means, the intercept constant in the regression line becomes zero, showing that the regression line goes through the origin. But this new origin is the point of means, that is, at the point $(\bar{X}, \bar{Y})$ on the former axis. Clearly the two regression lines must cross at this point of means.

SAMPLING THEORY OF REGRESSION: SAMPLING MODEL II

The regression analysis which has so far been expounded in this chapter must now be brought together with the sampling theory of the previous chapter. In order to do this, let us consider another population of numbered chips. Let each chip have two numbers on it: an X value and a Y value. But there will not be simply one of each kind; the frequencies are given in Table 4. There are 45 chips kept in 5 different bowls, according to their X values, and each bowl is sampled separately. A sample of 15 is drawn, 3 from each bowl, each chip being replaced after the numbers are noted, and the bowl being stirred again.

Let us suppose that the samples resulted as shown in Table 5. We should now compare the regression line derived from the sample with that from the population. But first we must pause to learn how to handle data that are in the form of a two-way frequency table, called a *correlation table*.

Table 4

Y \ X	1	2	3	4	5	
9				1	1	1
8				1	2	3
7			1	2	3	6
6		1	2	3	2	8
5	1	2	3	2	1	9
4	2	3	2	1		8
3	3	2	1			6
2	2	1				3
1	1					1
	9	9	9	9	9	45

These tables of figures should be studied carefully. They are examples of bivariate populations because there are two variables, X and Y. In an actual problem, the items might be individuals for each of whom we register two characteristics: X their height in inches, and Y their weight in pounds. Alternatively the items might be corporations, with

Table 5

Y \ X	1	2	3	4	5	
9						0
8				1	2	3
7						0
6				1	1	2
5		1	2			3
4	1	1	1	1		4
3	1	1				2
2	1					1
1						0
	3	3	3	3	3	15

X representing the number of employees and Y the amount of profit. Note that for such a bivariate distribution we can consider the distribution of the X value by itself without regard to the Y values, and we can consider the distribution of the Y values without regard to the X values.

Table 6

Distribution of X			Distribution of Y	
X	Frequency		Y	Frequency
1	9		1	1
2	9		2	3
3	9		3	6
4	9		4	8
5	9		5	9
	45		6	8
			7	6
			8	3
			9	1
				45

The two univariate distributions for the population that we are here considering can be seen in the marginal totals of Table 4, but are re-

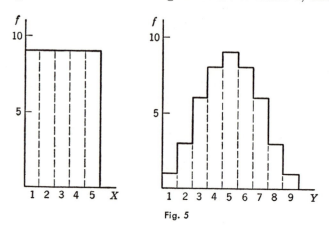

Fig. 5

peated in Table 6, with appropriate charts in Fig. 5. The reader should note and draw charts of the corresponding marginal distributions of the sample.

COMPUTATIONS FROM A CORRELATION TABLE

We wish to compute the regression of y on x so that we need to compute only two sums: $\sum (xy)$ and $\sum (x^2)$. The latter is a straightforward application of the frequencies of the x distribution, which frequencies are obtained by adding the columns. The computations are shown at the bottom of Table 7. We find that

$$\sum \{f(x^2)\} = 90$$

Table 7

Y \ X	1	2	3	4	5	f_Y	y	y^2	$f_Y y^2$
9					8 · 1 · 8	1	4	16	16
8				3 · 1 · 3	6 · 2 · 12	3	3	9	27
7			0 · 1 ·	2 · 2 · 4	4 · 3 · 12	6	2	4	24
6		−1 · 1 · −1	0 · 2 · 0	1 · 3 · 3	2 · 2 · 4	8	1	1	8
5	0 · 1 · 0	0 · 2 · 0	0 · 3 · 0	0 · 2 · 0	0 · 1 · 0	9	0	0	0
4	2 · 2 · 4	1 · 3 · 3	0 · 2 · 0	−1 · 1 · −1		8	−1	1	8
3	4 · 3 · 12	2 · 2 · 4	0 · 1 · 0			6	−2	4	24
2	6 · 2 · 12	3 · 1 · 3				3	−3	9	27
1	8 · 1 · 8					1	−4	16	16
f_x	9	9	9	9	9	45			150
x	−2	−1	0	1	2				
x^2	4	1	0	1	4				
$f_x x^2$	36	9	0	9	36	90			

The computation of the other sum is slightly more troublesome. Each box of Table 7 has an x value and a y value. These values are to be multiplied together, and entered at the top left-hand corner of each box. This product is then to be multiplied by the frequency in the box, and entered at the bottom right-hand corner of the box. All these final products are now to be summed:

$$\sum (fxy) = 90$$

The resulting value of β is

$$\beta = \frac{\sum (fxy)}{\sum (fx^2)} = \frac{90}{90} = 1$$

Similar computations made from the sample figures give us

$$b = \frac{\sum (fxy)}{\sum (fx^2)} = \frac{32}{30} = 1.07$$

All these computations are simplified because x and y are not just deviations from an arbitrary origin, but deviations from the means.

It would not be a major task to take ten or twenty more sets of samples from the population, compute the sample value of b in each case, and draw up a frequency distribution of the sample b's to appraise the variability. But the statisticians have worked out the theoretical distribution, which we shall proceed to apply.[9]

We first define $\sigma_{Y \cdot X}$ as the standard deviation from the regression of Y on X for the population. This corresponds to what above has been called the standard error of estimate, but, when sampling questions arise, estimating is found to be somewhat more complicated.

$$\sigma_{Y \cdot X}^2 = \frac{\sum (y - \beta x)^2}{N} = \frac{\sum (\delta_{Y \cdot X}^2)}{N} = 1.09$$

From the sample, an unbiased estimate of this value is

$$s_{Y \cdot X}^2 = \frac{\sum d_{Y \cdot X}^2}{N - 2} = \frac{\sum (y - bx)^2}{N - 2} = 1.16$$

where N is the number in the sample. The number 2 is subtracted from the number in the sample to obtain the number of degrees of freedom. This is done because there are two characteristics of the sample entailed: the mean of the Y's and the slope of the regression line. That is, in drawing a sample of 15 with given mean and given regression coefficient,

---

[9] G. W. Snedecor, *Statistical Methods*, 4th ed. (Ames, Iowa State Press, 1950), Chap. 6, pp. 117–120. Robert Ferber, *Statistical Techniques for Market Research* (New York, McGraw-Hill, 1949), Chap. VIII.

there are only 13 degrees of freedom. When 13 items have been chosen, the other two are fixed because of the values of $\bar{Y}$ and b.

The regression coefficient b is distributed with a variance estimated by

$$s_b^2 = \frac{s_{Y \cdot X}^2}{\sum (x^2)} = \frac{1.16}{30} = 0.039$$

and the quantity $(b - \beta)/s_b$ follows the t distribution with $N - 2$ degrees of freedom.

RELIABILITY OF THE SLOPE

In regression problems the following question is frequently asked: Can a knowledge of an X value be of any assistance in determining the Y value? This question can be re-phrased as follows: Can β reasonably be expected to differ from zero? We apply the t test in this way:

$$t = \frac{b - 0}{s_b} = \frac{1.07}{0.20} = 5.4$$

For 13 degrees of freedom, the value $t = 5.4$ is well beyond the 0.001 limit. Hence the value $b = 1.07$ is not likely to have arisen purely by chance from a population with $\beta = 0$.

RELIABILITY OF THE MEAN OF Y

Now consider the mean of Y. In simple univariate sampling, the variance of the mean[10] was estimated as s_Y^2/N where s_Y^2 is the variance of the sample. That is, if we ignore the X variable the variance in our present sample is 3.33. But we have found that there is a relation between the two variables X and Y, so that a considerable amount of the variation in Y can be accounted for by the variation in X. This means that Y tends to vary with X, so that, if we take the value of X to be $\bar{X}$, and then assess the variability of $\bar{Y}$, we use the sampling variance

$$\frac{s_{Y \cdot X}^2}{N} = \frac{1.16}{15} = 0.0773$$

VARIANCE OF ANY POINT ON THE REGRESSION LINE

This point of means, the point $(\bar{X}, \bar{Y})$ which was used in the previous paragraph, is but a single point on the regression line. As we move out

[10] See above, page 123.

along the regression line away from this point of means, the variability increases in accordance with the following formula:

$$s_{Yc}^2 = \frac{s_{Y \cdot X}^2}{N} + \frac{s_{Y \cdot X}^2 \cdot x^2}{\sum (x^2)} = \frac{s_{Y \cdot X}^2}{N} \left[1 + \frac{Nx^2}{\sum (x^2)} \right]$$

This formula is to be studied with care. s_{Yc}^2 is not a fixed value, but a function of the x value on the line where the estimate is to be made. The values $s_{Y \cdot X}^2$ and $\sum (x^2)$ are given by the sample, so that, in our case,

$$s_{Yc}^2 = \frac{1.16}{15} \left[1 + \frac{15x^2}{30} \right]$$

Now, if we wish to estimate Y for the mean value of X, the estimate is clearly the mean of the Y's which is $\bar{Y}$, and the variance of this estimate is simply

$$s_{Yc}^2 = \frac{1.16}{15} = 0.0773$$

as was found above. But, if we wish to estimate Y for any other value of X, the use of b in the regression formula entails an additional source of variation. The variance of such an estimate is therefore the sum of the two independent variances, that of $\bar{Y}$ and that of bx. Hence, if we wish to estimate the value of Y_c when $x = 2$,

$$s_{Yc}^2 = \frac{1.16}{15} \left(1 + \frac{4}{2} \right) = 0.232$$

It is clear that the variance increases rapidly if we move far out from the mean of the X's. This variability is shown in Fig. 6.

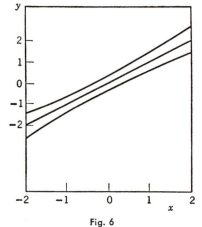

Fig. 6

VARIANCE OF THE INDIVIDUAL ITEMS

The variance just discussed applied to an estimate of an average value of Y for any particular value of X. Suppose, now, that we wish to estimate the range of variation of the individual items, which will fall above and below the line. These individual items therefore vary more widely than their average value for any given X. The variance is the sum of three independent variances, two of which we have already used, and the third is the variance of the items about the regression line.[11]

$$s_Y^2 = s_{Y \cdot X}^2 + \frac{s_{Y \cdot X}^2}{N} + \frac{x^2 \cdot s_{Y \cdot X}^2}{\sum (x^2)}$$

$$= \frac{s_{Y \cdot X}^2}{N} \left[N + 1 + \frac{N x^2}{\sum (x^2)} \right]$$

$$= \frac{1.16}{15} \left[15 + 1 + \frac{15 x^2}{30} \right]$$

$$= \frac{1.16}{15} \left[16 + \frac{x^2}{2} \right]$$

We leave as an exercise for the student the working out of the actual variabilities for various points along the line, and the construction of a variability chart similar to that of Fig. 6.

SAMPLING CONDITIONS

The statistical variability formulas just discussed in connection with the regression of Y on X are based upon two assumptions. First, the variance of the original population of Y is the same at all levels of X. In our sampling model this is obviously true, because each column has a distribution of identical size and shape. This assumption is known as "homogeneous variance," or "homoscedasticity."

The second assumption is that the variability is that of the Y variable for fixed values of X. Our experiment was designed to make this clear by keeping the X values in different bowls. One aspect of this assumption is that the X variable is measured without error. If there are such errors, then the tendency will be for the regression coefficient to be biased downward; that is, it will tend to be too low.[12] This is a consideration of some importance in economic problems inasmuch as the X variable may represent such variables as price, quantity, or an estimate of the national income.

If the first assumption appears from the data to be wrong, there are alternative ways of measuring the relationship.[13] But, if the second assumption does not hold, the situation is not so clear. In view of the difficulty in measuring the reliability of the constants when both X

[11] A. M. Mood, *Introduction to the Theory of Statistics* (New York, McGraw-Hill, 1950).

[12] G. W. Snedecor, *op. cit.* p. 106.

[13] G. W. Snedecor, *op. cit.* Chap. 6.

and Y are subject to variation, the above method is frequently applied, nevertheless, as an approximation.

SAMPLING MODEL III

This second assumption can be broken down into two parts. The assumption can be re-stated as (1) the assumption that the X values are known precisely, and (2) the assumption that they are held fixed. Consider now sampling model III, in which the X values are no longer held fixed. We take the same 45 chips that were used in sampling model II and mix all of them together in a single bowl. A sample of 15 is taken, one chip at a time, with replacement and thorough mixing after each drawing. Table 8 shows such a sample of 15 chips.

In sampling model III, the X values are known precisely (we can assume that they have been correctly observed and recorded) but they have not been kept under control; that is, fixed, as in sampling model II.

Both X and Y are now random variables. We could find the regression of Y on X as a means of predicting a Y value from an X value:

$$b = \frac{\sum f(xy)}{\sum f(x^2)} = 0.86$$

The regression of X on Y could be computed as a predictor of X for a given value of Y. But neither of these regressions may give a good approximation of "the relation" between X and Y. There are, however,

Table 8

Y \\ X	1	2	3	4	5
9					
8					1
7				1	1
6		2			1
5			2		2
4		1	1	1	
3					
2					
1	2				
	2	3	3	2	5

other techniques that could be used for this purpose. One of them is the "weighted regression" line, computed by assuming errors in both X and Y, and weighing these errors inversely as the assumed variance of these errors. Schultz used such a technique. He felt that there were errors of measurement in both the quantity variable and the price variable, but that the error in the quantity variable was considerably greater; hence he gave greater weight to the price variable, and his resulting weighted regression line was closer to the regression of q on p than to the regression of p on q. The mechanics of computation are a little too complicated to be discussed further here.

TRANSFORMATIONS

In many problems in economics that do not conform to any of the simple sampling models discussed, much caution and ingenuity are called for. Consider a set of sales and income data by counties for any considerable area. There are likely to be a few counties for which the figures are very large, and many counties with small figures. These data could be correlated in the usual way, but the meaning of such a coefficient would be limited, and indeed questionable. A more satisfying approach would be to express both variables in terms of their logarithms. The distribution of X and the distribution of Y should then be more balanced or symmetrical about their means, and hence a coefficient of the correlation of their logarithms would have more meaning. Similarly, the regression should be the regression of the logarithms of Y on the logarithms of X. The sampling variances are somewhat more difficult to work out, but will have more meaning than if they were computed directly without taking logarithms.[14]

RANK CORRELATION

In some cases the median is a better average, i.e., more representative, than the arithmetic mean. One such case is that of academic grades, where the actual figures are somewhat arbitrary, and the rankings are significant. Most indexes that purport to measure intelligence or aptitudes are also of this nature. Another class of data for which the median is more useful than the arithmetic mean is that for which the numerical values are very highly skewed as in a frequency distribution of incomes. One very high income figure can affect the arithmetic mean quite appreciably even though there are thousands of other individual items in the distribution that remain unchanged. The median is not so affected, and is recommended for such data.

For data of these types, the values should be ranked, and these ranks rather than the actual values should be correlated. The coefficient in

[14] An excellent example would be the population and income or sales data for the counties of the Province of Quebec, in Canada.

this case is

$$r_r = 1 - \frac{6\sum (D^2)}{N(N^2 - 1)}$$

where D is the difference between the ranks, and N is the number of items in each set.

NONLINEAR REGRESSION

It is to be expected that a straight line will not serve well in all cases.[15] At times curved lines are indicated. For example, the yield of a particular crop will tend to increase with increases in rainfall; but it is generally possible to have too much rainfall, so that the yield will tend to turn down if rainfall keeps on increasing. Here some sort of curve would be more suitable than a straight line.

One type of curve is obtained by transforming one of the variables into logarithms and leaving the other variable as it is. This results in a curve when plotted on an ordinary arithmetic grid, but it will always be monotonic because the logarithm of a variable will increase as the variable increases, and decrease only if the variable decreases.

A somewhat more flexible relation is the parabola

$$Y = a + bX + cX^2$$

The alert student who has mastered the least squares method for the straight line may be able to work out the normal equations that would be required to fit this curved regression. Since three constants are to be found, three normal equations will be needed, and these can be found as were the simpler ones. For those students who lack a knowledge of calculus, they can be found in any of the standard textbooks.

REGRESSION SLIPPAGE

The materials that are being handled should be given careful study to be sure that optimum use is made of them. One of the problems that can betray the careless researcher is that of regression slippage, which plays a somewhat similar role in regression analysis to that of spurious correlation[16] in correlation analysis. The problem may be

[15] Yule felt that the straight line was all that was needed, or could be used in actual cases. See *An Introduction to the Theory of Statistics* (London, Charles Griffin & Co., 1932), 10th ed.

[16] G. U. Yule, *An Introduction to the Theory of Statistics*, 10th ed. (London, Charles Griffin & Co., 1932), p. 215.

illustrated by taking the well-known consumption function which relates total consumption expenditures to total income, or better, disposable income. Consider the function $C = \alpha + \beta Y$, illustrated in Fig. 7, where C is total consumption expenditures and Y is total income. Alternatively we might consider the per capita figures, and the function

$$c = \frac{\alpha}{N} + \beta y$$

where $c = C/N$ and $y = Y/N$.

Now suppose that during the period under study the population has increased fairly steadily along with per capita income. Then, as y varies, N varies with it and α/N is not a constant. Suppose that, if N

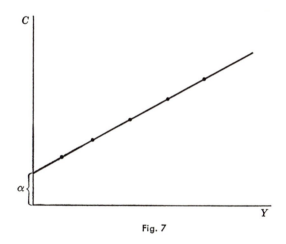

Fig. 7

were to double over the period, the α/N_2 is half as large as α/N_1. The relation between c and y can be seen to slip downward as the period progresses, as seen in Fig. 8. Since N is in the denominator of the intercept, the slipping will take place at a decreasing rate. Thus the data that appear as a straight line in Fig. 7 form a curved line in Fig. 8.

Now suppose further that during the period under study there was a considerable inflation. If the inflation proceeds steadily with the growth of population, then the curvature of the heavy line in Fig. 8 will be found to be still greater in a plotting of $c' = c/p$ against $y' = y/p$. But, since price inflations tend to be irregular, it will be more realistic to suppose that the general price rise took place suddenly and drastically in the middle of our period. Our heavy line now develops an extra wiggle as the inflation tends to offset the first curvature for a while, as in Fig. 9.

We conclude that a straight line regression between two compound variables like C and Y implies a curved relation between the adjusted variables, the curvature depending upon the behavior of the adjusting

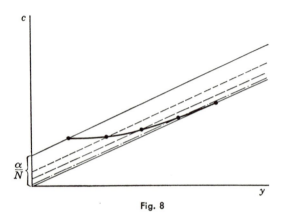

Fig. 8

variables; or, if the relation between the adjusted variables is straight, then the relation between the compound variables will not be straight unless (a) the adjusting variables have no correlation with the adjusted

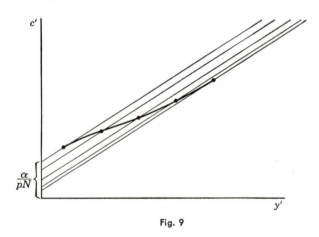

Fig. 9

variables, or (b) the adjusting variables offset each other. The reader might amuse himself by assuming that there is a linear relation between c' and y' and deducing the nature of the relation between C and Y.

EXERCISES

1. From the formula for the variability of a point on the regression line (page 146), compute the variability of the points where $x = \pm 1$ and also for the points $x = \pm 3$.

2. From the formula for the variability of an item above and below the regression line (page 147), compute the variability of an item at the following x values: $\pm 0, 1, 2, 3$, and construct a chart comparable to Fig. 6 for the variability of items.

READINGS

1. Paul G. Hoel, *Introduction to Mathematical Statistics*, 2nd ed. (New York, Wiley, 1954), Chaps. V, VI.
2. Elmer B. Mode, *Elements of Statistics* (New York, Prentice-Hall, 1951), Chap. XI.
3. Robert Ferber, *Statistical Techniques in Market Research* (New York, McGraw-Hill, 1949), Chap. XI.
4. Croxton & Cowden, *Practical Business Statistics* (New York, Prentice-Hall, 1948).
5. John E. Freund, *Modern Elementary Statistics* (New York, Prentice-Hall, 1952), Chaps. 12, 13, 14.
6. Edward E. Lewis, *Methods of Statistical Analysis in Economics and Business* (Boston, Houghton Mifflin Co., 1953), Chap. 12.
7. H. C. Fryer, *Elements of Statistics* (New York, Wiley, 1954), Chap. 7.

CHAPTER 9

Multivariate Regression

In the previous chapter, we studied relations between two variables. In some problems two variables are all that we need to consider; but in many problems there are more than two variables entailed, and to consider only two of them is to ignore the rest. Multiple or multivariate regression is a relation among three or more variables. We shall start with three variables, but the procedures can be extended readily to more variables.

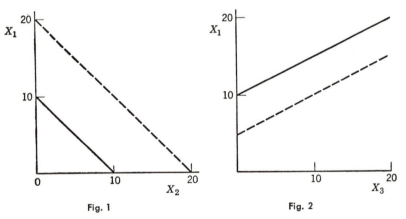

Fig. 1   Fig. 2

A REGRESSION PLANE

When three variables are entailed, there must be three dimensions. Thus we shall be concerned with a three-dimensional plane surface. Consider first a particular example:

$$X_1 = 10 - X_2 + \tfrac{1}{2}X_3 \qquad (1)$$

It may be somewhat confusing to try to visualize a plane surface all at once; it is easier to take it in easy steps. First let the variable X_3

154

take on a value of zero, so that the equation is reduced to $X_1 = 10 - X_2$. This simpler equation is represented by the solid line in Fig. 1. If we had assigned to X_3 a value of 20, then we should have obtained the equation $X_1 = 20 - X_2$, which is represented by the dashed line in Fig. 1. Either line has a slope of -1; that is, as X_2 increases, X_1 decreases by as many units. The intercept depends upon the arbitrary value assigned to the third variable.

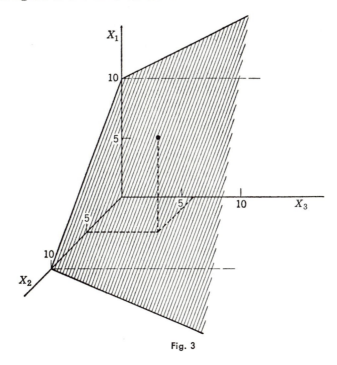

Fig. 3

Now let us assign a value to X_2 in the original equation, and study the relation between X_1 and X_3. If we let $X_2 = 0$, we get: $X_1 = 10 + \frac{1}{2}X_3$, which is the solid line in Fig. 2. If we had let $X_2 = 5$, we should have gotten $X_1 = 5 + \frac{1}{2}X_3$, which is the dashed line in Fig. 2.

These two partial representations may now be put together. The X_1X_2 plane of Fig. 1 is shown as a vertical plane in Fig. 3, going off to the left. The X_1X_3 plane of Fig. 2 becomes the vertical plane going off to the right in Fig. 3. The horizontal plane is the plane X_2X_3, which has not yet been examined. The complete plane of the original equation is now displayed in Fig. 3. It cuts the axes planes as shown in the previous charts, and it rises to the right as X_3 increases, and falls forward as X_2 increases. For any particular point in the base plane—

say $X_2 = 5$; $X_3 = 6$—we may move vertically to the plane for a value for X_1, which in this case is 8. As X_2 increases, X_1 decreases by an equal amount; as X_3 increases, X_1 increases by half as much. The regression slopes, coefficients, show the influence of that particular variable when the other variable is "adjusted for," or "taken into account," or held constant.

The "reductions" of the original equation as illustrated in Figs. 1 and 2 should be studied. When a fixed value is assigned to one of the variables, the result is a relation between the remaining variables. The constant or intercept value in this new relation depends upon the value assigned to the first variable. This bit of mathematical theory can be applied to economic theory. We find it useful, even necessary, to hold some variables constant while we examine the relation between or among the remaining variables. From the simple relation of a plane surface it can now be seen that it is not enough merely to keep other variables fixed in a *ceteris paribus* box; we should know at what level they are fixed. When we come to examine nonlinear relations, we shall find that this is very much more important, because, when the relations are nonlinear, then the slope will vary from one part of the function to another, whereas, in a linear function, the slope is constant throughout.

The general formula for a linear regression plane in three variables is:

$$X_1 = a_{1 \cdot 23} + b_{12 \cdot 3}X_2 + b_{13 \cdot 2}X_3$$

The terminology was originally devised by Yule, and has proved to be very useful. There are three variables, X_1, X_2, and X_3. The coefficients of the independent variables have subscripts to indicate the nature of the equation. There are two numbers before the dot to indicate first the dependent variable, and secondly the independent variable in question. After the dot there is only one number to indicate the remaining independent variable which is "allowed for." The constant term indicates the dependent variable to the left of the dot and all the independent variables to the right of it. To illustrate the terminology, the following is a four-variable equation with X_2 as the dependent variable:

$$X_2 = a_{2 \cdot 134} + b_{21 \cdot 34}X_1 + b_{23 \cdot 14}X_3 + b_{24 \cdot 13}X_4$$

We shall have occasion to use this terminology later.

SAMPLING MODEL IV

The data of Table 1 have been given by our fourth sampling model. Three variables are entailed, X_1, X_2, X_3, portraying a hypothetical demand function in which the quantity of a commodity demanded (X_1) is a linear function of the price of the commodity (X_2) and of the total income of the people in the market (X_3). Units are chosen so

Table 1

Item	X_1	X_2	X_3	e	X_1'
1	12	4	12	0	12
2	9	4	6	1	10
3	7	7	8	0	7
4	12	5	14	-1	11
5	15	5	20	0	15
6	10	1	2	-1	9
7	7	9	12	1	8
8	11	8	18	-2	9
9	11	3	8	0	11
10	8	7	10	0	8
11	17	2	18	0	17
12	10	10	20	0	10
13	12	7	18	0	12
14	14	5	18	2	16
15	7	4	2	1	8
16	13	6	18	2	15
17	7	7	8	-2	5
18	8	7	10	1	9
19	9	2	2	-1	8
20	15	5	20	0	15

that X_1 varies from 1 to 19, X_2 varies from 1 to 10, and X_3 from 2 to 20. Indeed, we are considering the plane surface discussed earlier in this chapter:

$$X_1 = 10 - X_2 + \tfrac{1}{2}X_3 \tag{1}$$

The sampling is undertaken in two steps: first, the points on the surface; and secondly the errors or deviations from the surface which are assumed to appear as errors in the X_1 variable.

The first part of the sampling model consists of 100 chips, each one with three figures on it, one figure for each variable. No two chips are duplicates. Table 2 shows 100 boxes, each box representing a chip, with the variables related so that each chip corresponds to a point on the plane surface (1). The X_2 values are given along the top, the X_3 values down the left-hand side, and the X_1 values in the body of the table. This sampling distribution is rectangular, since there is the same number of chips (i.e., one) for each point, and the points are evenly distributed over the area of the surface considered. The first half of the sampling operation consists in mixing these 100 chips, drawing one, noting the three figures on it, replacing it, mixing, and drawing again. In this manner 20 chips are drawn and noted, the details being shown in Table 1. From any three points (chips) which are not all in a straight

Table 2

X_3 \ X_2	1	2	3	4	5	6	7	8	9	10
20	19	18	17	16	15	14	13	12	11	10
18	18	17	16	15	14	13	12	11	10	9
16	17	16	15	14	13	12	11	10	9	8
14	16	15	14	13	12	11	10	9	8	7
12	15	14	13	12	11	10	9	8	7	6
10	14	13	12	11	10	9	8	7	6	5
8	13	12	11	10	9	8	7	6	5	4
6	12	11	10	9	8	7	6	5	4	3
4	11	10	9	8	7	6	5	4	3	2
2	10	9	8	7	6	5	4	3	2	1

line we could derive the equation of the plane surface (1) by substituting in a general formula the values noted on the three chips, and solving these three equations for the three parameters.

The second part of the sampling operation was performed by taking 12 more chips, and marking on them the numbers indicated in Table 3.

Table 3

Error	Frequency
2	1
1	3
0	4
−1	3
−2	1
	12

These twelve chips were then thoroughly mixed in the bowl, one drawn at a time, the digit noted, and the chip replaced. Twenty drawings were thus made, and the corresponding numbers attached as errors to the X_1 values in the previous sample; we shall call these the random errors.

A BEST–FITTING PLANE

Given the values of these variables found on the twenty chips, and the X_1 values modified so as to include a random error element, let us suppose that this is a typical batch of three-dimensional data, the data representing, respectively, quantity of a commodity purchased, the average price, and the total income of the people in this market area. We propose to fit a plane surface to these data much as we fitted a straight line to two-dimensional data in Chap. 8. We now seek the best-fitting plane which we take to be the least squares plane, i.e., that flat

Table 4

X_1'	X_2	X_3	$X_1'X_2$	$X_1'X_3$	X_2X_3	$X_2{}^2$	$X_3{}^2$
12	4	12	48	144	48	16	144
10	4	6	40	60	24	16	36
7	7	8	49	56	56	49	64
11	5	14	55	154	70	25	196
15	5	20	75	300	100	25	400
9	1	2	9	18	2	1	4
8	9	12	72	96	108	81	144
9	8	18	72	162	144	64	324
11	3	8	33	88	24	9	64
8	7	10	56	80	70	49	100
17	2	18	34	306	36	4	324
10	11	20	100	200	200	100	400
12	7	18	84	216	126	49	324
16	5	18	80	288	90	25	324
8	4	2	32	16	8	16	4
15	6	18	90	270	108	36	324
5	7	8	35	40	56	49	64
9	7	10	63	90	70	49	100
8	2	2	16	16	4	4	4
15	5	20	75	300	100	25	400
215	108	244	1118	2900	1444	692	3744

plane for which the sum of the squares of the deviations of the points from the plane, the deviations measured in the X_1 direction, will be less than for any other noncurved three-dimensional plane. It will be noted that in seeking such a plane there are 3 degrees of freedom. There is, first of all, the height of the plane above (or below) the base plane; secondly, there is the slant of the plane in the X_2 direction, and, thirdly, there is the slant of the plane in the X_3 direction. These three degrees of freedom correspond to the three constants to be evaluated in the general equation:

$$X_1 = a + bX_2 + cX_3$$

From the nature of the problem, one of the three variables is decided upon as a dependent variable, and the other variables are classed as independent. The dependent variable is here taken to be X_1. The normal equations turn out to be:[1]

$$\sum(X_1) = Na + b \cdot \sum(X_2) + c \cdot \sum(X_3)$$

$$\sum(X_1 X_2) = a \cdot \sum(X_2) + b \cdot \sum(X_2^2) + c \cdot \sum(X_2 X_3)$$

$$\sum(X_1 X_3) = a \cdot \sum(X_3) + b \cdot \sum(X_2 X_3) + c \sum(X_3^2)$$

it will be noted that eight different sums are used in these three equations, as follows: $\sum(X_1)$, $\sum(X_2)$, $\sum(X_3)$, $\sum(X_1 X_2)$, $\sum(X_1 X_3)$, $\sum(X_2^2)$, $\sum(X_3^2)$, $\sum(X_2 X_3)$. These sums can be computed from the data, as shown in Table 4.

RELIABILITY OF THE CONSTANTS

The plane surface fitted to the sampled points turns out to be

$$X_1' = 9.76 - 1.007 X_2 + 0.527 X_3$$

These three constants are statistical estimates of the corresponding parameters of the population equation 1. Note how close they are. Their values depend upon the particular chips that happen to have been picked in the random selection process. Another sample under the same general conditions would give somewhat different values, and we are interested in finding out how different they might have been in another sample. If the sampling were truly random (as our system presumably is), and if the sample were large enough (a sample of 50 would be better, but 20 should be fairly good), then the numbers obtained in another sample should not be much different. The amount of variation to be expected here is given by the standard errors. The formula for these standard errors, now that we are dealing with three variables, is rather more complicated and will not be given here. The general principles are, however, the same as those of the previous chapter.

---

[1] These normal equations can be derived, as were the normal equations in the previous chapter, by setting up an expression for the sum of the squares of the deviations and differentiating in turn by each of the constants to be computed, namely, a, b, and c. These resulting normal equations should be compared with the normal equations for two-variable regression, given on page 134. The student should attempt to derive general rules by which he can guess at the four normal equations that would be needed for a four-variable regression equation.

SOME THREE–DIMENSIONAL GEOMETRY

The plane surface represented by the equation

$$X_1 = 10 - X_2 + \tfrac{1}{2}X_3$$

is shown in Fig. 3. Let us examine its projections on to the three axis planes. The student may amuse himself by calculating the dimensions of a piece of plywood or cardboard that could be used to represent the

Table 5

X_1	1	2	3	4	5	6	7	8	9	10	T X_2
20											
19	/										1
18	/	/									2
17	/	/	/								3
16	/	/	/	/							4
15	/	/	/	/	/						5
14	/	/	/	/	/	/					6
13	/	/	/	/	/	/	/				7
12	/	/	/	/	/	/	/	/			8
11	/	/	/	/	/	/	/	/	/		9
10	/	/	/	/	/	/	/	/	/	/	10
9		/	/	/	/	/	/	/	/	/	9
8			/	/	/	/	/	/	/	/	8
7				/	/	/	/	/	/	/	7
6					/	/	/	/	/	/	6
5						/	/	/	/	/	5
4							/	/	/	/	4
3								/	/	/	3
2									/	/	2
1										/	1

surface in question. Indeed, if his imagination does not serve him adequately, he may actually cut out such a piece and fit it into the corner of a box, the bottom of which could form the X_2X_3 plane. For these computations, it may be convenient (though certainly not necessary) to let the units of X_3 be half-inches, and the units of the other two variables be 1 inch. The part of the X_2X_3 plane that will be relevant will then be a square illustrated in Fig. 4. This square is the projection of the plane on to the X_2X_3 axis plane. That is, each point in the base plane corresponds to a point directly above it in the fitted plane.

In Table 2 we see what is essentially the base square, with the value of X_1 indicated for each subsquare (actually for a point in each subsquare). Figure 5 is a plotting of the X_2X_3 points drawn in the sample of 20 chips.

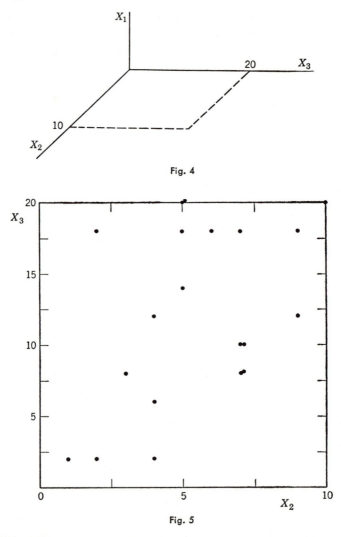

Fig. 4

Fig. 5

The projection of our fitted plane on to the X_2X_1 axis plane is seen in Fig. 6. Table 5 gives an array of the population of chips to correspond to it. The chips actually drawn have their X_2 and X_1 values plotted in Fig. 7.

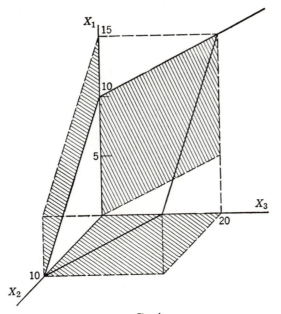

Fig. 6

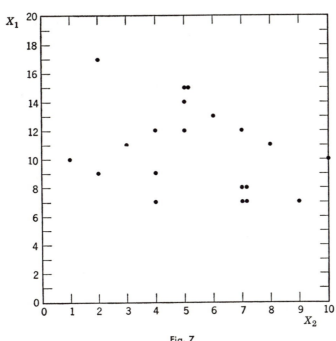

Fig. 7

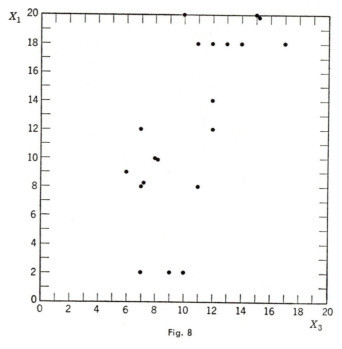

Fig. 8

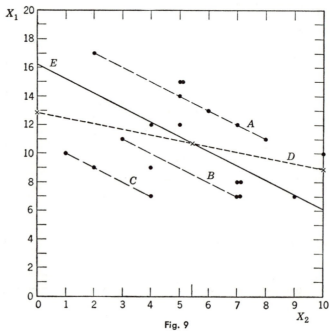

Fig. 9

The third projection of our plane is shown in Fig. 6, and the plotting of the X_1 and X_3 values on the chips actually drawn is given in Fig. 8.

Now it should be clear that a drawing of 20 chips at random from the sampling model IV without any "errors" added will produce 20 points on the plane surface; but, if the X_3 values on these chips are ignored, and only the X_2 and X_1 values are noted, there will probably be some relation between the X_2 and X_1 values; a straight regression line would probably have a negative slope, but the points would not cluster about the line very closely. The gross correlation between X_2 and X_1 would not be very high,[2] even though we know that there is a precise relation between these two variables when a third variable is allowed for. Note, for example, the five points for which the X_3 value is 18; it will be found that all of them lie on a straight line A in Fig. 9. Similarly, there are two points with an X_3 value of 8 (line B) and three points with an X_3 value of 2 (line C). All three of these lines have the same slope. Indeed, when all the points have had their q values adjusted for the income variable, they lie on a line which represents the bottom line of the quadrilateral in the X_1X_2 plane shown in Fig. 6.

FITTING A PLANE BY THE GRAPHIC METHOD

Let us suppose that we have been given 20 sets of numbers, each set consisting of a value for each of the three variables, X_1, X_2, and X_3. Our economic theory suggests that there is probably a relation among these variables, so that the variations in X_1, the quantity of a commodity sold in a given period, can be explained, at least in part, by variations in X_2, the average price for the period, and X_3, the total income of the people in the market area. If there is reason to believe that the relationship is linear in both independent variables, X_2 and X_3, then we can proceed directly to fit by least squares the general plane

$$X_1 = a + bX_2 + cX_3$$

But if we cannot be at all certain as to the shape of the surface, if, for example, the relationship with respect to X_2 may not be linear but parabolic or logarithmic, then the prospect of fitting a number of planes mathematically and testing each with regard to fit can be a laborious and wasteful procedure. An alternative approach is to use the graphic method [3] to seek out the nature of the relationship, if there be any, which we now illustrate.

[2] The student should compute the value of r, the correlation coefficient in this case.
[3] M. Ezekiel, *Methods of Correlation Analysis* (New York, Wiley, 1941).

We shall take X_1 as the dependent variable, i.e., the one whose variations are to be explained by the variations in the other two variables. We then proceed to draw a scatter chart with X_1 on the vertical axis and X_2 on the horizontal axis, as in Fig. 7. There appears to be some relation, with a negative slope, but it is not sharp, clear, or obvious. Next, draw up a scatter chart of X_1 on X_3 (Fig. 8). Here we can see some relation, positive in slope, but again it is not sharp.

It is a good idea at this stage to draw a third scatter chart showing the distribution of the X_2X_3 points, as in Fig. 5. We find that the points are well scattered over the square, and this is very satisfying. If they tend to cluster about a line, say a diagonal, we can expect trouble because then it will be more difficult to isolate the effects of each independent variable.[4]

Now return to the X_1X_2 chart, and pick out a group of points that have the same value of X_3. We note that there are 5 points that have an X_3 value of 18, and that all these points lie on a straight line of negative slope. We then find 2 points for which the X_3 value is 2. Joining these two points, we get a line of the same slope as the line joining the five points. This slope is further corroborated by finding two more points for which $X_3 = 8$, and these give us the same slope. Clearly when X_3 is held constant, the relation between X_2 and X_1 is a straight line of negative slope.

We may now proceed as follows: knowing that a regression line goes through the point of means,[5] we can compute the arithmetic mean of the X_1 values and the arithmetic mean of the X_2 values, and mark this point of means on the scatter chart. An experienced eye might estimate such a point without working out the arithmetic means. Now, through this point of means we draw a straight line with the slope indicated by the lines already drawn for the subgroups of points. The slope of line A of Fig. 9 can be computed by noting that the five points in question range over a distance 6 units along the X_2 scale, and over a distance of 6 units along the X_1 scale. This A line therefore falls $6X_1$ units over a distance of $6X_2$ units, and the slope is $-6/6$ which equals -1. Our partial regression line will therefore pass through the point of means, with a slope of -1.

Now suppose that we had proceeded in a different manner, ignoring the X_3 variable, and computing the simple, or gross, regression of X_1 on X_2. We would have obtained the equation:

$$X_1{}^c = 12.88 - 0.395X_2$$

[4] See below, page 183.
[5] See above, page 140.

which is represented by the line D on Fig. 9. Such a regression line gives us an altogether misleading idea of the slope of the ultimate three-dimensional regression plane in the X_2 direction because the influence of X_3 is very important in the scatter of the points.

We have now measured the relationship between the X_2 variable and the X_1 variable as indicated by the line E on Fig. 9. We wish now to eliminate the influence of the X_2 variable from the X_1 values so as to get an estimate of the slope of the regression plane in the X_3 direction. We do this by taking the deviations of the X_1 variable from the partial regression line, which we have already found (line E). That is, we measure the vertical distance of each point from the line. The measurement can be done graphically or arithmetically. The graphic method is more rapid; it consists of measuring along the edge of a piece of paper the distances of the points above or below the line, and then marking these deviations off on a new chart, above or below a zero line, but placed according to their X_3 values. See Figs. 10 and 11. The resulting points are found to lie precisely on a straight line whose slope can be estimated as 9.2/18 which equals 0.51.

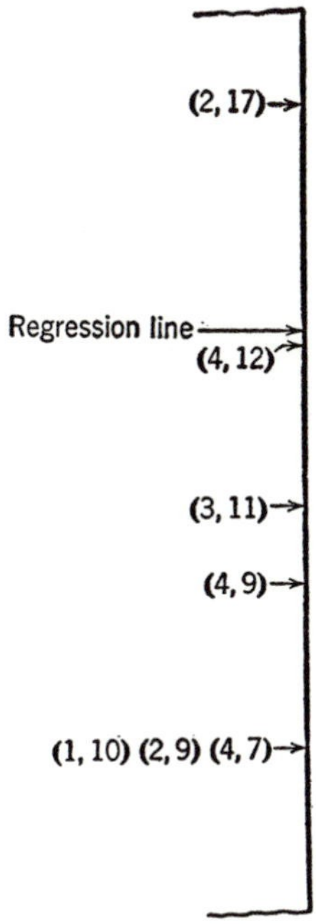

Instead of measuring these deviations graphically, the equation of the partial regression line can be estimated. We know that the slope is -1 and the intercept value at the mean of the X_2 would be the mean of the X_1's. From Table 4, this is computed as 10.8. Then our equation becomes

$X_1^c = 10.8 - X_2$. From this equation line an X_1^c value can be computed for each X_2 value, and this computed value can be subtracted from the observed X_1^o value for that point to give the deviations: $d_1 = X_1^o - X_1^c$. These d_1 values can now be plotted according to their X_3 values. The result will be about the same as before. The precision of the numerical method should be greater.

We have now estimated the slope with respect to each of the independent variables, and these may be put together to make the general equation. The student is now advised to repeat this procedure, being careful to draw all the scatter charts, using the X_1' values (including random errors) instead of the X_1 values as we have done. Most of the points will now be found to deviate from the plane by the extent of the error element, and the resulting equation may be expressed as

(2, 17)→

Regression line →
(4, 12)↗

(3, 11)→

(4, 9)→

(1, 10) (2, 9) (4, 7)→

Fig. 10

follows:

$$X_1' = \alpha + \beta X_2 + \gamma X_3 + e$$

where e is the error. The student should be able to isolate the errors with this graphical method, and he should compare his estimated errors with the errors actually introduced in Table 3.

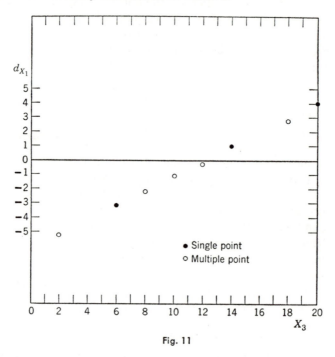

Fig. 11

The general procedure is essentially the same even with three independent variables. We could first classify the items by their X_4 values. That is, we could take a group of items for which the X_4 values were high, a second group with about average X_4 values, and a third group for which the X_4 values were low. Within each of these three groups, we should try to get a minimum variation of X_4 even to the extent of excluding some points from all groups. With each group, we then proceed as before, considering three variables on the assumption that the fourth variable is held constant. It is clear that we should start with about three times as many items as we had before when we considered three variables alone, so that each of our three groups will have a sufficient number with which to work satisfactorily. We ought to have at least 15 points to investigate a three-variable relation, and hence we need about 50 points for an investigation of a four-variable relation.

In economics this is a serious problem because (*a*) frequently we do not have enough data, and (*b*) we can hardly expect our relations to remain unchanged for such long periods when we are dealing with a time series.

The approach is usable for nonlinear relations; indeed, here is where it is most useful, as explained in the introduction to this section. With more complicated relations, however, we should have more points, and they should show wide scatter on scatter charts of any two of the independent variables.

PARTIAL CORRELATION ANALYSIS

In a set of two-variable data there are two possible regression lines, depending upon which variable is regarded as dependent and which independent. In three-variable data there are three regression planes. Sometimes the nature of the problem indicates which one of the variables is to be regarded as the dependent one, and the other two will be independent. However, there are other problems in which the indications are not so clear, and we may wish to compute all three regression planes.

There is also the question of how many and which variables to include in the analysis. We have already found that the gross or simple correlation is not alone an adequate indication. We must therefore look more carefully into the question of the relation between two variables, making allowances for other variables.

Yule developed a partial correlation analysis for this purpose, and we follow his presentation.[6] He computed the three regression equations among the three following variables: (1) the average earnings of agricultural laborers, (2) the percentage of the population in receipt of poor-law relief, and (3) the ratios of the numbers of individuals in receipt of outdoor relief to the numbers relieved in the workhouse, in each of 38 rural districts. We are interested here only in using the variables as deviations from their means, and the equations are therefore:[7]

$$x_1 = -1.21x_2 + 0.23x_3$$

$$x_2 = -0.45x_1 + 0.22x_3$$

$$x_3 = +0.85x_1 + 2.18x_2$$

These slope coefficients may be compared with the two-variable slope

---

[6] G. U. Yule, *An Introduction to the Theory of Statistics* (London, Charles Griffin, 1932), Chap. XII.

[7] See above, page 140.

coefficients:

$$x_1 = -0.87x_2 \qquad x_1 = -0.07x_3 \qquad x_2 = 0.25x_3$$

$$x_2 = -0.50x_1 \qquad x_3 = -0.23x_1 \qquad x_3 = 1.44x_2$$

It may be noted that with two exceptions these coefficients differ considerably from the corresponding coefficients of the previous group. For example, b_{12} is -0.87, whereas $b_{12 \cdot 3}$ is -1.21.

It should be recalled that the coefficient of correlation r was found to be a function of the slope coefficients (page 140). In the terminology of the present chapter we may write:

$$r_{12}^2 = b_{12} \cdot b_{21}$$

Yule defines a *partial correlation coefficient:*

$$r_{12 \cdot 3}^2 = b_{12 \cdot 3} \cdot b_{21 \cdot 3}$$

Substituting the appropriate numerical values from the above equations:

$$r_{12 \cdot 3} = [(-1.21)(-0.45)]^{\frac{1}{2}} = -0.73$$

where the sign is taken from the b values as in simple correlation. An alternative method of computation that gives the sign as well as the numerical value is:

$$r_{12 \cdot 3} = \frac{r_{12} - r_{13}r_{23}}{(1 - r_{13}^2)^{\frac{1}{2}}(1 - r_{23}^2)^{\frac{1}{2}}}$$

Here the partial correlation coefficient is given in terms of the simple or gross correlation coefficients. This is, in fact, the way in which Yule suggests that they be computed. The results are:

$$r_{12} = -0.66 \qquad r_{12 \cdot 3} = -0.73$$

$$r_{13} = -0.13 \qquad r_{13 \cdot 2} = +0.44$$

$$r_{23} = +0.60 \qquad r_{23 \cdot 1} = +0.69$$

The difference in sign between r_{13} and $r_{13 \cdot 2}$ should be emphasized. When the second variable is ignored, there is a small negative correlation between the first and third variables. When the second variable is taken into account, and an allowance made for it, the correlation is distinctly positive. Yule finds this of considerable practical significance in assessing the arguments that were current at that time over the effects of the poor laws. The second formula given above shows that it is quite possible for the gross and the net correlation coefficients to be of opposite sign. The limits of the net correlation coefficients are plus and minus 1, as for the gross correlation coefficients.

It must be remembered that the allowance for the third variable is in terms of a linear relation alone, although the logarithmic and other transformations are available to supplement primary linearity. Yule himself was convinced that, even without such transformation, linear relations were all that were needed.

The method can be extended to any number of variables. That is, the correlation can be measured between any two variables, net of any number of other variables that can be taken into account. The term "net correlation" seems more appropriate than "partial correlation," but the latter term is firmly entrenched in the literature. Similarly, the term "gross correlation" fits well the two-variables coefficient.

The concept of partial correlation will become a little clearer if it is presented somewhat differently. Returning to equation 1 and re-writing it, we have

$$X_1 - \tfrac{1}{2}X_3 = 10 - X_2$$

Now let

$$X^*_1 \equiv X_1 - \tfrac{1}{2}X_3$$

giving us a simple linear relation between two variables X^*_1 and X_2:

$$X^*_1 = 10 - X_2$$

Clearly there is now a perfect correlation between X_2 on the one hand and X^*_1 on the other, which is X_1 adjusted for X_3.

Consider now Yule's data on pauperism. Here the correlation is not perfect, and hence any adjustment by a regression coefficient will be imperfect. We now adjust both variables for the effects of a third. Using the first elementary regression equation:

$$x_1 = -1.21x_2 + 0.23x_3$$

we form a new variable:

$$x^*_1 = x_1 - 0.23x_3$$

and, from the second elementary regression equation,

$$x_2 = -0.45x_1 + 0.22x_3$$

we form a new variable:

$$x^*_2 = x_2 - 0.22x_3$$

The net correlation coefficient $r_{12.3}$ indicates the correlation between these two adjusted variables x^*_1 and x^*_2.

CONFLUENCE ANALYSIS

Yule's concept of adjusting for other variables has been extended by Frisch. His method is to compute all regression equations in a set of variables, and, in addition, all regression equations in all subsets of these variables. Thus, in a group of four variables, there are four regression equations to be found by taking each variable in turn as the dependent variable, and minimizing the sum of squares of the deviations measured in that direction; there are then four subsets of three variables each, and each of these subsets will supply three regression equations; finally there are twelve subsets of two variables each, each of these subsets giving us two regression equations. In all there are forty regression relations, four in terms of four variables, twelve in terms of three variables, and twenty-four in terms of two variables. The regression slopes are "normalized" for better comparison, and then displayed graphically in "bunch maps," as will now be explained. Frisch is particularly interested in the effect upon a group of regression slopes of the addition of another variable.

The three-variable pauperism illustration of Yule will again be used in this discussion. Recall his three regression equations:

$$x_1 = -1.21x_2 + 0.23x_3$$

$$x_2 = -0.45x_1 + 0.22x_3$$

$$x_3 = 0.85x_1 + 2.18x_2$$

These equations may be re-written in three different ways, bringing each variable in turn to the left-hand side:

$$x_1 = -1.21x_2 + 0.23x_3$$
$$x_1 = -2.2x_2 + 0.5x_3$$
$$x_1 = -2.5x_2 + 1.2x_3$$

$$x_2 = -0.8x_1 + 0.2x_3$$
$$x_2 = -0.45x_1 + 0.22x_3$$
$$x_2 = -0.39x_1 + 0.45x_3$$

$$x_3 = +4.3x_1 + 5.3x_2$$
$$x_3 = +2.1x_1 + 4.5x_2$$
$$x_3 = +0.85x_1 + 2.18x_2$$

The information given by these three groups of equations is given twice, so that we need take only half the numbers:

Direction of Minimization	$b_{12 \cdot 3}$	$b_{13 \cdot 2}$	$b_{23 \cdot 1}$
1	-1.21	0.23	0.2
2	-2.2	0.5	0.22
3	-2.5	1.2	0.45

These slopes may be compared with the lower-order slopes:

Direction of Minimization	b_{12}	b_{13}	b_{23}
direct	-0.87	-0.07	$+0.25$
inverse	-2.00	-4.35	$+0.69$

These figures were obtained from the two-variable equations just as the figures in the previous table were obtained from the three-variable regression equations. For example, for the first two variables we have the regression equations $x_1 = -0.87x_2$; $x_2 = -0.50x_1$. The first slope is taken directly; the second equation is transformed to $x_1 = -2.00x_2$, from which we get the second or inverse value b_{12}.

It may be noted that a striking change takes place from the b_{13} slopes to the $b_{13 \cdot 2}$ slopes. That is, when the variable x_2 is taken into account, the nature of the relation between x_1 and x_3 changes sharply.[8] The slopes of the gross relations are far apart and negative. The net relations are positive and are much closer together.

The slope coefficients are necessarily expressed in terms of the units of the relevant variables. For purposes of comparison with slopes relating another pair of variables, it is desirable to adjust the slopes so as to remove the effect of the units. This is best done by using the standard deviations to transform the slopes into "a constants,"[9] a process known as "normalizing":

$$a_{ij} = b_{ij} \frac{s_j}{s_i}$$

Yule gives the standard deviations of the variables used here: $s_1 = 1.71$ shillings; $s_2 = 1.29$ per cent; and $s_3 = 3.09$, and hence the a constants are as follows:

$a_{12 \cdot 3}$	$a_{13 \cdot 2}$	$a_{23 \cdot 1}$
-0.90	0.42	0.48
-1.65	0.90	0.53
-1.88	2.17	1.08

[8] See above, page 170.

[9] In the literature these "a constants" are generally called β's, but this use of a Greek letter is inconsistent with our use of Greek letters for the parameters of a population.

It will be noted that the normalizing of the two-variable regression slopes by the method suggested produces the values of the corresponding correlation coefficients:

$$a_{12} = r_{12} = -0.66 \qquad a_{13} = r_{13} = -0.13 \qquad a_{23} = r_{23} = 0.60$$

We may now compare these results graphically. First we show r_{ij} and its reciprocal in the top row of charts in Fig. 12. The second row shows the $a_{ij \cdot k}$ of the three-variable equations. The main point to note is the change in the slopes from a_{13} to $a_{13 \cdot 2}$ and the drawing together of the $a_{13 \cdot 2}$ group. That is, by taking variable x_2 into account, the relation between the variables x_1 and x_3 is very different from what it is when we do not take x_2 into account. There is also a drawing together of the $a_{23 \cdot 1}$ group over the a_{23} in which variable x_1 is ignored.

There is still another element in the Frisch analysis. He is interested not only in the slope but also in the numerator and denominator as derived from the simple correlation coefficients. He defined the a's as follows:

$$a_{12 \cdot 3} = \frac{r_{12} - r_{13}r_{23}}{1 - r_{23}^2} = \frac{-0.66 - (-0.13 \times 0.60)}{1 - (0.60)^2} = \frac{-0.58}{0.64}$$

The computations give us:

$a_{12 \cdot 3}$	$a_{13 \cdot 2}$	$a_{23 \cdot 1}$
$-\dfrac{0.58}{0.64}$	$-\dfrac{-0.27}{0.64}$	$-\dfrac{-0.27}{0.58}$
$-\dfrac{0.98}{0.58}$	$-\dfrac{-0.51}{0.58}$	$-\dfrac{-0.51}{0.98}$
$-\dfrac{-0.51}{-0.27}$	$-\dfrac{0.58}{-0.27}$	$-\dfrac{0.56}{-0.51}$

The coefficients are now shown by beams or vectors out of the origin. We note their length as well as their slopes. We note the compactness of the bunch and the changes in these aspects as another variable is taken into consideration and allowed for. In moving from 13 to 13.2, in particular, the slopes change, the bunch closes, and the lines shorten. Thus are we able to assess the effect of the addition of a new variable to our set. "A new variate is judged *useful* if (a) it tightens the bunch of regression coefficients, (b) it changes the slope of the bunch, and (c) the coefficient obtained by minimizing the sum of squares in the direction of the new variate lies between those already derived. On the other hand, if the opposites of these changes are brought about by the introduction of a new variate, it is considered *superfluous* from this point of view. Other criteria of superfluity are that the new beam is much shorter than the others and that the other beams are not appreciably shortened by the introduction of the new variate. Finally, if the slopes of the beams are scattered by the introduction of a new variate, or if the tightness of the bunch is diminished without any appreciable change in the average direction of the beams, the variate is said to be detrimental."[10]

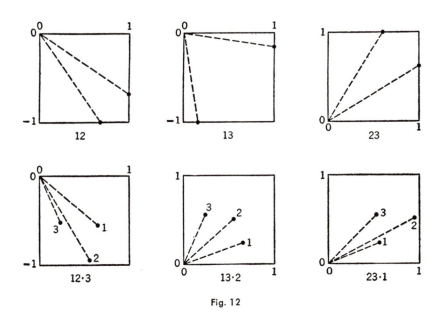

Fig. 12

These criteria are not simple to apply; moreover they sometimes conflict. But experience with this type of analysis provides information that can be obtained in no other way. The technique can be used in determining which variables should be included in a group for analysis.[11] Frisch devised his confluence analysis because of the inadequacy he felt in the standard errors of regression coefficients when the independent variables are highly correlated with each other. His method is not so much a substitute for the use of standard errors as it is a complement to it.

[10] R. Stone, "The Analysis of Market Demand," *Journal of the Royal Statistical Society, 108:* 309. The italics are mine. See also his multitude of applications.

[11] C. Clark, "A System of Equations Explaining the United States Trade Cycle, 1921 to 1941," *Econometrica, 17:* 93–124.

THE NUMBER OF RELATIONS

The work of this chapter has been devoted to the searching for a functional or structural relation among a set of variables. If it so happens that there are two or more relations operating simultaneously, the problem is more difficult. The discovery of several relations at once is the subject of the final chapter in this book; but first we should study the problems of serial correlation.

AUTOCORRELATION

The data with which we are primarily[12] concerned in model building are time series data. The values of the variables need not, of course, be taken for the same period of time. The correlation of a lagged series with a nonlagged series has long been the object of study, and indeed is an essential part of the sequence models of Chap. 6. When, however, a variable is correlated with itself after a fixed lag, problems of very considerable importance are presented to the model builder. Residuals from regression lines are supposed to be random, and when they tend to form a pattern the fit of our model is suspect. Though commonly called "serial" correlation, this is more properly known as *autocorrelation*. When there is autocorrelation in a series, it generally implies that the data are cyclical, or more strictly, periodic. Such cycles have long been sought for by means of the periodogram, but more recently two statistical tests have been devised which provide more complete testing for the absence of randomness.

One of these tests has been devised by R. L. Anderson[13] who proposed that we compute the coefficient of correlation of successive items:

$$r_s = \frac{\sum\limits_{i=1}^{N} (x_i x_{i+1})}{\sum\limits_{i=1}^{N} x_i^2}$$

where x_i is the deviation from the mean of the items. The significance of any particular value of r_s is determined by reference to a table that Anderson supplied. The value of r_s may be positive or negative, but the distribution is not symmetrical. As an illustration, a value of

---

[12] An exception is the study of cross-section data such as that by J. Marschak and William H. Andrews, Jr., "Random Simultaneous Equations and the Theory of Production," *Econometrica, 12:* 143–205.

[13] *Annals of Mathematical Statistics, 13:* 1–13.

$r_s = 0.25$ based on a sample of 15 items is not significant, whereas a value of $r_s = 0.50$ is significant for such a number even at the 0.01 probability level, and autocorrelation is to be presumed.

An alternative test of autocorrelation, devised by B. I. Hart,[14] is known as the mean-square-successive-difference method. The following statistic is computed:

$$K = \frac{\sum_{i=1}^{N} (X_{i-1} - X_i)^2 / N - 1}{\sum_{i=1}^{N} (X_i - \bar{X})^2 / N}$$

The denominator is, of course, merely the variance of the series. The numerator is the sum of the squares of successive differences divided by the number of degrees of freedom. The value of K is necessarily positive. If the successive differences are small, there is a trend, cycle, or other pattern in the series. This is positive correlation in ordinary parlance, where each item is close to its neighbor. If each item is very far from the one preceding, the numerator will be large; this is negative correlation. Thus both very low and very high values of K are significant. A table is supplied in the original article, from which we read that, in a series of 15 items, if we obtain a value for K of 1.52, there is no significant indication of autocorrelation. However, in a series of that length, a value of $K = 0.90$ would indicate a significant positive correlation at the 0.01 level, and $K = 3.30$ or more indicates negative correlation at the 0.01 level.

These two tests are designed to test whether a significant degree of correlation exists. If an extreme value is obtained from either test, this is unlikely to have arisen from a population with no autocorrelation. We thus infer that the series is not random. These tests are not designed, however, to measure the amount of correlation that may exist. An important use is to test the results of a regression fitting, for the standard errors are to be used only if the residuals are random. If it turns out that the residuals are not random, some other form of regression should be sought.

Either test may be used, but the latter one (mean-square-successive difference) is somewhat more powerful. Both are equally efficient in indicating the absence of autocorrelation when in fact none exists; but the latter is more likely to indicate correlation if in fact some does exist.[15]

[14] "Significance Levels for the Rates of the Mean Square Successive Difference to the Variance," *Annals of Mathematical Statistics, 13:* 446.

[15] Robert Ferber, *Statistical Techniques in Market Research* (New York, McGraw-Hill, 1949).

Table 6

Gross National Product of Canada, 1926–1954		Daily Maximum Temperatures McGill Observatory, Montreal, month of April, 1954	
Year	Tens of Millions of Dollars	April	Degrees
1926	529	1	37.5
1927	565	2	37.7
1928	611	3	23.2
1929	617	4	21.4
1930	555	5	43.5
1931	456	6	44.2
1932	377	7	53.2
1933	355	8	54.8
1934	403	9	37.7
1935	435	10	54.9
1936	470	11	48.9
1937	536	12	46.0
1938	523	13	51.1
1939	571	14	39.5
1940	687	15	50.4
1941	852	16	46.8
1942	1054	17	49.2
1943	1118	18	58.7
1944	1194	19	56.4
1945	1185	20	51.7
1946	1203	21	62.9
1947	1377	22	78.7
1948	1561	23	58.4
1949	1646	24	51.7
1950	1820	25	62.2
1951	2147	26	53.0
1952	2319	27	45.9
1953	2435	28	58.4
1954	2400	29	69.5
		30	76.3

Source of Gross National Product of Canada is *The Canadian Statistical Review*, Dominion Bureau of Statistics, Ottawa; source daily maximum temperatures is McGill Observatory, McGill University, Montreal.

SOME EXAMPLES OF AUTOCORRELATION

In the examples offered here (Table 6) the Anderson test has been used to contrast the nature of economic data with meteorological data. The economic data consist of annual Gross National Product figures for Canada from 1926 to 1954, and the meteorological data are daily maximum temperature readings at the McGill Observatory, Montreal, for the month of April 1954. In numbers of items the two series are not far apart, the first consisting of 29 items, and the second of 30 items. Each series was handled in the same way: the whole series was tested, then two subseries consisting of every second item in the full series, one subseries starting with the first item, and the other subseries starting with the second item. Then a still further set of subseries was taken, consisting of every third item. The results are shown in Tables 7 and 8.

Table 7

Autocorrelation in Maximum Temperatures, Montreal, April 1954

		Series	r_s	5 %	1 %	Answer
A	30	items	0.490	0.257	0.370	correlation
B	15	alternate items	0.198	0.328	0.475	no correlation
C	15	alternate items	0.193	0.328	0.475	no correlation
D	10	third items	0.365	0.360	0.525	?
E	10	third items	−0.106	−0.564	−0.705	no correlation
F	10	third items	−0.186	−0.564	−0.705	no correlation

The test figures for the 5 per cent and the 1 per cent significance points are taken from Table 17, page 524, of Ferber, *Statistical Techniques in Market Research*.

The correlation coefficient for the series of 30 temperature readings is 0.490, and the coefficient for the 29 G.N.P. figures is 0.844. Both

Table 8

Autocorrelation in Canadian G.N.P.   Figures 1926–1954

		Series	r_s	5 %	1 %	Answer
G	29	items	0.844	0.257*	0.370*	correlation
H	15	alternate items	0.686	0.328	0.475	correlation
I	14	alternate items	0.64	0.335	0.485	correlation
J	10	third items	0.464	0.360	0.525	?
K	10	third items	0.60	0.360	0.525	correlation
L	9	third items	0.425	0.366	0.533	?

*Taken for 30 items.

series have positive autocorrelation, because both coefficients exceed even the 1 per cent level. If these coefficients had fallen short of the 5 per cent level, we should say that such results could have been obtained fairly easily by chance, even if there were no correlation in the series. However, our two coefficients are beyond what could normally be expected by chance from series of similar length with no correlation in them.

It would seem as if the economic series has more correlation since its coefficient is so very much higher; but let us test these correlation propensities further by dropping every second item and correlating the remainder. For the meteorological data, the two series that we get in this way, series B starting with the first item, and series C starting with the second item, each consist of 15 items, and both correlation coefficients are so low that they do not even come close to the 5 per cent level. There is therefore no evidence of autocorrelation remaining in these series. When we proceed further, by taking every third item, the correlation coefficients become erratic, suggesting that our samples are dangerously small. What evidence there is certainly confirms the earlier report of no correlation.

The economic series contrasts sharply with the meteorological data. Not only is there a much higher coefficient to start with but in each subseries the positive correlation remains, with some doubt only in the two short series J and L, and even in these the actual coefficients are well beyond the 5 per cent level. These economic data have more definite and persistent cycles than the temperature readings, and these cycles can be confirmed by comparing charts of the data in question.

SUMMARY AND ASSESSMENT

It has been shown that correlation and regression techniques are not simple tools. The first question is the choice of variables to be used. A series of scatter charts, each chart showing two variables at a time, can be very helpful. The complete tilling technique of Frisch is thorough, but unfortunately it is limited to linear relationships. Clearly this question cannot be firmly and finally answered without becoming involved in the second question, which is the nature of the relationship among the variables. The graphic techniques devised by Bean and Ezekiel are helpful. It must be kept in mind that a perfect curvilinear relationship can exist between two variables that show a zero linear correlation.

The rules of this game are neither simple nor clear. In any particular problem we should like to build a specific theory to which we apply the data as a test. But the theory turns out to be not specific enough, and the data turn out to be inadequate, so that we specify and modify our theory on the basis of the data at hand. When we do this, the data do not give a complete test of our theory, and a close fit is not enough to justify the theory. We should test the theory with a completely new batch of data. Fortunately the data are growing in quantity, precision, and appropriateness, and more "proving" should be possible in the future.

EXERCISES

1. Make up another sampling model which might be called sampling model V as follows: Take 1200 chips, 12 for each of the boxes of Table 2, and on these twelve add to the X_1 values the deviations shown in Table 3. The results of such a model should in general be the same as those for sampling model IV.

2. Choose a set of three-variable data which has some relevance to problems with which you have had some experience, and analyze it with the techniques discussed in this chapter. For handling the computations, further guidance should be sought in the textbooks of Ezekiel, Ferber, or Croxton and Cowden.

READINGS

1. M. Ezekiel, *Methods of Correlation Analysis* (New York, Wiley, 1941). A standard text on multiple correlation techniques, with an especially good presentation of graphic analysis.
2. J. Tinbergen, *Statistical Testing of Business Cycle Theories* (Geneva, League of Nations, 1939). See especially Vol. I, Chap. II, for an unusually good presentation of correlation and regression methods in simple language. J. M. Keynes reviewed Tinbergen's work critically in the *Economic Journal*, September 1939, pp. 558–569, and again in March 1940, pp. 141–155.
3. G. U. Yule and M. Kendall, *An Introduction to the Theory of Statistics* (London, Charles Griffin & Co., 12th ed., revised, 1940). A famous textbook of many editions, the last of which have been prepared by the junior author.
4. Richard Stone, "The Analysis of Market Demand," *Journal of the Royal Statistical Society*, *CVIII*, Parts III–IV: 386–391 (1945). An excellent example of the application of multiple correlation and the use of confluence analysis. The introductory discussion is very good, but requires some acquaintance with statistical theory.
5. Richard Stone, *Measurement of Consumers' Expenditure and Behaviour in the United Kingdom, 1920–1938*, Vol I (Cambridge: At the University Press, 1954).
6. B. Chait, *Sur l'econométrie* (Bruxelles, J. Lebegue & Cie, 1949). (Reprinted from *Revue de l'institut de sociologie*, No. 2, Avril–Juin, 1949.)
7. Robert Ferber, *Statistical Techniques in Market Research* (New York, McGraw-Hill, 1949).
8. F. E. Croxton and D. J. Cowden, *Applied General Statistics* (New York, Prentice-Hall, 1955) 2nd ed.

CHAPTER 10

Multiple Relations

In the preceding chapter, correlation and regression techniques are used to find those variables that are significantly related and to seek out the type of relationship among them. In this search we have been assuming that there is only one relationship among these variables; but there may be more than one relationship existing at any time among the variables under study. In a particular market a demand relation and a supply relation are two different relations existing simultaneously connecting the price and quantity variables. Obviously any technique that considers only one of these relations and ignores the other can lead to trouble. Indeed, the whole discussion of Part I of this book is devoted to the study of a number of relations existing among a number of variables, which is what we call a model.

We now consider such multiple relations in two different groups. First, we consider additional relations which may exist among the independent or explaining variables alone. This is a problem that can be bothersome in any multiple correlation problem. It raises questions of the adequacy of our techniques, but it need not be discussed at great length here. The second group will concern us throughout most of this chapter. This is the case of more than one relationship existing among the dependent variables, as illustrated by the example of a competitive market just mentioned.

MULTIPLE RELATIONS AMONG INDEPENDENT VARIABLES

Frisch made extensive studies of correlation and regression, and found that, when there was a close relationship among the explaining variables, the standard errors of the estimated parameters were very large. This may be understood in the extreme case: if there were perfect correlation between any two explaining variables that are used in a regression equation, then either of these two correlated variables could be used as well as the other, and there would be no reason to use both. We seldom find perfect correlation, but quite often we have high correlation among the independent or explaining variables. In problems in economics, we may even say that correlation among the explaining variables is the general rule. When Klein[1] sets up a consumption function by explaining expenditures on consumption goods in terms of two variables: (a) the wage bill, and (b) nonwage income (profit), there is certain to be some correlation between these two explaining variables over the years. Here we have the problem that Frisch christened "multicollinearity,"[2] in which the suitability of the probable error technique[3] is called into question.

This concept of multicollinearity may be illustrated geometrically. Recall the three-variable plane surface of Chapter 9 (equation 1). It is possible that variation does not take place freely over a large area of the plane surface. If the correlation between X_2 and X_3 were perfect, then variation in the X_2X_3 plane would be limited to some such positive[4] sloped straight line as V, illustrated in Fig. 1. As a consequence, variation in the three-dimensional plane surface is also limited to a straight line in space, W. Now, there are an infinite number of three-dimensional planes that can pass through any straight line in space such as W, and hence, if we are trying to estimate a plane from points in $X_1X_2X_3$ space that are very nearly on the line W, rather slight difference in the positions of the points could make a considerable difference in the plane selected. Hence the reliability of the estimated plane is not great when the explaining variables X_2 and X_3 are closely related. A considerable change in the slope of the plane could be brought about by a relatively slight change in the position of one of the points, because these points are so close to the pivotal line. If the point were farther away from this pivotal line, a given change, say, in the height of the point above the base plane would make less percentage difference. It was this weakness in the use of the probability analysis that caused Frisch to devise his confluence analysis. This weakness remains even in the more sophisticated technique to be explored presently.

[1] L. R. Klein, *Economic Fluctuations in the United States 1921–1941* (New York, Wiley, 1950), Cowles Commission for Research in Economics, Monograph 11, p. 59.

[2] Tinbergen took an arbitrary combination of the two as a single variable at one time. See J. Tinbergen, *Statistical Testing of Business Cycle Theories* (Geneva, League of Nations, 1939), Vol. 1, p. 29.

[3] Richard Stone, "The Analysis of Market Demand," *Journal of the Royal Statistical Society, 108*, section 3.

[4] If the correlation between X_2 and X_3 is negative, the slope of the line V will be negative.

This multicollinearity is an inherent weakness in the statistics about which little can be done. If the data are experimental, then the experimenter should see that he has a wide selection of points in the $X_2 X_3$ plane and so avoid the problem; but, when observational data are used,

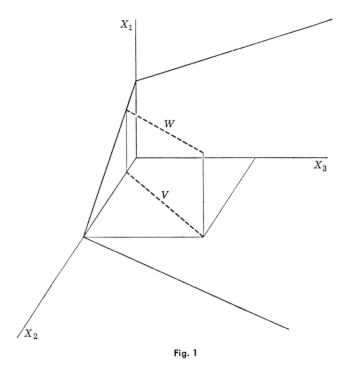

Fig. 1

the data come to us as a by-product of some other activity and we have no control over them. We can only try to select explaining variables that show little correlation among themselves. If we cannot find any such variables, our statistical technique is of limited help, and can result even in misleading indications, if it is not used with care.

MULTIPLE RELATIONS INVOLVING DEPENDENT VARIABLES

While Frisch was working out these implications of the statistical technique, E. J. Working was thinking about the economic theory, and raised a somewhat different point in his now classic article, "What Do Statistical Demand Curves Show?"[5] He made the point that, in searching for one relation, we must take into account other possible relations.

[5] *Quarterly Journal of Economics, 41* (1927).

We cannot ignore other relations without serious damage to our results.[6]
Consider the following model:

Demand relation: $q = 10 - p + t$

Supply relation: $q = p + 2t$

XXXI

In this model XXXI, t is an exogenous variable time, moving on in its inexorable fashion. Each equation has a t in it, and therefore each relation will shift over time as follows:

Assume $t = 0$, giving model XXXI_0:

$$q = 10 - p$$

$$q = p$$

Solving:

$$p = 5; \qquad q = 5$$

Assume $t = 1$, giving model XXXI_1:

$$q = 10 - p + 1$$

$$q = p + 2$$

Solving:

$$p = 4.5; \qquad q = 6.5$$

Assume $t = 2$, giving model XXXI_2:

$$q = 10 - p + 2$$

$$q = p + 4$$

Solving:

$$p = 4; \qquad q = 8$$

Continuing in this way, giving successive numerical values to t, it can be seen that p will change over time as follows: 5, 4.5, 4, 3.5, 3, ⋯. This is a moving equilibrium value of p. The changing values of q will be: 5, 6.5, 8, 9.5, 11, ⋯. These points are plotted in Fig. 2. Clearly a regression of p on q, or of q on p, using these numerical values will result in an exact relation between p and q, namely,

$$p = 6\tfrac{2}{3} - \tfrac{1}{3}q$$

but this is neither a demand nor a supply relation. It is therefore clear that, if the supply and demand relations shift over time, in some regular pattern, they will generate a definite relation between p and q, but this relation will be neither a demand curve nor a supply curve.

---

[6] See also above, page 166, for the effect of ignoring an important variable in a single relation.

Now, if only one of the relations shifts with time, while the other is independent of time, all the points that are generated will fall on the

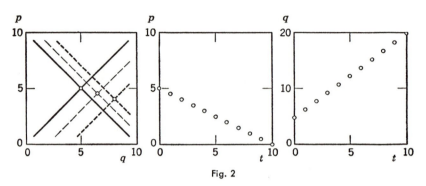

Fig. 2

unchanging curve, and regression analysis will derive this line for us. Consider the model:[7]

Demand:	$q = 10 - p$	
Supply:	$q = p + t$	XXXII

which gives us successive equilibrium values of p as: 5, 4.5, 4, 3.5,···

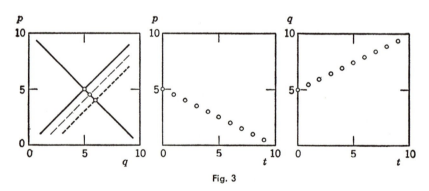

Fig. 3

and q as: 5, 5.5, 6, 6.5,····. These are shown in Fig. 3. More generally, we may write:

Demand:	$q = \alpha + \beta p$	
Supply:	$q = \gamma + \delta p + \epsilon t$	XXXIII

[7] This model is not strictly the one that Working had in mind. He thought of the supply curve as shifting back and forth over time, much as if the coefficient of t were replaced by a sine function. See Exercise 2.

Solving, we get $\alpha + \beta p = \gamma + \delta p + \epsilon t$

$$p(\beta - \delta) = \gamma - \alpha + \epsilon t$$

$$p = \frac{\gamma - \alpha}{\beta - \delta} + \frac{\epsilon}{\beta - \delta} t$$

$$q = \alpha + \beta \left(\frac{\gamma - \alpha}{\beta - \delta} + \frac{\epsilon}{\beta - \delta} t \right)$$

$$= \frac{\alpha\beta - \alpha\delta + \beta\gamma - \alpha\beta}{\beta - \delta} + \frac{\beta\epsilon}{\beta - \delta} t$$

$$= \frac{\beta\gamma - \alpha\delta}{\beta - \delta} + \frac{\beta\epsilon}{\beta - \delta} t$$

Now, for any particular value of t such as $0,1,2,\cdots$, the equilibrium values of p and q will be found to lie on the demand curve. Thus we see that a demand curve appears from a linear regression of q on p because the supply curve shifts regularly with time. Similarly, if the demand curve were to shift, we should obtain a supply curve.[8] It is clear, then, that, in searching for a relation among a group of variables, we must take cognizance of other possible relations among these variables.

Many of the problems posed by the existence of multiple relations are still unsolved, but econometricians have developed a method of attack. There are two foundation stones now in place, which we may call the principle of Haavelmo and the principle of Koopmans. The former states that we must work from a model, and the second states that the model must be of a certain kind.

The Haavelmo principle: The statistical method used must be derived from a model that specifies the relations among the jointly dependent variables.

On historical grounds, this principle should be named after E. J. Working, but the phrase "Working principle" is unfortunate. Moreover, Haavelmo fully merits the distinction, because he laid out the problem as it relates to modern statistical theory, and applied the principle in practical applications.

The Schultz approach violates this principle in that it is an attempt to estimate a single relation among a group of variables, ignoring all other possible relations among these variables. Haavelmo showed that a bias is to be expected in such cases, and estimated the amount of bias in a specific case.[9] He estimated the marginal propensity to consume

[8] See Exercise 1 at the end of this chapter.
[9] "Methods of Measuring the Marginal Propensity to Consume," *Journal of the*

in two different ways; the usual least squares estimate was 0.732, whereas, by devising a simple and not inappropriate model of two relations, he estimated the value at 0.672, which is a difference of 9 per cent of the former estimate.

Let us examine Haavelmo's approach in a little more detail. The least squares equation

$$c = ay + b + v \qquad\qquad \text{A}$$

where v is the random variable, c is consumption expenditures, and y is income, was computed as

$$c = 0.732y + 84.0$$

This was obtained by minimizing the sum of the squares of the vertical deviations from the line (those in the c direction).

The simple Haavelmo model consisted of two equations:

$$c = \alpha y + \beta + u$$
$$y = c + z \qquad\qquad \text{B}$$

in which c and y are endogenous or mutually dependent variables, z is an exogenous or independent variable, and u is a random variable. The second equation defines y (income) as the sum of c (consumption) and z (investment). The first equation expresses c as a linear function of y, with random deviations presumably caused by a multitude of other factors not taken into account by this simple model. α and β are parameters whose numerical values we wish to estimate. Henceforth we shall be dealing with econometric models—with random variables— and these will be given letters.

Now, if this model is reasonably correct, we should not estimate the parameters by taking the regression of c on y, because we cannot take y as given[10]—it is one of the dependent variables. We must solve the equations so as to express them in reduced form.[11]

$$c = \alpha(c + z) + \beta + u$$
$$= \alpha c + \alpha z + \beta + u$$
$$c = \frac{\alpha}{1 - \alpha} z + \frac{1}{1 - \alpha} \beta + \frac{1}{1 - \alpha} u$$

American Statistical Association, 1947, reprinted in Wm. C. Hood, and T. Koopmans, *Studies in Econometric Method* (New York, Wiley, 1953), Cowles Commission for Research in Economics, Monograph 14, Chap. IV.

[10] E. G. Bennion, "The Cowles Commission's Simultaneous Equations Approach: A Simplified Explanation," *Review of Economics and Statistics*, *XXXIV*: 49–56 (1952).

[11] See above, page 31.

and

$$y = z + \alpha y + \beta + u$$

$$y = \frac{1}{1 - \alpha} z + \frac{1}{1 - \alpha} \beta + \frac{1}{1 - \alpha} u$$

We may now proceed to find the regression of c on z and the regression of y on z, since z is an exogenous variable and can be taken as fixed or determined outside the model. In this way Haavelmo found:

$$\frac{1}{1 - \alpha} = 3.048 \quad \text{(the "multiplier")}$$

$$\alpha = 0.672 \quad \text{(the marginal propensity to consume)}$$

$$\beta = 113.1$$

From the formulas derived, Haavelmo expected α to be lower than a, and β to be greater than b; that is, he expected an upward bias in a, the least squares estimate of slope, and a downward bias in b, the least squares intercept. These results were confirmed by the computations. There was a 9 per cent difference in the slope, but the difference was even greater in the multiplier, 3.048 as against 3.731 by least squares, a difference of 22 per cent.

The bias referred to here exists on the assumption that the Haavelmo model is appropriate, which implies that the direct least squares approach is not. If, as is likely to be true, neither model is entirely appropriate, then the bias is not measured here exactly. The more complete model has some chance of fitting the situation better, but there are stalwart defenders of the least squares approach.[12] More will be said on this point below.

The Working model (XXXIII) illustrates the Haavelmo principle further. The results of the direct least squares method are misunderstood unless Working's more complete model is laid out. In that particular case, if the assumptions of the model are correct (i.e., the supply line shifts with time while the demand line does not), the least squares regression of q on p is not necessarily incorrect; indeed it is correct if we can assume further that errors in measuring p are negligible and that the model is complete in that no significant variables have been omitted.

The Haavelmo principle tells us that we must set up a model in order that we may plan our statistical method rationally. This model specifies what variables are to be considered, and which of these are endogenous

---

[12] E. g., Stone, Wold, and Fox.

and which exogenous. It specifies the relations among the variables; that is, which variables are in which equation, and exactly how they enter, as in a linear, quadratic, logarithmic, or another form. In some cases, indeed, in quite a number of cases, the model will allow the use of the least squares technique, and it will tell us how it is to be used, i.e., which is the variable to be explained, and which are the explaining ones. Thus, the least squares technique is certainly not to be discarded, but we have come a long way from a universal and undiscriminating use of it.

We are ready now to proceed to the next general principle of the application of statistical methods in economics. Consider the following model:

$$\text{Demand:} \qquad q = 10 - p + t$$
$$\text{Supply:} \qquad q = \tfrac{5}{2} + \tfrac{1}{2}p + \tfrac{7}{4}t \qquad\qquad \textbf{XXXIV}$$

Here t is again exogenous, and the demand and supply relations shift over time.

Assuming $t = 0$, we get model

$$q = 10 - p$$
$$q = \tfrac{5}{2} + \tfrac{1}{2}p \qquad\qquad \textbf{XXXIV}_0$$

Solving:
$$p = 5; \qquad q = 5$$

Assuming $t = 1$, we get model

$$q = 11 - p$$
$$q = \tfrac{17}{4} + \tfrac{1}{2}p \qquad\qquad \textbf{XXXIV}_1$$

Solving:
$$p = 4.5; \qquad q = 6.5$$

Assuming $t = 2$, we get model

$$q = 12 - p$$
$$q = 6 + \tfrac{1}{2}p \qquad\qquad \textbf{XXXIV}_2$$

Solving:
$$p = 4; \qquad q = 8$$

Continuing in this way, we find the very interesting result that model XXXIV gives us exactly the same intersection points as does model XXXI. Thus, from the statistical data alone, regardless of how long a period we study, we have no way of knowing whether these points were generated by model XXXI, by model XXXIV, or by any of an infinity of other models that could be found to generate this series of points. We conclude that a general model such as the following:

Demand: $q = \alpha + \beta p + \theta t$

Supply: $q = \gamma + \delta p + \epsilon t$

XXXV

is inadequate for statistical purposes. If we know the slopes of these lines, for example, if $\beta = -1$ and $\delta = +1$ as in model XXXI, then we can find the values of the other parameters, α, θ, γ, and ϵ. If, as in model XXXIV, $\beta = -1$ and $\delta = +\frac{1}{2}$, the values of α, θ, γ, and ϵ which

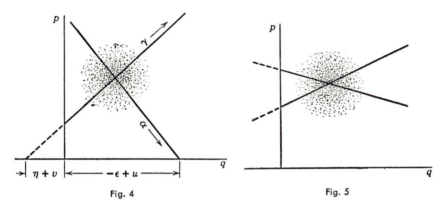

Fig. 4   Fig. 5

we found would be different. But, if we are not given any information about the slopes of these lines, we cannot find the values of the six parameters even if we had a very large number of intersection points. The reason for the difficulty is that the equations are not identified, and this brings us to the second principle of econometrics:

Koopmans' principle: The hypothetical model specifying the relations among the variables should be such as to allow for identification of the parameters.

This question of identification is presented clearly by Koopmans himself.[13] Assuming straight-line demand and supply schedules in a competitive market:

$$q + \alpha p + \epsilon = u \quad \text{(demand)}$$

$$q + \gamma p + \eta = v \quad \text{(supply)}$$

C

where u and v are random variables, and given a set of observed points as in Fig. 4 (the same points are shown in Fig. 5). If we know beforehand the two slopes α and γ, we can compute ϵ and η by assuming that

[13] "Identification Problems in Economic Model Construction," *Econometrica, 17*: 125–144; reprinted with minor modifications in *Studies in Econometric Method,* ed. Wm. C. Hood and T. C. Koopmans (New York, Wiley, 1953), Chap. 2.

u and v will average out to zero. Then all our parameters are known. But, if we do not know the slopes α and γ, there is not enough information supplied so far to find them, because straight lines of any other slopes could be drawn through these observed points as in Fig. 5, and intercepts could be found for them in the same way. There would be no way of telling which of these two pairs of lines is the more correct.

Koopmans re-states the problem in algebraic terms as follows:[14] "Let the numerical values of the 'true' parameters α, γ, ϵ, $\eta \cdots$ be known to an individual who, taking delight in fraud, multiplies the demand equation by $\frac{2}{3}$, the supply equation $\cdots$ by $\frac{1}{3}$, and adds the result to form an equation

$$q + \frac{2\alpha + \gamma}{3} p + \frac{2\epsilon + \eta}{3} = u^*$$

which he proclaims to be the demand equation $\cdots$. Similarly he multiplies the same equations by $\frac{2}{5}$ and $\frac{3}{5}$, respectively, say, to produce an equation

$$q + \frac{2\alpha + 3\gamma}{5} p + \frac{2\epsilon + 3\eta}{5} = v^*$$

$\cdots$which he presents as if it were the supply equation. If our prankster takes care to select his multipliers in such a manner as not to violate the sign rules ($\alpha > 0$, $\gamma < 0$)$\cdots$the deceit cannot be discovered by statistical analysis of any number of observations."

Koopmans then proposes a second model with a new exogenous variable, r (rainfall):

$$q + \alpha p + \epsilon = u \quad \text{(demand)}$$
$$q + \gamma p + \delta r + \eta = v \quad \text{(supply)}$$

D

in which the demand equation is identified, but the supply equation is not, since we can derive any number of additional equations by combining these two, as was done above, all of which are statistically similar to the supply equation, but different from the demand equation. This model is comparable to our model XXXII above.

Thus, in a particular model, some equations may be identified, and some not identified. A model will, of course, be completely identified only if each of its equations is. An individual equation is identified

---

[14] *Studies in Econometric Method*, ed. Wm. C. Hood and T. C. Koopmans (New York, Wiley, 1953), p. 30.

when some of the variables are missing from that equation, so that a duplicate or twin cannot be created by combining other equations in the model. Sometimes identification can be established by other *a priori* information on the values of the parameters or on the variabilities of the random "shift" variables. These details will not be considered further here, but one important point will be noted. When a model is completely identified, the statistical procedure is to obtain the reduced forms of the "structural" equations, and use the least squares method to find the parameters of these reduced-form equations. Then we may solve for the parameters of the original structural equations. When the original equations are identified, such solving back is possible; but when equations are not identified, then it is not possible to solve for the parameters of the original equations, because then there are not enough relations connecting the original parameters to the reduced-form parameters. The student should work out the reduced forms for all the models just discussed to see the procedure for himself.[15]

It is possible to have an *overidentified* model for which there are too many connecting relations between the parameters of the original model and the parameters of the reduced form. In this case, conflicting answers can result, and special procedures are needed.[16]

The Koopmans principle suggests that we use models that are just identified. He has shown also that lagged endogenous variables may be used as exogenous variables. Since they are not strictly exogenous in a set of data covering a considerable period, he has used the term *predetermined* to include truly exogenous and lagged endogenous variables. The statistical theory is much more complicated when lagged endogenous variables are entailed, but the approach is the same as that suggested above for the purely exogenous variables.

---

[15] A necessary condition for identification of a given equation in a given model is that there must be excluded from that equation at least $G - 1$ variables, where G is the number of equations and the number of endogenous variables in the model. The reader should apply this test to each of the equations of each of the models discussed in this chapter. For a thorough, yet readable treatment of identification, see G. Tintner, *Econometrics* (New York, Wiley, 1952), pp. 155–166. More details are given in L. R. Klein, *Econometrics* (Evanston, Row, Peterson, 1953), pp. 92–99. See also W. W. Leontief, "Econometrics," Chap. 11 of *A Survey of Contemporary Economics*, ed. H. S. Ellis (Philadelphia, Blakiston, 1948), pp. 393–403. There are some errors in the last one: (1) p. 400, l. 14, v_t should be u_t and correspondingly in the next few lines; and (2) p. 401, l. 12 from bottom, p_t should be p_{t-1}.

[16] "Statistical Analysis of the Demand for Food: Examples of Simultaneous Estimation of Structural Equations," M. A. Girshick and T. Haavelmo, *Econometrica*, *15;* 79–110 (April 1947), reprinted in *Studies in Econometric Method*, ed. Wm. C. Hood and T. C. Koopmans (New York, Wiley, 1953), as Chap. V. See also Tintner, *Econometrics*, pp. 167–168.

AN ILLUSTRATION

We offer a simple manufactured illustration of the principles that
have been discussed. Suppose that we have the data of the accompany-
ing table on the price and quantity of a certain commodity traded in a

Table I

q	p
5	5
4	5
6	5
5	4
5	6
4	6
6	4
$7\overline{)35}$	$7\overline{)35}$
5	5

given market. Now, to find a relation between these two variables,
p and q, by straightforward least
squares, we could compute the
regression of q on p, getting

$$q = 7\tfrac{1}{2} - \tfrac{1}{2}p$$

If we computed the regression
of p on q, we should get

$$p = 7\tfrac{1}{2} - \tfrac{1}{2}q$$

which can be written in the form:

$$q = 15 - 2p$$

Both of these regression lines
are plotted with the original data
in Fig. 6.

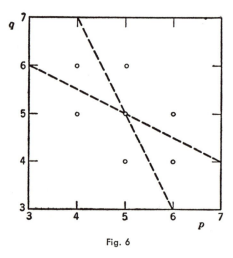

Fig. 6

Suppose, now, that we follow
Haavelmo's principle, and formulate a model explaining these two variables by means of two market relations:

Demand: $q = \alpha + \beta p + u$

Supply: $q = \gamma + \delta p + v$

Solving, to derive the reduced forms, we get

$$p = \frac{\gamma - \alpha}{\beta - \delta} + \frac{v - u}{\beta - \delta}$$

and

$$q = \frac{\beta\gamma - \alpha\delta}{\beta - \delta} + \frac{\beta v - \delta u}{\beta - \delta}$$

Now, the Koopmans' principle states that our model should be identified. Our model clearly is not identified, and this can be shown in two different ways. First, if, like Koopmans' prankster, we multiply our demand equation by $\frac{1}{3}$ and our supply equation by $\frac{2}{3}$, and add, we get

$$q = \frac{\alpha + 2\gamma}{3} + \frac{\beta + 2\delta}{3} p + \frac{u + 2v}{3}$$

which may be written as

$$q = \alpha' + \beta'p + u'$$

and there is no way to distinguish statistically between α and α' or between β and β'.

The second test concerns the reduced forms. If u and v are random, so are $(v - u)/(\beta - \delta)$ and $(\beta v - \delta u)/(\beta - \delta)$ and we can assume them to be zero on the average. Now, if we compute an average value for p equal to, say, p_a, and an average value for q, equal to q_a, we can say

$$p_a = \frac{\gamma - \alpha}{\beta - \delta}$$

and

$$q_a = \frac{\beta\gamma - \alpha\delta}{\beta - \delta}$$

but there is no way of solving for α, β, γ, and δ from these equations. Hence we cannot find the structural parameters.

Let us suppose, however, that, from some additional information, such as budget data, we were able to find out that $\beta = -1$, and from another source we judged that $\delta = +1$. Then the reduced forms become

$$p = \frac{\gamma - \alpha}{-2} + \frac{v - u}{-2}$$

and

$$q = \frac{-\gamma - \alpha}{2} + \frac{-v - u}{-2}$$

We are now able to proceed. If we average our price data, we can assume that the random variable vanishes (although seven items is hardly enough to assure this vanishing; thirty or forty would be much better), and we write

$$p_a = 5 = \frac{\gamma - \alpha}{-2}$$

Similarly, averaging the quantity data, we write

$$q_a = 5 = \frac{-\gamma - \alpha}{-2}$$

Now, subtracting the one from the other, we get

$$p_a - q_a = 5 - 5 = \frac{\gamma - \alpha}{-2} - \frac{-\gamma - \alpha}{-2}$$

$$0 = \frac{-2\gamma}{-2} = \gamma$$

Substituting this value of γ, we find

$$p_a = 5 = \frac{0 - \alpha}{-2}$$

$$\alpha = 10$$

The original structural equations can now be written:

Demand: $q = 10 - p$

Supply: $q = p$

These equations, with which we are already familiar, should be compared with the regression lines. The differences are considerable.

AN EVALUATION

Klein constructed a sixteen-equation model of the United States in which he attempted to employ these principles.[17] He found that he could not specify his model completely on the basis of economic theory alone, and hence calculated various trial regressions in an attempt to let the data suggest relationships that might be satisfactory. This, of course, is dangerous, because it is merely a searching for regularities in the data at hand which may not be found in similar data for a different period. This was the fatal weakness of the Harvard indexes of business activity. Hence Klein brings to light the inadequacy of economic theory when faced with a task so great.

[17] L. R. Klein, *Economic Fluctuations in the United States, 1921–1941* (New York, Wiley, 1950).

In estimating his parameters, Klein did not in general use the most complete statistical technique, the full-information maximum-likelihood method. Such a method is very costly since it requires much computation, and the precision of the data and the adequacy of the model would not justify the expenditure. He usually chose instead to estimate the parameters by two cheaper methods, and to compare the results. One method was least squares; the other was the limited-information method, which is a maximum-likelihood method of estimating the parameters of one equation at a time. After securing estimates of the parameters, he applied several tests. He computed the standard errors of the parameters. In general, we should expect that a parameter might be several times its standard error;[18] but Klein found a number of his parameters less than their standard errors, and he found himself testing the parameters by asking whether they were greater than their standard errors.

Klein also computed the residuals, and noted their size in relation to the size of the original variables. Thirdly, Klein tested these residuals for autocorrelation. If such residuals are not random, then there is likely to be some regularity left in them not captured by the model. Estimation procedures generally assume that such residuals are random.[19]

These tests proved the model to be a disappointing one. Parameters were not large relative to standard errors (and, even if they had been, it may be noted that Frisch has criticized the standard error method for this purpose),[20] residuals were in many cases still large, and seldom were they random.

Klein's model was subsequently improved by Marshall, and then by Christ. The equations were fitted to re-worked data for the years 1921–1947, and various tests were made. The most interesting test was the prediction of the 1948 values for the endogenous variables, and the comparison of these predictions with those made by two "naive" models. The first "naive" model consisted simply in assuming no change in the variables from 1947. The second "naive" model consisted in assuming that the amount of change between the years 1946–1947 was duplicated for the years 1947–1948.[21]

The results of the Christ model were again disappointing. To quote from Christ: "For 1948, each of the two naive models predicts 7 out of 13 endogenous variables better, i.e., it has smaller errors, than do the

[18] See above, Chap. 7, page 119.

[19] See above, Chap. 9, page 176.

[20] See above, page 174.

[21] *Conference on Business Cycles*, held under the auspices of Universities-National Bureau Committee for Economic Research, Special Conference Series, 2 (New York, National Bureau of Economic Research, Inc., 1951).

equations of the reduced form as estimated by the ordinary least-squares method. Naive model I predicts better in 15 cases out of 21 than the reduced form as estimated by the restricted least-squares method, and naive model II predicts better in 13 cases out of 21 than the reduced form as estimated by the restricted least-squares method. The econometric model used here has failed, at least in our sample consisting of the one year 1948, to be a better predicting device than the incomparably cheaper naive models, even though almost every structural equation performs as well, i.e., has just as small an error, in extrapolation to 1948 as it does in the sample period."

The failure of an econometric model to make good predictions is not a complete test of its usefulness. Indeed, Tinbergen and Clark were satisfied merely to display the "computed" series against the actual, so that the differences, or "residuals," could be seen and judged. It is felt to be of considerable value to show that certain relations do not hold, so that theorists will not too readily assume that they do. On the positive side, Daly and Brown[22] have pointed out that econometric relations can be useful in government policy decisions, along with other data, if interpreted with care.

In evaluating the difficulties facing anyone who would build a model of simultaneous relations and fit these relations simultaneously to the data, it may be noted that there have been two major studies of demand, one in Britain and one in Sweden, and in neither study has the simultaneous equations approach been used.[23] Each has used least squares regression; but their reasons are very different.

Stone gives four reasons: (1) The use of a system of equations rather than a single equation entails much more work. "The construction of a system around a single equation can only be expected to improve the estimates of the parameters in the single equation by bringing into account in a realistic fashion some related phenomena with which the relationship under investigation is closely connected. A formal system built to satisfy conditions for identifiability is not likely to be helpful." (2) We may obtain more consistency at the cost of greater variance.

[22] D. J. Daly, "The Christ and Canadian Econometric Models—Some Comparisons in Approach," Cowles Commission Discussion Paper (*Statistics*, No. 374). T. M. Brown, "Habit Persistence and Lags in Consumer Behavior," *Econometrica*, *20*: 355–371.

[23] Richard Stone, *The Measurement of Consumers' Expenditure and Behaviour in the United Kingdom, 1920–1938*, I (Cambridge: At the University Press, 1954); and Herman Wold, in association with Lars Jureen, *Demand Analysis: A Study in Econometrics* (Stockholm, Almqvist and Wiksell; New York, Wiley, 1953). See also Wm. C. Hood, "Empirical Studies of Demand," *Canadian Journal of Economics and Political Science*, *21*: 309–327.

(3) So long as the determining variables are subject to some error of measurement, all the good results promised cannot be obtained. (4) It is necessary that the determining variables in the transformed equations should be distributed independently of the disturbances in those equations. This assumption is likely to be severe.

Stone concludes: "In fact single equation methods are used throughout this study. Although the aim of simultaneous equation methods is clear there remains some doubt as to their practical value in the applications made here . . . there are other dangers to be guarded against, the presence of which in part places a greater burden on the investigator and in part diminishes the advantages of estimation by means of a system of equations." Stone realizes that, in using least squares regression when in fact some of the variables used are jointly dependent, his estimates will be biased; and he has no way of knowing how much the bias might be. He hopes, however, that such biases are not great, and believes that he would not have been much closer if a more complicated method had been used.

Wold, with the help of Jureen in the actual calculation, has made a thorough study of demand in Sweden. He also uses least squares regression, but his approach is different from that of Stone. Wold suggests that systems of equations used to express dependent situations can quite generally be of the recursive type[24] which form a causal chain, so that only one endogenous variable at a time is the dependent variable. Such recursive systems have the valuable property that for them least squares estimates are not biased. Haavelmo apparently overlooked this type of system. However, such systems are not really *jointly dependent*, and, whenever a true case of joint dependence occurs, Wold offers us no solution.[25]

PREDICTION AND POLICY

The elaborate method developed in this chapter is necessary if we wish to discover the structural relations existing in the economy. These relations are important both for economic theory and public policy. There is no guarantee, however, that these methods will produce the results sought. The success so far has not been great. As the data

[24] The Cobweb model is a recursive system.

[25] It would appear that time divisions are of some importance here. If the time units are taken as very short, then a one-at-a-time causal force might be regarded as more helpful; but, if substantial periods of time are taken, such as a year, joint determination would appear to have more place. See also Karl A. Fox, "Structural Analysis and the Measurement of Demand for Farm Products," *Review of Economics and Statistics, 36:* 57–66.

increase in quantity and improve in quality, and computation procedures become more manageable, we should expect some steady improvement. It is damaging to note, however, that, although an examination of the statistics suggested to one econometrician that the acceleration principle is of little significance,[26] it still forms an important part in business cycle theory.[27]   On the other hand, theorists are paying considerable attention to statistical evidence on such aspects of the economy as the consumption function and the multiplier.

It should be pointed out, also, that the Schultz regression approach is far from useless. The relations among economic variables that have been discovered by Schultz himself, as well as those by Ezekiel, Dean, Tinbergen, Roos, and others, are helpful information.   Furthermore, such relations can be used for prediction on the assumption that the structural parameters remain unchanged. If they remain unchanged, we do not need to know them—we need merely to note relations that exist. It is a little safer to use the reduced equations which have only one endogenous variable in each, but probably not much safer.

The simultaneous relations approach is not restricted to time series. Marschak and Andrews have applied it to cross-section production data. The fact that the results are not obviously superior to those dealing with time series suggests that our slow progress in this field of multiple relations is not due solely to the difficulties of handling time series.

One further difficulty is, of course, our inability to control some of the data as experimenters can.   But, in this, we are not different from meteorologists and even astronomers, in whose fields great advances have been made. What is there about economic data that makes them so recalcitrant?

RECALCITRANCE OF ECONOMIC STATISTICS

The quantity of economic data is tremendous.   The number of economic statisticians is so large that other statisticians sometimes feel called upon to point out that noneconomic statisticians exist.   Yet, despite this wealth of men and information, fundamental achievements in this field seem to be less numerous than in astronomy, on the one hand, or agronomy, on the other.   Why should this be?

It is, of course, possible that our economic theory itself is inadequate.

[26] J. Tinbergen, "An Acceleration Principle for Commodity Stockholding and a Short Cycle Resulting from It," in *Studies in Mathematical Economics and Econometrics*, ed. by O. Lange, F. McIntyre, and T. O. Yntema (Chicago, University of Chicago Press, 1942).

[27] J. R. Hicks, *A Contribution to the Theory of the Trade Cycle* (Oxford: At the Clarendon Press, 1950).

Indeed the revolution in economic thought brought about by Keynes's ideas suggests that our foundations may not yet be broad enough. It is important to keep in mind that economic dependence is highly relative. When we speak of determination of prices and quantities in terms of purely economic factors, this is an abstraction. We dismiss sociological, legal, and other factors which also play a part. In fact, there are situations in which the economic factors seem to play a minor role. The importance of the economic factors lie in their fundamental nature in that they underlie or limit the scope of other factors. This is clear when economic factors limit the achievements of a war effort, or when a plague like the Black Death changes the labor situation. Indeed it should be clear in every struggle with a budget. But in any human situation there are so many factors presumably having some influence on the result that in a sense every situation is "overdetermined" and only those forces that are powerful enough to overwhelm the others become the true determinants; by and large, the economic forces are able to hold their own. Furthermore, the model builders are not restricted to economic variables; they may use any factor that can be reduced to quantitative terms.

This last qualification is an important limitation. There are factors that cannot be reduced to measurement in any quantitative terms; speculative factors are notorious. Only a limited number of the aspects of dynamic or historical change can be so measured. We are only partly successful in finding related factors to which numbers can be attached.

Even those concepts that are measurable have fuzzy margins. Any discussion of national income concepts should leave econometricians feeling a bit uneasy. And the precision of the idea of a market is not as great as we should like. Many of our quantities are nonprecise.

Finally, there is the difficulty of isolation. In astronomy, the influence of the other planets can be neglected as a first approximation in examining the relation between the sun, earth, and moon, and this approximation is very good. In economics, we have difficulty in finding a set of relations that stand out from the others so that a first approximation of this type is at all good. The relations seem to be more equal in importance, and to be less permanent in nature.

This list of difficulties in dealing with economic relations is distressingly formidable though probably not complete. In all fairness, however, it should be recognized that government policy makers and economists do make much good use of the wealth of data available, and each year adds to our knowledge, slow though the progress be.

EXERCISES

1. Consider model **XXXVI**:

   Demand: $q = 10 - p + t$

   Supply: $q = p$

Plot the changes over time in the equilibrium values of p and q, assuming values of t as 0, 1, 2, 3, $\cdots$. Illustrate with a chart showing the successive positions of the demand line.

2. Consider model **XXXVII**:

   Demand: $q = 10 - p$

   Supply: $q = p + \cos \dfrac{\pi}{2} t$

Here again the time variable t may be assumed to vary discretely as 0, 1, 2, 3, $\cdots$ so that the last element in the supply equation becomes, respectively:

$$\cos 0 = 1$$

$$\cos \frac{\pi}{2} = 0$$

$$\cos \pi = -1$$

$$\cos \frac{3\pi}{2} = 0$$

$$\cos 2\pi = 1$$

Illustrate with a chart as in Exercise 1.

3. Examine the models of Exercise 1 and 2 again, giving fractional values to t.

4. In the illustration on page 195, assume $\beta = -1$ and $\delta = \frac{1}{2}$, and compute α and γ.

5. Apply the techniques of the illustration on page 195 to the following data:

	q	p
	5	5
	4	6
	6	4
	5.5	5
	4.5	5
	5	4.5
	5	5.5
av.	5	5

READINGS

A. FOR THE NONMATHEMATICAL STUDENT (Items from which the nonmathematician can derive benefit):

1. E. G. Bennion, "The Cowles Commission's Simultaneous Equations Approach: A Simplified Explanation," *Review of Economics and Statistics, XXXIV:* 49–56 (1952).
2. G. Cooper, "The Role of Econometric Models in Economic Theory," *Journal of Farm Economics, 30:* 101–116 (1948).
3. T. Haavelmo, "Quantitative Research in Agricultural Economics, the Interdependence between Agriculture and the National Economy," *Journal of Farm Economics, 29:* 910–924 (1947).
4. W. C. Hood, and T. C. Koopmans, *Studies in Econometric Method,* Cowles Commission for Research in Economics, Monograph 14 (New York, Wiley, 1953).
5. L. R. Klein, "The Use of Econometric Models as a Guide to Economic Policy," *Econometrica,* April 1947, pp. 111–151.
6. L. R. Klein and A. S. Goldberger, *An Econometric Model of the United States, 1929–1952* (Amsterdam, North-Holland Pub. Co., 1955).
7. T. C. Koopmans, "The Econometric Approach to Business Fluctuations," *Papers and Proceedings, American Economic Review, XXXIX,* No. 3: 64–72 (May 1949).
8. T. C. Koopmans, "Statistical Estimation of Simultaneous Economic Relations," *Journal of the American Statistical Association, 40,* No. 232, Part I: 448–466 (1945).
9. T. C. Koopmans, "Measurement without Theory," *Review of Economics and Statistics, XXIX:* 161–172 (Aug. 1947).
10. W. W. Leontief, "Econometrics," Chap. II of *A Survey of Contemporary Economics,* H. S. Ellis, ed. (Philadelphia, Blakiston, 1948).
11. J. Tinbergen, *Econometrics* (New York, Blakiston, 1951).
12. J. Tinbergen "Econometric Business Cycle Research," *Review of Economic Studies, 7:* 73–90 (1939–1940).
13. Rutledge Vining, "Methodological Issues in Quantitative Economics: Koopmans on the Choice of Variables to be Studied and of Methods of Measurement," *Review of Economics and Statistics,* May 1949, pp. 77–86. See also Koopmans' "A Reply," *ibid.,* pp. 86–91, and Vining's "A Rejoinder," *ibid.,* pp. 91–94.

B. FOR THE MATHEMATICAL STUDENT:

14. T. Haavelmo, "The Probability Approach to Econometrics," *Econometrica,* supplement, 1944.
15. L. R. Klein, *Econometrics* (Evanston, Row, Peterson, 1953).
16. T. C. Koopmans, ed., *Statistical Inference in Dynamic Economic Models,* Cowles Commission for Research in Economics, Monograph 10 (New York, Wiley, 1950).
17. G. Tintner, *Econometrics* (New York, Wiley, 1952).

Glossary

PART I

X, Y, Z are variables or variates.

x, y, z are variables expressed as deviations from their respective means.

α, β, γ are Greek letters used as constants or parameters; that is, they stand for some particular numbers which are to be held fixed. A specific number like five or eight would be too restrictive.

a, b, c are also used as constants or parameters, sometimes as estimates of α, β, γ, respectively.

Δx is an expression for a small addition to or increment in x.

$\dfrac{\Delta y}{\Delta x}$ is a ratio of two increments.

$\dfrac{dy}{dx}$ is a limit of the changes in the ratio $\Delta y/\Delta x$ as both Δx and Δy tend toward zero, y being a certain function of x. This ratio will in general not vanish, but be some specific value which we call "the derivative of y with respect to x."

$Y(t)$ or Y_t represents a variable Y at time t.

PART II

$P(X)$ probability of an event X.

σ standard deviation of population.

$\sigma_Y{}^2$ variance of population of Y's.

$\sigma_{\bar{X}}$ standard error of mean of X_i.

N number is sample.

n degrees of freedom.

$\bar{X}$ arithmetic mean of X_i.

$\hat{\sigma}$ estimate of standard deviation of population.

s standard deviation of sample.

$s_Y{}^2$ variance of sample of Y's.

$\sum(X)$ sum of all X's, i.e., $\bar{X} = \dfrac{\sum(X)}{N}$.

Y_c is Y value computed from line of regression.

$\sigma_{Y \cdot X}$ standard error of estimate in population.

$\sigma_E{}^2$ variance "explained" by regression line.

$s_b{}^2$ variance of b regression coefficient.

$s_{Y \cdot X}^2$ variance of sample points about regression line.

s_{Yc}^2 variance of point on regression line.

r_r coefficient of rank correlation.

r_s coefficient of autocorrelation.

X_1 $= a_{1 \cdot 23} + b_{12 \cdot 3}X_2 + b_{13 \cdot 2}X_3$ is regression equation in three variables.

$X_1{}^o$ observed values of variable X_1.

$X_1{}^c$ computed values of variable X_1.

$X^*{}_1$ values of X_1 adjusted for another variable.

r_{12} coefficient of correlation between X_1 and X_2.

$r_{12 \cdot 3}$ coefficient of correlation between X_1 and X_2 with X_3 taken into account and allowed for.

$a_{12 \cdot 3}$ normalized partial regression coefficient.

MATHEMATICAL SIGNS

$=$ equality.

$\neq$ nonequality.

$\equiv$ identity.

$\approx$ nearly equal.

$<$ less than, as $a < b$: a less than b.

$>$ greater than, as $a > b$: a greater than b.

$\sum$ summation sign. Frequently it is used as $\sum X$ to mean the sum of all X's, or $\sum(XY)$ to mean the sum of all products (XY). More specifically, it could be written as

$$\sum_{i=1}^{n}(X_iY_i) \equiv X_1Y_1 + X_2Y_2 + \cdots + X_iY_i + \cdots + X_nY_n.$$

$|a|$ absolute or numerical value of a.

$\int$ sign for integration, which is in calculus the reverse operation to that of taking the derivative dy/dx.

Answers to Exercises

CHAPTER 2

EX. 1

x	y
1	68.36
10	48.02
20	25.42
35	−8.48
$5\frac{1}{2}$	58.19
7.23	54.28

EX. 2 $y = 3 + 5x$

x	y
1	8
3	18
17	88
2.3	14.5

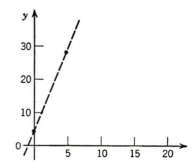

EX. 4 $y = 2 + 0.5x + 1.2w$
$$y = 1 - 0.5x + 1.2w$$

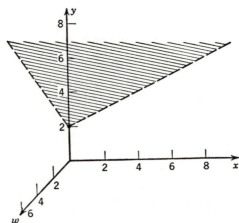

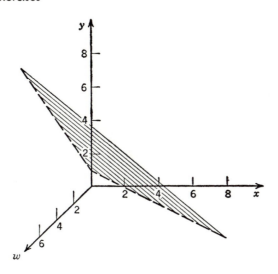

EX. 5 Some examples are:

    (a) Polynomial $y = \alpha_0 + \alpha_1 x + \alpha_2 x^2 + \cdots + \alpha_n x^n$

    (b) Fractional $y = \dfrac{\alpha_0 + \alpha_1 x + \cdots + \alpha_n x^n}{\beta_0 + \beta_1 x + \cdots + \beta_n x^n}$

    (c) Logarithmic $y = \dfrac{\alpha_0 + \alpha_1 \log n}{\beta_0 \log (x^2 - 7)}$

    (d) Trigonometric $y = \alpha_0 \cos x + \alpha_1 \sin^2 (x - 3)$

    (e) Exponential $y = \alpha e^x$

EX. 6 $d = \alpha_0 + \alpha_1 p + \alpha_2 Y + \alpha_3 n$

EX. 7

p	Y	d
0	0	0
0	1	0
1	0	0
1	1	1
1	2	20
2	1	20
2	2	40

EX. 8 A logarithmic curve:

$$y = \log x$$

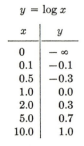

x	y
0	$-\infty$
0.1	-0.1
0.5	-0.3
1.0	0.0
2.0	0.3
5.0	0.7
10.0	1.0

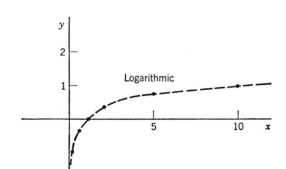

The student should plot

$$y = 2 \log (x - 1).$$

An exponential curve:

$$y = e^x$$

x	y
-2	$1/e^2 = 0.14$
-1	$1/e = 0.37$
0	$1 = 1.00$
1	$e = 2.72$
2	$e^2 = 7.40$

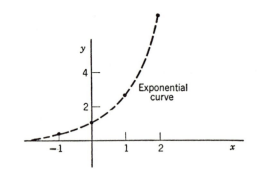

The student should plot

$$y = \tfrac{1}{2} \cdot 2^x$$

CHAPTER 3

EX. 1 One general approach is to impose the three following requirements:

$$(1)\ \delta \neq \beta, \qquad (2)\ \frac{\alpha - \gamma}{\delta - \beta} \geq 0, \qquad (3)\ \frac{\delta\alpha - \beta\gamma}{\delta - \beta} \geq 0$$

EX. 2 $d = 10 - \tfrac{1}{2}p$

$s = 2 + 2p$

$d = s$

$p = 3\tfrac{1}{5};\ s = d = 8\tfrac{2}{5}$

EX. 4 Solving:

$2x - 3y = 5$

$x + 2y = 4$

$x = 3\tfrac{1}{7};\ y = \tfrac{3}{7}$

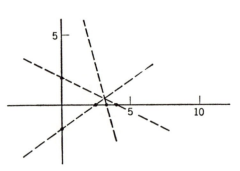

By solving any other pair of equations the solution will be found to be the same.

EX. 5

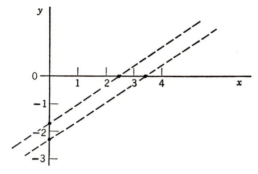

EX. 7 The solution is: $x = \frac{7}{9}$; $y = -\frac{5}{9}$; $z = \frac{7}{9}$.

EX. 9 The reduced forms are:

$$p = \frac{\gamma - \alpha}{\beta - \delta} + \frac{\epsilon}{\beta - \delta} r - \frac{\zeta}{\beta - \delta} t$$

$$d = s = \frac{\beta\gamma - \alpha\delta}{\beta - \delta} + \frac{\beta\epsilon}{\beta - \delta} r - \frac{\delta\zeta}{\beta - \delta} t$$

The dependence matrix is:

	r	t
p	$\dfrac{\epsilon}{\beta - \delta}$	$\dfrac{-\zeta}{\beta - \delta}$
$d = s$	$\dfrac{\beta\epsilon}{\beta - \delta}$	$\dfrac{-\delta\zeta}{\beta - \delta}$

EX. 10 (a) $\quad Y = \dfrac{20}{1 - \frac{3}{4}} + \dfrac{1}{1 - \frac{3}{4}} \times 20 + \dfrac{1}{1 - \frac{3}{4}} \times 20 = 240$

(b) If $Y = \dfrac{20}{1 - \frac{3}{4}} + \dfrac{1}{1 - \frac{3}{4}} \times 20 + \dfrac{1}{1 - \frac{3}{4}} G = 250$

$$G = \frac{90}{4} = 22.5$$

(c) The general formula:

$$Y = 160 + 4G$$

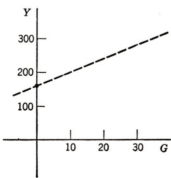

EX. 11

	F	G	P
C	$\dfrac{ea}{1-a-d}$	$\dfrac{a}{1-a-d}$	$\dfrac{(1-d)b}{1-a-d}$
I	$\dfrac{e(1-a)}{1-a-d}$	$\dfrac{d}{1-a-d}$	$\dfrac{bd}{1-a-d}$
Y	$\dfrac{e}{1-a-d}$	$\dfrac{1}{1-a-d}$	$\dfrac{b}{1-a-d}$

The numerical values from model VA can now be inserted.

EX. 12 Both functions pass through the points $(1, 1)$ and $(2, 4)$. The values and errors are as follows:

x	$3x - 2$	x^2	Error	Percentage Error
1	1	1	0	0
$1\frac{1}{4}$	$1\frac{3}{4}$	$1\frac{9}{16}$	$\frac{3}{16}$	12
$1\frac{1}{2}$	$2\frac{1}{2}$	$2\frac{1}{4}$	$\frac{1}{4}$	11
1.63	2.89	2.66	0.23	9
$1\frac{3}{4}$	$3\frac{1}{4}$	$3\frac{1}{16}$	$\frac{3}{16}$	6
2	4	4	0	0
3	7	9	-2	22

EX. 13 One way is to find the points through which the function $y = \log x$ passes when x equals, respectively, 5 and 10. When $x = 5$, $\log x = 0.7$; when $x = 10$, $\log x = 1.0$. Now pass a straight line through these two points. The formula for the straight line is $y = \alpha + \beta x$, and, if these points are to be on the line, their x and y values should satisfy this equation. Hence, by substituting these x and y values into the equation, we get

$$0.7 = \alpha + \beta(5)$$

$$1.0 = \alpha + \beta(10)$$

Now solve these two equations for the parameters α and β, getting $\alpha = 0.4$ and $\beta = 0.06$. Therefore the straight line of approximation is $y = 0.4 + 0.06x$. When $x = 7.5$, this line gives 0.850, whereas the log function gives 0.875, giving an error of 0.025, which is a relative error of $0.025/0.875$ or 2.9 per cent.

CHAPTER 4

EX. 1 Substituting (2) and (3) into (1) gives:

$$\beta_0 + \beta_1 p = \alpha_0 + \alpha_1 p + \alpha_2 p^2$$

$$\alpha_2 p^2 + (\alpha_1 - \beta_1)p + (\alpha_0 - \beta_0) = 0$$

$$p = \frac{-(\alpha_1 - \beta_1) - [(\alpha_1 - \beta_1)^2 - 4\alpha_2(\alpha_0 - \beta_0)]^{1/2}}{2\alpha_2}$$

We omit the larger root as being outside our range. By substituting this value for p in equation 2 the equilibrium value for d and s can be found.

EX. 2 $100 - 20p + p^2 = \frac{1}{2}p^2$

$\qquad$ $100 - 20p + \frac{1}{2}p^2 = 0$

$\qquad$ $p = \dfrac{20 - (400 - 200)^{\frac{1}{2}}}{1} = 20 - 10\sqrt{2}$

$\qquad$ $s = \frac{1}{2}p^2 = \frac{1}{2}(20 - 10\sqrt{2})^2$

$\qquad\qquad$ $= \frac{1}{2}(400 + 200 - 400\sqrt{2})$

$\qquad\qquad$ $= \frac{1}{2}(600 - 400\sqrt{2})$

$\qquad\qquad$ $= 300 - 200\sqrt{2}$

EX. 3 $d = 3 - 2\log p = 3 - 2p'$

$\qquad$ $s = 3\log p \qquad = 3p'$

$\qquad$ $d = s$

Solving: $3p' = 3 - 2p'$

$\qquad\qquad$ $p' = \frac{3}{5}$

Thus $\log p = 0.60$

and $p = 3.98$

$\qquad\qquad$ $s = d = 3p'$

$\qquad\qquad\qquad$ $= \frac{9}{5} = 1.80$

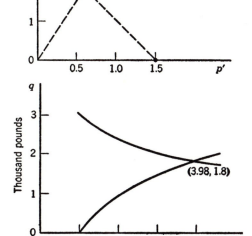

EX. 4   If $d_1 = s_1$, then

$$\alpha_0 + \alpha_1 p_1' + \alpha_2 p_2' = \gamma_0 + \gamma_1 p_1' + \gamma_2 p_2'$$

i.e., $(\alpha_1 - \gamma_1)p_1' + (\alpha_2 - \gamma_2)p_2' + (\alpha_0 - \gamma_0) = 0$

If $d_2 = s_2$, then

$$\beta_0 + \beta_1 p_1' + \beta_2 p_2' = \delta_0 + \delta_1 p_1' + \delta_2 p_2'$$

i.e., $(\beta_1 - \delta_1)p_1' + (\beta_2 - \delta_2)p_2' + (\beta_0 - \delta_0) = 0$

$$\frac{(\alpha_1 - \gamma_1)}{(\beta_1 - \delta_1)} \times \{(\beta_1 - \delta_1)p_1' + (\beta_2 - \delta_2)p_2' + (\beta_0 - \delta_0)\} = 0$$

or $\qquad (\alpha_1 - \gamma_1)p_1' + \dfrac{(\alpha_1 - \gamma_1)(\beta_2 - \delta_2)}{(\beta_1 - \delta_1)}\, p_2' + \dfrac{(\alpha_1 - \gamma_1)(\beta_0 - \delta_0)}{(\beta_1 - \delta_1)} = 0$

Subtracting this equation from the third equation:

$$\left[(\alpha_2 - \gamma_2) - \frac{(\alpha_1 - \gamma_1)(\beta_2 - \delta_2)}{(\beta_1 - \delta_1)}\right] p_2' + \left[(\alpha_0 - \gamma_0) - \frac{(\alpha_1 - \gamma_1)(\beta_0 - \delta_0)}{(\beta_1 - \delta_1)}\right] = 0$$

$$p_2' = \frac{\dfrac{(\alpha_1 - \gamma_1)(\beta_0 - \delta_0)}{(\beta_1 - \delta_1)} - (\alpha_0 - \gamma_0)}{(\alpha_2 - \gamma_2) - \dfrac{(\alpha_1 - \gamma_1)(\beta_2 - \delta_2)}{\beta_1 - \delta_1}}$$

Now, to solve for p_1':

$$\frac{(\alpha_2 - \gamma_2)}{(\beta_2 - \delta_2)} \times \{(\beta_1 - \delta_1)p_1' + (\beta_2 - \delta_2)p_2' + (\beta_0 - \delta_0)\} = 0$$

or $\qquad \dfrac{(\alpha_2 - \gamma_2)(\beta_1 - \delta_1)}{\beta_2 - \delta_2}\, p_1' + (\alpha_2 - \gamma_2)p_2' + \dfrac{(\alpha_2 - \gamma_2)(\beta_0 - \delta_0)}{(\beta_2 - \delta_2)} = 0$

Subtracting this equation from the third equation:

$$\left[(\alpha_1 - \gamma_1) - \frac{(\alpha_2 - \gamma_2)(\beta_1 - \delta_1)}{(\beta_2 - \delta_2)}\right] p_1' + \left[(\alpha_0 - \gamma_0) - \frac{(\alpha_2 - \gamma_2)(\beta_0 - \delta_0)}{(\beta_2 - \delta_2)}\right] = 0$$

$$p_1' = \frac{\dfrac{(\alpha_2 - \gamma_2)(\beta_0 - \delta_0)}{(\beta_2 - \delta_2)} - (\alpha_0 - \gamma_0)}{(\alpha_1 - \gamma_1) - \dfrac{(\alpha_2 - \gamma_2)(\beta_1 - \delta_1)}{(\beta_2 - \delta_2)}}$$

Somewhat similar expressions can be worked out for d_1 and s_1 from the first equation of the model, and for d_2 and s_2 from the second equation of the model simply by substituting the values of p_1' and p_2' found above into these equations.

Now suppose first that $\alpha_2 = \beta_1 = \gamma_2 = \delta_1 = 0$. The demand and supply relations of the model now become:

$$d_1 = \alpha_0 + \alpha_1 p_1'$$
$$d_2 = \beta_0 \qquad\qquad + \beta_2 p_2'$$
$$s_1 = \gamma_0 + \gamma_1 p_1'$$
$$s_2 = \delta_0 \qquad\qquad + \delta_2 p_2'$$

and the equilibrium values:

$$p_1' = \frac{-(\alpha_0 - \gamma_0)}{(\alpha_1 - \gamma_1)}$$

$$p_2' = \frac{(\alpha_1 - \gamma_1)(\beta_0 - \delta_0) - \cancel{(\alpha_0 - \gamma_0)(\beta_1 - \delta_1)}}{\cancel{(\alpha_2 - \gamma_2)(\beta_1 - \delta_1)} - (\alpha_1 - \gamma_1)(\beta_2 - \delta_2)}$$

$$= -\frac{\cancel{(\alpha_1 - \gamma_1)}(\beta_0 - \delta_0)}{\cancel{(\alpha_1 - \gamma_1)}(\beta_2 - \delta_2)} = -\frac{\beta_0 - \delta_0}{\beta_2 - \delta_2}$$

Thus, when the cross elasticities of price are all zero, that is, when each price affects only its own supply and demand, we have merely two separate models each identical with model I. Suppose, now, we allow one of the elasticities to have a value, so that $\alpha_2 = \frac{1}{10}$ and we assume that $\alpha_0 = 3$, $\alpha_1 = -2$, $\gamma_0 = 0$, $\gamma_1 = 3$, as in Exercise 3. The equilibrium value of p_1' thus becomes

$$p_1' = \frac{\frac{\frac{1}{10}(\beta_0 - \delta_0)}{\beta_2 - \delta_2} - 3}{-5 - \frac{\frac{1}{10}(\beta_1 - \delta_1)}{\beta_2 - \delta_2}} = -\frac{1}{5}\left[\frac{1}{10}\left(\frac{\beta_0 - \delta_0}{\beta_2 - \delta_2}\right) - 3\right]$$

Thus the equilibrium value of p_1' depends on the equilibrium value of p_2'. Let us now assume such an equilibrium value for p_2' as 5, from which it follows that p_1' has an equilibrium value of $\frac{1}{2}$. Then $p_1 =$ antilog $0.5 = 3.16$. We have assumed that $p_2' = 5$, so that $p_2 = 25$, but we have made no specific assumptions about the parameters β_0, β_2, δ_0, and δ_2. The student should amuse himself by doing so.

EX. 5 From page 239 of the Neisser article, we take two equations:

$$Y = C(Y) + I(r)$$

$$M = M_1(Y) + M_2(r)$$

in two endogenous variables, Y (aggregate income) and r (interest rate). M can be considered an exogenous variable. The other letters can be thought of as representing functions. If, for example, all these functions were linear:

$$C = \alpha_0 + \alpha_1 Y$$

$$I = \beta_0 + \beta_1 r$$

$$M_1 = \gamma_0 + \gamma_1 Y$$

$$M_2 = \delta_0 + \delta_1 r$$

Then the equations of the model become

$$Y = (\alpha_0 + \beta_0) + \alpha_1 Y + \beta_1 r$$

$$M = (\gamma_0 + \delta_0) + \gamma_1 Y + \delta_1 r$$

Of course, an important element in Keynesian theory is that these relations are not linear. In particular, M_2 should better be expressed as a parabolic function of r. The student should do so, and then insert plausible values of the parameters, chart, and study.

CHAPTER 5

EX. 1
$$v = \frac{ds}{dt} = gt + c_1$$

$$v(0) = g \times 0 + c_1 = c_1$$

Therefore
$$c_1 = 1$$

and
$$s = \tfrac{1}{2}gt^2 + c_1 t + c_2$$

$$s(0) = \tfrac{1}{2}g \times 0 + c_1 \times 0 + c_2 = c_2$$

Therefore
$$c_2 = 1$$

EX. 2   (a) $D'(t) = \alpha Y$

$$Y = \beta$$

where Y does not vary with time, since β is a constant. Therefore

$$Y_0 = \beta$$

and $D'(t) = \alpha\beta$

Therefore $D(t) = \int \alpha\beta \, dt = \alpha\beta t + c$

Ratio: $\dfrac{D(t)}{Y} = \dfrac{\alpha\beta t + c}{\beta} = \alpha t + \dfrac{c}{\beta}$

which increases over time in a linear fashion.

(b) $D'(t) = \alpha Y(t)$

$$Y(t) = \beta + \gamma t$$

Therefore $D'(t) = \alpha\beta + \alpha\gamma t$

$$D(t) = \int \alpha\beta \, dt + \int \alpha\gamma t \, dt$$

$$= \alpha\beta t + \tfrac{1}{2}\alpha\gamma t^2 + c$$

Ratio: $\dfrac{D(t)}{Y(t)} = \dfrac{\alpha\beta t + \tfrac{1}{2}\alpha\gamma t^2 + c}{\beta + \gamma t}$

$$= \dfrac{\dfrac{\alpha\beta}{t} + \tfrac{1}{2}\alpha\gamma + \dfrac{c}{t^2}}{\dfrac{\beta}{t^2} + \dfrac{\gamma}{t}}$$

Obviously, as t increases, this ratio approaches a constant value $\tfrac{1}{2}\alpha\gamma$. All other elements become smaller and smaller as t increases.

EX. 3   The differential equation is

$$p'(t) = Ap(t) + B$$

where $B = (\alpha_0 - \beta_0)/(\beta_2 - \alpha_2)$ and $A = (\alpha_1 - \beta_1)/(\beta_2 - \alpha_2)$.

By following the steps on page 83, we obtain a solution of the differential equation as follows:

$$p(t) = \left(p_0 + \frac{B}{A}\right)e^{At} - \frac{B}{A}$$

which will be found to be identical with the solution on page 83.

CHAPTER 6

EX. 1   The solution of the Harrod model is

$$Y(t) = \left(\frac{\beta}{\beta - \alpha}\right)^t Y_0$$

Case   (a): $Y(t) = (\frac{10}{9})^t 100$
    (b): $Y(t) = (\frac{10}{11})^t 100$
    (c): $Y(t) = (\frac{1}{3})^t 100$
    (d): $Y(t) = -(\frac{10}{9})^t 100$

t	0	1	2	3	$\cdots$
Case (a)	100	111	123	137	$\cdots$
Case (b)	100	91	83	75	$\cdots$
Case (c)	100	33	11	3.7	$\cdots$
Case (d)	-100	-111	-123	-137	$\cdots$

EX. 2   The last two cases are not plausible, since we cannot consider aggregate income negative, or vanishing altogether. The second case might continue for a limited time only. The first case is therefore the only plausible one for any extended time. Additional cases are: (1) $-\frac{1}{5}$, 2, -100; (2) 4, 2, 100.

EX. 3   If the slope of the demand curve is negative, $\delta < 0$; and, if the slope of the supply curve is negative, $\beta < 0$, so that $\beta' < 0$ also; then the approach to equilibrium will not be oscillatory. The stability condition $\left|\dfrac{\delta}{\beta'}\right| < 1$ indicates that the demand curve must be flatter than the supply curve, both slopes being with respect to the quantity axis. A diagram may help the student to visualize the situation.

EX. 4   The solution of the interaction model in the cyclical case is given on page 108 as follows:

$$Y(t) = A^t(g \cos tB + h \sin tB) + \frac{\gamma}{1 - \alpha}$$

Now, at time $t = 0$:

$$Y_0 = (g \cos (0) + h \sin (0)) + \frac{\gamma}{1 - \alpha} = g + \frac{\gamma}{1 - \alpha}$$

and at time $t = 1$:

$$Y_1 = A (g \cos B + h \sin B) + \frac{\gamma}{1 - \alpha}$$

Solving for g and h:

$$g = Y_0 - \frac{\gamma}{1 - \alpha}$$

$$h = \frac{\dfrac{1}{A}\left(Y_1 - \dfrac{\gamma}{1 - \alpha}\right) - g \cos B}{\sin B}$$

$$= \frac{\dfrac{1}{A}\left(Y_1 - \dfrac{\gamma}{1 - \alpha}\right) - \left(Y_0 - \dfrac{\gamma}{1 - \alpha}\right) \cos B}{\sin B}$$

$$= \frac{Y_1 - \dfrac{\gamma}{1 - \alpha}}{A \sin B} - \left(Y_0 - \dfrac{\gamma}{1 - \alpha}\right) \cotan B$$

EX. 5 The difference equation is

$$Y(t) - \alpha Y(t-1) + \beta + I = 0$$

which is a first-order nonhomogeneous equation identical with (40) when $A = \alpha$ and $-B = \beta + I$. The solution, taken from Equation 52, is

$$Y(t) = \alpha^t \left(Y_0 + \frac{\beta + I}{1 - \alpha} \right) - \frac{\beta + I}{1 - \alpha}$$

CHAPTER 8

EX. 1 When $x = \pm 1$,

$$s_{Y_c}^2 = \frac{1.16}{13} (1 + \tfrac{1}{2}) = 0.13$$

When $x = \pm 3$,

$$s_{Y_c}^2 = \frac{1.16}{13} (1 + \tfrac{9}{2}) = 0.49$$

EX. 2

When $x = 0$, $\qquad s_Y^2 = \dfrac{1.16}{13} \times 16 = 1.43 = (1.20)^2$

When $x = \pm 1$, $\qquad s_Y^2 = \dfrac{1.16}{13} (16 + \tfrac{1}{2}) = 1.47 = (1.21)^2$

When $x = \pm 2$, $\qquad s_Y^2 = \dfrac{1.16}{13} (16 + \tfrac{4}{2}) = 1.61 = (1.27)^2$

When $x = \pm 3$, $\qquad s_Y^2 = \dfrac{1.16}{13} (16 + \tfrac{9}{2}) = 1.83 = (1.35)^2$

CHAPTER 10

EX. 1 Solving for p:

$$p = 10 - p + t$$
$$p = 5 + \tfrac{1}{2}t$$

Therefore

t	p	q
0	5	5
1	$5\frac{1}{2}$	$5\frac{1}{2}$
2	6	6
3	$6\frac{1}{2}$	$6\frac{1}{2}$

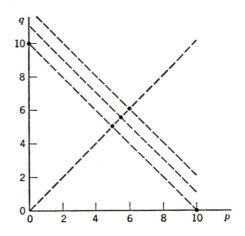

EX. 2 Solving for p:

$$10 - p = p + \cos\frac{\pi}{2}t$$

$$p = 5 + \tfrac{1}{2}\cos\frac{\pi}{2}t$$

t	p	q
0	$5\frac{1}{2}$	$4\frac{1}{2}$
1	5	5
2	$4\frac{1}{2}$	$5\frac{1}{2}$
3	5	5
4	$5\frac{1}{2}$	$4\frac{1}{2}$

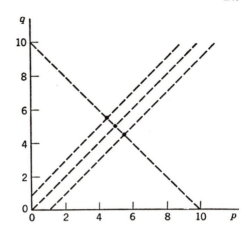

EX. 4 If $\beta = -1$ and $\delta = \frac{1}{2}$, then

$$p = \frac{\gamma - \alpha}{-1 - \frac{1}{2}} = \frac{\gamma - \alpha}{-\frac{3}{2}}$$

and

$$q = \frac{-\gamma - \frac{1}{2}\alpha}{-\frac{3}{2}}$$

Now, if

$$\tfrac{2}{3}\alpha - \tfrac{2}{3}\gamma = 5$$

and

$$\tfrac{1}{3}\alpha + \tfrac{2}{3}\gamma = 5$$

then adding,

$$\alpha = 10$$

and

$$\gamma = (5 - \tfrac{10}{3})\tfrac{3}{2} = 2\tfrac{1}{2}$$

EX. 5 To compute the regression equations, set up a table:

q	p	qp	q^2	p^2
5	5	25	25	25
4	6	24	16	36
6	4	24	36	16
5.5	5	27.5	30.25	25
4.5	5	22.5	20.25	25
5	4.5	22.5	25	20.25
5	5.5	27.5	25	30.25
35	35	173.0	177.5	177.5

For the regression of p on q, we need the normal equations

$$\sum p = na + b\sum q$$

$$\sum (pq) = a\sum q + b\sum q^2$$

Substituting the sums in the proper places:

$$35 = 7a + 35b$$

$$173 = 35a + 177.5b$$

Solving the two equations, we get $b = -0.8$; $a = 9.0$. Hence the regression of p on q is $p = 9 - 0.8q$. In much the same way, it can be found that the regression of q on p is $q = 9 - 0.8p$. The former regression equation can be rewritten as

$$q = 11\tfrac{1}{4} - 1\tfrac{1}{4}p$$

If now we use the model and assume that $\beta = -1$ and $\delta = +1$, since we have the same average price (5) and the same average quantity (5) as in the illustration, we find that $\gamma = 0$ and $\alpha = 10$. If, on the other hand, we assume that $\beta = -1$ and $\delta = +\tfrac{1}{2}$, as in Exercise 4, we find that $\gamma = 2\tfrac{1}{2}$ and $\alpha = 10$.

Table A. Student's *t* Distribution[*]

Degrees of freedom *n*	Probability of a deviation greater than *t*					
	.005	.01	.025	.05	.1	.15
1	63.657	31.821	12.706	6.314	3.078	1.963
2	9.925	6.965	4.303	2.920	1.886	1.386
3	5.841	4.541	3.182	2.353	1.638	1.250
4	4.604	3.747	2.776	2.132	1.533	1.190
5	4.032	3.365	2.571	2.015	1.476	1.156
6	3.707	3.143	2.447	1.943	1.440	1.134
7	3.499	2.998	2.365	1.895	1.415	1.119
8	3.355	2.896	2.306	1.860	1.397	1.108
9	3.250	2.821	2.262	1.833	1.383	1.100
10	3.169	2.764	2.228	1.812	1.372	1.093
11	3.106	2.718	2.201	1.796	1.363	1.088
12	3.055	2.681	2.179	1.782	1.356	1.083
13	3.012	2.650	2.160	1.771	1.350	1.079
14	2.977	2.624	2.145	1.761	1.345	1.076
15	2.947	2.602	2.131	1.753	1.341	1.074
16	2.921	2.583	2.120	1.746	1.337	1.071
17	2.898	2.567	2.110	1.740	1.333	1.069
18	2.878	2.552	2.101	1.734	1.330	1.067
19	2.861	2.539	2.093	1.729	1.328	1.066
20	2.845	2.528	2.086	1.725	1.325	1.064
21	2.831	2.518	2.080	1.721	1.323	1.063
22	2.819	2.508	2.074	1.717	1.321	1.061
23	2.807	2.500	2.069	1.714	1.319	1.060
24	2.797	2.492	2.064	1.711	1.318	1.059
25	2.787	2.485	2.060	1.708	1.316	1.058
26	2.779	2.479	2.056	1.706	1.315	1.058
27	2.771	2.473	2.052	1.703	1.314	1.057
28	2.763	2.467	2.048	1.701	1.313	1.056
29	2.756	2.462	2.045	1.699	1.311	1.055
30	2.750	2.457	2.042	1.697	1.310	1.055
∞	2.576	2.326	1.960	1.645	1.282	1.036

The probability of a deviation *numerically* greater than *t* is twice the probability given at the head of the table.

[*] This table is reproduced from *Statistical Methods for Research Workers*, with the generous permission of the author, Professor R. A. Fisher, and the publishers, Messrs. Oliver and Boyd.

Student's *t* Distribution

Degrees of freedom *n*	Probability of a deviation greater than *t*					
	.2	.25	.3	.35	.4	.45
1	1.376	1.000	.727	.510	.325	.158
2	1.061	.816	.617	.445	.289	.142
3	.978	.765	.584	.424	.277	.137
4	.941	.741	.569	.414	.271	.134
5	.920	.727	.559	.408	.267	.132
6	.906	.718	.553	.404	.265	.131
7	.896	.711	.549	.402	.263	.130
8	.889	.706	.546	.399	.262	.130
9	.883	.703	.543	.398	.261	.129
10	.879	.700	.542	.397	.260	.129
11	.876	.697	.540	.396	.260	.129
12	.873	.695	.539	.395	.259	.128
13	.870	.694	.538	.394	.259	.128
14	.868	.692	.537	.393	.258	.128
15	.866	.691	.536	.393	.258	.128
16	.865	.690	.535	.392	.258	.128
17	.863	.689	.534	.392	.257	.128
18	.862	.688	.534	.392	.257	.127
19	.861	.688	.533	.391	.257	.127
20	.860	.687	.533	.391	.257	.127
21	.859	.686	.532	.391	.257	.127
22	.858	.686	.532	.390	.256	.127
23	.858	.685	.532	.390	.256	.127
24	.857	.685	.531	.390	.256	.127
25	.856	.684	.531	.390	.256	.127
26	.856	.684	.531	.390	.256	.127
27	.855	.684	.531	.389	.256	.127
28	.855	.683	.530	.389	.256	.127
29	.854	.683	.530	.389	.256	.127
30	.854	.683	.530	.389	.256	.127
∞	.842	.674	.524	.385	.253	.126

The probability of a deviation *numerically* greater than *t* is twice the probability given at the head of the table.

Table B. χ² Distribution

Degrees of freedom	P = 0.99	0.98	0.95	0.90	0.80	0.70	0.50	0.30	0.20	0.10	0.05	0.02	0.01
1	0.000157	0.000628	0.00393	0.0158	0.0642	0.148	0.455	1.074	1.642	2.706	3.841	5.412	6.635
2	0.0201	0.0404	0.103	0.211	0.446	0.713	1.386	2.408	3.219	4.605	5.991	7.824	9.210
3	0.115	0.185	0.352	0.584	1.005	1.424	2.366	3.665	4.642	6.251	7.815	9.837	11.341
4	0.297	0.429	0.711	1.064	1.649	2.195	3.357	4.878	5.989	7.779	9.488	11.668	13.277
5	0.554	0.752	1.145	1.610	2.343	3.000	4.351	6.064	7.289	9.236	11.070	13.388	15.086
6	0.872	1.134	1.635	2.204	3.070	3.828	5.348	7.231	8.558	10.645	12.592	15.033	16.812
7	1.239	1.564	2.167	2.833	3.822	4.671	6.346	8.383	9.803	12.017	14.067	16.622	18.475
8	1.646	2.032	2.733	3.490	4.594	5.527	7.344	9.524	11.030	13.362	15.507	18.168	20.090
9	2.088	2.532	3.325	4.168	5.380	6.393	8.343	10.656	12.242	14.684	16.919	19.679	21.666
10	2.558	3.059	3.940	4.865	6.179	7.267	9.342	11.781	13.442	15.987	18.307	21.161	23.209
11	3.053	3.609	4.575	5.578	6.989	8.148	10.341	12.899	14.631	17.275	19.675	22.618	24.725
12	3.571	4.178	5.226	6.304	7.807	9.034	11.340	14.011	15.812	18.549	21.026	24.054	26.217
13	4.107	4.765	5.892	7.042	8.634	9.926	12.340	15.119	16.985	19.812	22.362	25.472	27.688
14	4.660	5.368	6.571	7.790	9.467	10.821	13.339	16.222	18.151	21.064	23.685	26.873	29.141
15	5.229	5.985	7.261	8.547	10.307	11.721	14.339	17.322	19.311	22.307	24.996	28.259	30.578
16	5.812	6.614	7.962	9.312	11.152	12.624	15.338	18.418	20.465	23.542	26.296	29.633	32.000
17	6.408	7.255	8.672	10.085	12.002	13.531	16.338	19.511	21.615	24.769	27.587	30.995	33.409
18	7.015	7.906	9.390	10.865	12.857	14.440	17.338	20.601	22.760	25.989	28.869	32.346	34.805
19	7.633	8.567	10.117	11.651	13.716	15.352	18.338	21.689	23.900	27.204	30.144	33.687	36.191
20	8.260	9.237	10.851	12.443	14.578	16.266	19.337	22.775	25.038	28.412	31.410	35.020	37.566
21	8.897	9.915	11.591	13.240	15.445	17.182	20.337	23.858	26.171	29.615	32.671	36.343	38.932
22	9.542	10.600	12.338	14.041	16.314	18.101	21.337	24.939	27.301	30.813	33.924	37.659	40.289
23	10.196	11.293	13.091	14.848	17.187	19.021	22.337	26.018	28.429	32.007	35.172	38.968	41.638
24	10.856	11.992	13.848	15.659	18.062	19.943	23.337	27.096	29.553	33.196	36.415	40.270	42.980
25	11.524	12.697	14.611	16.473	18.940	20.867	24.337	28.172	30.675	34.382	37.652	41.566	44.314
26	12.198	13.409	15.379	17.292	19.820	21.792	25.336	29.246	31.795	35.563	38.885	42.856	45.642
27	12.879	14.125	16.151	18.114	20.703	22.719	26.336	30.319	32.912	36.741	40.113	44.140	46.963
28	13.565	14.847	16.928	18.939	21.588	23.647	27.336	31.391	34.027	37.916	41.337	45.419	48.278
29	14.256	15.574	17.708	19.768	22.475	24.577	28.336	32.461	35.139	39.087	42.557	46.693	49.588
30	14.953	16.306	18.493	20.599	23.364	25.508	29.336	33.530	36.250	40.256	43.773	47.962	50.892

For degrees of freedom greater than 30, the expression $\sqrt{2\chi^2} - \sqrt{2n'-1}$ may be used as a normal deviate with unit variance, where n' is the number of degrees of freedom.

Reproduced from *Statistical Methods for Research Workers*, 6th ed., with the permission of the author, R. A. Fisher, and his publisher, Oliver and Boyd, Edinburgh.

Index of Names

Subject Index